Dr Judy Davis has created a powerful book examining the challenges, roles, and contributions of Mad Black Women in the advertising industry, preserving a previously unchartered piece of history. Her comprehensive cultural research and true narrative accounts of shocking racial diversity struggles offer lessons for students, scholars, practitioners, and readers. This 'behind the scenes' approach prompts honest discourse and dialogue on issues of race and gender that are still highly relevant. Such compelling stories of how these rare women rose to success, in spite of tremendous obstacles, offer hope, yet questions why such diversity issues and barriers still exist today. Together, we will all rise through better understanding such history!

Sheila Sasser, *Ph.D., Professor of Marketing, Eastern Michigan University, SWOCC Fellow, University of Amsterdam, Adcraft Lifetime Member, AAF, AAA, EAA, Former Advertising Industry Veteran, Senior Vice President, and Managing Director*

Dr Judy Davis has crafted a fantastic book that fills a significant gap in the historiography of the advertising industry. The experiences and contributions of African-American women to the industry have long been an overlooked aspect of advertising. Yet as Dr. Davis so expertly demonstrates, black women have been some of the most impactful professionals, entrepreneurs, and top creative forces in advertising. As such they have been a force in challenging many of its most demeaning characterizations of African-Americans as a group and black women in particular. This book should be required reading for advertising professionals and students of advertising around the country.

Jason P. Chambers, *Ph.D., Associate Professor, University of Illinois*

Pioneering African-American Women in the Advertising Business

Much has been written about the men and women who shaped the field of advertising, some of whom became legends in the industry. However, the contributions of African-American women to the advertising business have largely been omitted from these accounts. Yet, evidence reveals that some trailblazing African-American women who launched their careers during the 1960s *Mad Men* era went on to achieve prominent careers. This unique book chronicles the nature and significance of these women's accomplishments, examines the opportunities and challenges they experienced, and explores how they coped with the extensive inequities common in the advertising profession.

Using a biographical narrative approach, this book examines the careers of these important African-American women who not only achieved managerial positions in major mainstream advertising agencies but also established successful agencies bearing their own names. Based on their words and memories, this study reveals experiences which are intriguing, triumphant, bittersweet, and sometimes tragic. These women's stories comprise a vital part of the historical narrative on women and African-Americans in advertising and will be instructive not only to scholars of advertising and marketing history but to future generations of advertising professionals.

Judy Foster Davis is a Professor of Marketing at Eastern Michigan University, USA. Her research interests concern integrated marketing communications (IMC) strategies and policies, historical and multicultural marketing topics, and online pedagogy. She is a graduate of Howard University and Michigan State University.

Routledge Studies in the History of Marketing

Edited by Mark Tadajewski
and Brian D. G. Jones

It is increasingly acknowledged that an awareness of marketing history and the history of marketing thought is relevant for all levels of marketing teaching and scholarship. Marketing history includes, but is not limited to, the histories of advertising, retailing, channels of distribution, product design and branding, pricing strategies, and consumption behavior – all studied from the perspective of companies, industries, or even whole economies. The history of marketing thought examines marketing ideas, concepts, theories, and schools of marketing thought including the lives and times of marketing thinkers.

This series aims to be the central location for the publication of historical studies of marketing theory, thought, and practice, and welcomes contributions from scholars from all disciplines that seek to explore some facet of marketing and consumer practice in a rigorous and scholarly fashion. It will also consider historical contributions that are conceptually and theoretically well-conceived, that engage with marketing theory and practice, in any time period, in any country.

Pioneering African-American Women in the Advertising Business

Biographies of MAD Black WOMEN

Judy Foster Davis

Routledge
Taylor & Francis Group
LONDON AND NEW YORK

First published in paperback 2018

First published 2016
by Routledge
2 Park Square, Milton Park, Abingdon, Oxon OX14 4RN

and by Routledge
711 Third Avenue, New York, NY 10017

Routledge is an imprint of the Taylor & Francis Group, an informa business

British Library Cataloguing-in-Publication Data
A catalogue record for this book is available from the British Library

Library of Congress Cataloging-in-Publication Data
Names: Davis, Judy Foster, author.
Title: Pioneering African-American women in the advertising business : biographies of mad black women / by Judy Foster Davis.
Description: New York : Routledge, 2016. | Series: Routledge studies in the history of marketing ; 3 | Includes bibliographical references and index.
Identifiers: LCCN 2016030170| ISBN 9781138918313 (hardback : alk. paper) | ISBN 9781315688619 (ebook)
Subjects: LCSH: Advertising executives–United States–Biography. | African American women executives–United States–Biography. | Advertising–United States–History.
Classification: LCC HF5810.A2 .D39 2016 | DDC 659.1092/520973–dc23 LC record available at https://lccn.loc.gov/2016030170

ISBN: 978-1-138-91831-3 (hbk)
ISBN: 978-0-8153-6992-9 (pbk)
ISBN: 978-1-315-68861-9 (ebk)

Typeset in Bembo
by Wearset Ltd, Boldon, Tyne and Wear

This book is dedicated to the memory of the three extraordinary women who raised me – my mother, Mrs. B. Janice Merritt; my aunt, Dr. E. Barbara Wilson; and my great-grandmother "Mee-Mee", Bessie R. Wilson. They instilled in me a love of the knowledge of the history of our people, often passed down to the family through Mee-Mee's great gift for storytelling. Their memories sustained and encouraged me through this journey. May they Rest in Heaven.

Contents

Figures

Tables

Acknowledgments

Publication of this book would not have been possible without the help of some wonderful people and institutions. I am very grateful for their support and encouragement of this project. I apologize in advance if I have overlooked anyone in this acknowledgment.

First, I thank Dr. Brian Jones and Dr. Mark Tadajewski, editors of the *Studies in the History of Marketing* series, who appreciated my work submitted to the CHARM (Conference on Historical Analysis and Research in Marketing) meetings and encouraged me to write this book. I am also humbled at how the CHARM Association and the Macromarketing Society embraced my research over the years, inspiring me to continue to do research in this topic area.

I am also very appreciative of the support provided to me by the Graduate School and Provost's Office of Eastern Michigan University (EMU), which provided me with financial support and much needed release time in the form of a Faculty Research Fellowship and sabbatical in order to complete this book. I am especially thankful for the assistance provided by the EMU Faculty Development Center and its Director, Dr. Peggy Leggit, who gave valuable feedback allowing me to obtain institutional support on my first attempt. I am also indebted to my EMU department and College of Business colleagues who shared helpful advice and insights, including Dr. Sheila Sasser and the late Dr. Dawn Pearcy. I also thank my graduate assistant, Kim David, who worked diligently doing proofreading, copy editing, and formatting of the chapter drafts and citations, while providing valuable commentary.

Historical research cannot be conducted without access to primary documents and information which are often rare and hard to find. Since 2002, I have been fortunate to be able to work with the staffs of some of the best archival depositories in the world, including the National Museum of American History at the Smithsonian Institution, the Schomberg Center for Research in Black Culture in New York City, the Chicago Historical Society, and the Hartman Center for Sales, Advertising & Marketing History at Duke University. Since documentation concerning the history of African-Americans in advertising is not centrally located, I am particularly grateful for the insights of Jacqueline Reid Wachholz, Director of the Hartman Center collections. I am appreciative to the staff at the CBS-TV network which provided materials concerning the *60 Minutes* segment featuring Barbara Proctor. I also acknowledge the assistance of the late Bill Sharp, who provided me with background information and articles concerning the Basic Advertising Course and a copy of his 1969 book *How to be Black and Get a Job in the Advertising Agency Business Anyway*. These materials allowed me to accurately recreate personal histories.

This research could not be completed without the cooperation of a number of individuals. I thank the living subjects profiled in this book, along with subjects' family members and ad industry colleagues who helped to "fill in the gaps" when the materials trail was exhausted. To that end, I thank Carol H. Williams and Joel P. Martin for sharing with me firsthand about their experiences in the advertising business; Morgan Proctor, Tony R. Jones, and Carol Hood, Jr. for providing important insights about their mothers; Suzanne Stantley, Sarah Burroughs, and several other anonymous women who provided important perspective regarding the subjects, the advertising industry, and their own experiences in advertising. I also thank Brian Welburn, Gracie Turner, Tesha Williams, Carol Wyatt, and Jordan Bizell of the Carol H. Williams Advertising agency for facilitating timely access to critical information and materials. I also thank my friend and fellow Cass Technician, Pamela R. Hall Purifoy, for cheerleading this work and introducing me to Tony Jones; along with my sisters in Delta Sigma Theta Sorority, Inc. who championed this project.

I am very appreciative to the advertisers who allowed their brands to be showcased in this unique study, including: New Albertson's for Jewel Food Stores; Kraft Foods; the Prudential Insurance Company; Anheuser-Busch, Inc.; Procter & Gamble; and the General Motors (GM) Corporation. I am also thankful to Adriane Gaines, Terrie Williams, and Joel Martin, former Executive Directors with the CEBA Awards program and journal and the Black-Owned Communications Alliance (BOCA), respectively, for helping me to access and include CEBA and BOCA materials in this publication.

Finally, I appreciate the support and patience of my family, especially my husband Raymond P. Davis, when I traveled to collect information for this research and spent long hours engaged in writing the manuscript; my son Christopher, who helped with the digital photographs which appear in this book; and my daughter Elena, who supported me with smiles and hugs.

I love you all!

Abbreviations

4 A's	American Association of Advertising Agencies
AAF	American Advertising Federation
AARP	American Association of Retired Persons
BAC	Basic Advertising Course
BBD&O	Batten Barton Durstine and Osborne agency
BCG	Black Creative Group
BOCA	Black Owned Communications Alliance
CEBA	Communications Excellence for Black Audiences
CHWA	Carol H. Williams Advertising agency
CORE	Congress for Racial Equality
CPUC	California Public Utilities Commission
DDB	Doyle Dane Bernbach agency
EMU	Eastern Michigan University
FCB	Foote, Cone and Belding agency
FCC	Federal Communications Commission
GAP	Group for Advertising Progress
GM	General Motors
IPG	Interpublic Group of Companies
JMCT	Jordan, McGrath, Case and Taylor
JWT	J. Walter Thompson agency
KFC	Kentucky Fried Chicken
NAACP	National Association for the Advancement of Colored People
NAMD	National Association of Market Developers
NYCCHR	New York City Commission on Human Rights
O&M	Ogilvy & Mather agency
R&B	rhythm and blues
SBA	Small Business Administration
SMG	Starcom MediaVest Group
STEM	science, technology, engineering, and math
WASP	white, Anglo-Saxon Protestant
WRG	Wells, Rich, Greene agency
Y&R	Young & Rubicam agency

Introduction

Black women and Madison Avenue

Mad Men, the popular award-winning television series which dramatizes the lives and careers of men and women who work in a fictional 1960s-era New York City advertising agency, ended its seven-season run on the AMC-TV network in May 2015. Praised by many observers for its historical authenticity and stylistic accuracy of the period, the series offered an intriguing look into the workplace culture of the advertising business up until the early 1970s. A particularly interesting aspect of *Mad Men* was the show's treatment of women and ethnic minorities, including the very limited role of African-American women in the advertising workplace. The final episodes of *Mad Men* were greeted with great fanfare and widespread publicity as many viewers mourned the program's conclusion. However, while nostalgic retrospectives flowed freely, some reminiscences about the show and its setting were unsettling. On the occasion of the series finale, *Mad Men* creator Matthew Weiner was asked by trade publication *Advertising Age* to provide his opinion about the most surprising aspects of the advertising business. Weiner responded (Bruell, 2015):

> "You know what was shocking to me? How late African-Americans came into the game, and how they're still not there. There were black agencies, and I could've focused on that segregated aspect, which I didn't, but it never happened. And it still hasn't happened. And there are pioneers, and there are obviously plenty of talented African-Americans. All of my feelings about how white it was, and how male it was, were understatements."

Mad Men's fictional setting illuminated a harsh truth about the real-world advertising business: historically, professional career opportunities for people of color and women – especially in managerial and executive roles – have been extremely low. Although contemporary advertising is more than a $540 billion global industry (eMarketer, 2014), its poor track record regarding diversity among its professional ranks has been called its "dirty little secret" (Winski, 1992, p. 16). The low rates of black participation in the advertising industry have drawn particular scrutiny and little seemed to change over time. For example, in the mid-1960s, *Advertising Age* ran a headline declaring:

"Negro Has Precarious Foothold in Agency Field" (Feehery, 1966) and, 42 years later, *Adweek* magazine referred to the industry as "a poster child for a dearth of diversity" (Newman, 2008). Employment statistics published in 1968 concerning 35 large New York ad agencies placed the overall "Negro" and "Puerto Rican" employment rates at 5.1 percent and 1.8 percent, respectively; among 16,062 total employees, with most positions concentrated in clerical jobs; moreover, African-Americans held less than 1 percent of managerial roles – or just four jobs out of a total of 415 management positions (City of New York, 1968, p. 5). By 2009, a report showed that black advertising professionals and managers combined accounted for 5.3 percent of the industry's total employment (Bendick and Egan, 2009) and a 2012 *New York Times* article showed that of the 78,000 Americans working as advertising and promotion managers, 9.6 percent were Hispanic, 2.3 percent were Asian, and fewer than 1 percent were African-American (Vega, 2012). These figures underscored a low rate of industry participation and nearly no improvement for African-Americans over 40-plus years. Since the 1960s, various stakeholders and activist groups, including members of the U.S. Congress, the U.S. Equal Employment Opportunity Commission, the New York City Commission on Human Rights (NYCCHR), the National Urban League, and the NAACP (National Association for the Advancement of Colored People) repeatedly confronted Adland's diversity problem. Over the years these efforts prompted the establishment of numerous industry-sponsored, university and independent programs to encourage, recruit, train, and retain diverse peoples for advertising careers. In 2009, the NAACP and a prominent civil rights attorney launched the Madison Avenue Project – an initiative intended to prompt changes in employment practices in advertising firms – including the threat of a class action discrimination lawsuit aimed at the advertising industry (Patel, 2010). While there has been recent improvement in placements of young college graduates of color in entry-level advertising jobs, it is acknowledged that black advertising professionals often encounter significant challenges in their career trajectories (Bush, 2011; Vega, 2012).

In addition to diversity issues concerning people of color, academic and trade sources revealed long-standing concerns regarding gender equality in the advertising industry, resulting in restricted career opportunities for women, especially with respect to high-level managerial positions (Mallia, 2009; Maclaran, Stephens, and Catterall, 1997; Still, 1986). Claiming that women comprised only 3 percent of advertising Creative Directors, in 2012 adwoman Kat Gordon founded the "3% Conference" – an organization which champions women to assume high-level creative positions and leadership roles in advertising firms (3% Conference, 2015). According to industry insiders, these and other efforts helped the proportion of women in creative leadership to rise to 11 percent by 2015, a significant increase (Batthany, 2015). Although white women fared better than African-Americans in advertising careers, a 2013 industry survey published in *Advertising Age* revealed considerable levels of dissatisfaction among women in the industry, in contrast to the attitudes of men (Liesse, 2013). The survey included nearly 1,000 responses – 55 percent from men and 45 percent from women – with about 70 percent of the respondents working at agencies and 30 percent working for client organizations. Statistically, women represented half of the advertising workforce while men held 68 percent of the management jobs. Interestingly, 75 percent of the women believed that gender issues were a problem in the industry, and analysis suggested that the relative paucity of women in top executive positions was obscured by the overall high participation rate of women in advertising jobs. Heide Gardner, Senior Vice President for Diversity and Inclusion for the Interpublic Group, noted that men may not view gender parity as an issue in advertising, explaining (Liesse, 2013, p. 10):

> "I am not surprised that men don't see this as a problem. Unlike racial or ethnic diversity, they see plenty of women working in marketing, and, when they do, they aren't thinking about the level or titles of the women. They think the system is a pure meritocracy and it works as it should."

Concerns about diversity in advertising careers are not limited to the United States. Research by Arnberg and Svanlund (2016), Davis (2015), Knight (2013), and the United Kingdom's Institute of Advertising Practitioners (Hall, 2011) reveals low employment levels and/or restrictions in professional roles among women and people of color in Europe and South Africa, suggesting that the problem is a widespread and vexing global issue. Taken together, the background on people of color and women in advertising suggest that opportunities for high-level positions in the industry for black women have been and remain extremely rare.

Mad Men's black women

The roles of women who work in advertising are a conspicuous and much-discussed aspect of the *Mad Men* television series. Set in the fictitious Sterling Cooper advertising agency, most women's characters are limited to clerical positions, except for office manager "Joan Harris" – the agency's ace problem-solver – and "Peggy Olsen" – the naïve secretary who evolves into ambitious copywriter and Creative Department supervisor. About mid-way through the series, the real-world minority hiring issue surfaces in *Mad Men*. In response to Civil Rights pressures exerted upon the advertising industry in the 1960s, two African-American female characters named "Dawn" and "Shirley" are eventually hired as secretaries by the Sterling Cooper agency. While other black people appear in the *Mad Men* series – usually in domestic or servant capacities – Dawn and Shirley are the only black employees of Sterling Cooper. Dawn is the first black person hired around 1966 and remained the sole black employee for a few years. While Dawn is highly competent at her job, she is repeatedly put into uncomfortable work situations by white colleagues who ask her to perform dubious tasks such as punching another's time card or acting as an informant. These treatments subtly indicate that Dawn is viewed as powerless and subject to exploitation, leaving her in a perpetual state of fear that she might be terminated at any time over some real or alleged infraction. Outside of the office, Dawn confides to her best friend about the dysfunctional work climate and how she feels lonely and alienated as the only black agency employee (*Mad Men*, 2013). However, Dawn eventually learns to shrewdly navigate the politics of the office and uses these insights to slightly improve her position at the agency.

Shirley, hired toward the end of the 1960s, is very different from Dawn. While both women are competent and articulate, Dawn is mild-mannered and conservative in appearance – wearing modest dresses and a straightened and softly curled hairstyle. Shirley is more expressive and opinionated. She wears brightly colored mini-dresses and an Afro hairstyle – a look popular among liberal black people and proponents of the Black Power movement. Despite their obvious differences, many of the agency colleagues seem not to distinguish between the two women, as if they are interchangeable, and Dawn and Shirley create an inside joke out of this situation. In one scene where they both happen to be in the coffee break room along with a white co-worker, Dawn repeatedly calls Shirley "Dawn" and Shirley calls Dawn "Shirley" in a pronounced and affected manner (*Mad Men*, 2014). The co-worker does not notice the name mix-up or acknowledge Dawn and Shirley's presences. In this setting, Dawn and Shirley appear to be marginalized as invisible women, unworthy of respect or even mere recognition as individuals by their peers. In another similarly awkward situation, Shirley's fiancé sends her flowers at the office, but Shirley's white supervisor, Peggy Olsen, mistakenly assumes they are for her and makes a fuss about them. This scenario suggests that Peggy fails to see Shirley as an individual with a life outside of the office. When the flower delivery snafu is finally straightened out, Peggy – embarrassed and angry – demands that Shirley be reassigned to another supervisor. This sets up a bizarre sequence of "musical desks" among several secretaries including Dawn – who had no role in the flower mix-up – being assigned to the only desk still available in the office: the main reception desk. However, when Cooper, one of the principals of the agency, learns that a black woman is to be seated at the entrance to the agency, he immediately declares the new arrangement "unsuitable" (*Mad Men*, 2014). The conclusion drawn from *Mad Men* is that the professional role of black women in advertising is to remain inconspicuous, accepting inferior status in the workplace.

In a final episode of *Mad Men*, Shirley makes a profound statement from a black woman's perspective. The Sterling Cooper agency has been acquired by the real-life McCann Erickson agency and most of the principals and staff are relocating to new offices. However, Shirley has resigned to take a job with an insurance company. Speaking with her boss, Roger Sterling, she explains that it is her last day and she will not be joining the others at the new agency. Incredulous, Roger asks why she is not going. Shirley replies matter-of-factly: "Advertising is not a very comfortable place for everyone" (*Mad Men*, 2015). Hearing Shirley's comment, Roger's expression is one of stunned perplexity. Shirley exits the scene, the last black agency employee to appear in the *Mad Men* series. Yet, her final and revealing statement underscored an unpleasant truth for African-American women in the advertising workplace.

Adland's real-life black women

Despite Dawn and Shirley's limited roles in *Mad Men* and the real-world diversity issues in the advertising business, a small number of African-American women entered advertising in the 1960s and led very prominent advertising careers. They served in pioneering executive and entrepreneurial roles, culminating in the establishment of their own respected advertising agencies. These women's stories are important to the study of the history of advertising, yet scholars have paid limited attention to their experiences and contributions. Living at the intersection of race and gender, their circumstances were unique given Adland's institutional culture. However, their roles have not been fully documented or understood, but they offer valuable insights for scholars and practitioners. While advertising is a relatively small industry in terms of the number of people it employs, it is an influential profession which projects cultural norms and social values. Thus, the creators of advertising are as important as advertising content itself with respect to the ad industry's history, impact and reflections of society. As such, the stories of black women's participation in the advertising business must be included in the historical narrative.

This study provides a comprehensive examination of the professional careers of pioneering African-American women who served in prominent managerial and entrepreneurial roles in the advertising business over a 50-year period from the early 1960s to about 2010. This research chronicles the nature and significance of these women's accomplishments, examines the opportunities and challenges they experienced, and explores how they coped with inequities common in the advertising profession. The main subjects of this research are: Barbara Gardner Proctor (1932–), Caroline Robinson Jones (1942–2001), Joel P. Martin (1944–), and Carol H. Williams (1950–). These four women are recognized as having achieved exceptional success in the advertising business, serving in ground-breaking roles in corporate and entrepreneurial settings against a backdrop of systemic discrimination. Proctor was the first African-American woman to establish an advertising agency, founded in Chicago in 1970. Her career accomplishments were recognized by the Smithsonian Institution and by former U.S. President Ronald Reagan. Jones, in the mid-1970s, was the first black woman hired as a Vice President at a major general-market advertising agency and later founded her own agency in New York City. Jones was named, posthumously, by *Advertising Age* in 2012 as one of the "100 most influential women in advertising." Martin was one of the first black female Creative Directors at a general-market agency in the 1960s and was the first African-American women to open a full-service ad agency, in New York City in 1974. Williams, who remains active as CEO of her own advertising agency, was the first black woman to serve as Creative Director and Senior Vice President at two large general-market advertising agencies. Since setting up her own agency in the late 1980s, Williams' firm has consistently ranked among the top earning black-owned advertising agencies in the business (*Black Enterprise*, 2012) and she is widely considered an icon within the advertising industry. Beyond the main subjects, other pioneering black adwomen are referenced in this study.

Significance of this study

This research fills a gap in the scholarship which has mostly ignored the experiences of black women in the advertising profession. While there are many studies on the history of advertising and biographies of important advertising practitioners, African-American women have been largely left out of the literature. For example, Applegate's (1994) biographical dictionary of 54 important historical advertising figures includes nine women and one black man, but no black women. Widely cited advertising historian Stephen Fox (1984) provides passing references to black adwoman Joyce Hamer in his popular book *The Mirror Makers*, but makes no mention of other important African-American adwomen of the era. Scholars Dates and Barlow (1990) and Walker (1998) briefly reference Proctor and Jones in their discussions of African-Americans in advertising. Professor Jason Chambers (2008) supplied the most comprehensive scholarly examination of the experiences and contributions of black advertising professionals in his exemplary and groundbreaking book, *Madison Avenue and the Color Line: African-Americans in the Advertising Industry*. However, the subjects of his research are overwhelmingly male and less attention was focused on black adwomen and their unique experiences in the industry. Sivulka (2009) discusses Jones, Proctor, and Williams, respectively, over less than a dozen pages in *Ad Women: How They Impact What We Need, Want, and Buy*. In sum, Proctor, Jones, and Williams have received limited attention in the academic literature and Martin has not been studied. I have conducted much of the other scholarship in this topic area, including a study of the development of black-owned advertising agencies between 1940 and 2000 (Davis, 2002), the role of black professionals in cultivating the black consumer market among mainstream corporations (Davis, 2013b), and earlier studies concerning pioneering adwoman Caroline Jones (Davis, 2003; Davis, 2007; Davis, 2013a).

African-American adwomen have not only been overlooked by most advertising scholars and historians, but among industry practitioners as well. Although they received numerous industry awards and recognitions, over the time frame addressed in this study – 1960–2010 – no black adwoman was ever inducted into the Advertising Hall of Fame, which is considered "the most prestigious award bestowed in the advertising industry honoring individuals" (AAF.org, 2015). Sponsored by the American Advertising Federation (AAF), by 2010, only 14 women and ten African-American men were included in this esteemed group out of a total of more than 200 inductees (see Table I.1). This omission prompted questions: (1) On what basis are individuals bestowed this prestigious recognition? and (2) Have black adwomen been ignored, dismissed, or forgotten? According to the AAF, Advertising Hall of Fame invitations are based on the following criteria (AAF.org, 2015):

> "Induction into the Advertising Hall of Fame is reserved for men and women from the United States or abroad who have had exceptionally distinguished and extraordinary careers, have completed their primary careers or have had careers spanning at least 35 years, and who, through and in their professional lives and community involvement, have made outstanding and notable contributions to the profession of advertising and its reputation, have consistently practiced the highest ethical standards, and have contributed substantially to their communities."

Advertising Hall of Fame inductees are nominated and selected by industry peers. After 2010, six more African-Americans were inducted – including the first woman – in 2015. As this book was being written, the Hall of Fame *finally* inducted its first African-American woman – Catherine "Cathy" Hughes, prominent founder of the Radio One and TV One companies. Hughes, the first black woman in the U.S. to head a publicly traded company (History Makers.com, 2015), is unquestionably qualified and deserving of this recognition. However, she rose through the media ownership ranks, not advertising. Therefore, it remains at this writing that no black adwoman has been invited to the Advertising Hall of Fame.

Research method and justification

This study applies a biographical narrative method approach to study the subjects' lives and careers using primary sources as much as possible. Described by professors Jones (2012) and Savitt (2011), this method is used by marketing historians to conduct research concerning the experiences, practices, and ideas of marketing practitioners. This approach requires the systematic collection, synthesis, and analysis of relevant primary and secondary information obtained from the subjects and other appropriate sources. Typically, the information falls into four categories pertaining to the subjects: (1) personal data such as information about their backgrounds, family structure, and upbringing; (2) intellectual data relating to education, professional training, and experience; (3) professional data, including career-related events, activities, and experiences; and (4) environmental data which indicate social and economic conditions during the subjects' lives. With this type of research, historical books, and trade and newspaper articles are important primary

Table I.1 Women and African-American members of the AAF Advertising Hall of Fame, 1948–2015*

Women inducted	*African-Americans inducted*
1952 – Erma Perham Proetz (posthumously)	1996 – Frank Mingo (posthumously)
1967 – Helen Landowne Resor (posthumously)	2002 – John H. Johnson
1980 – Shirley Polykoff	2004 – Thomas J. Burrell
1981 – Bernice Fitz-Gibbon	2006 – Robert L. Johnson
1989 – Jean Wade Rindlaub	2007 – Vincent T. Cullers (posthumously)
1996 – Jo Foxworth	2007 – Billy Davis (posthumously)
1997 – Gertrude Crain (posthumously)	2007 – Bruce Gordon
1998 – Janet L. Wolff	2009 – Clarence Holte (posthumously)
1999 – Mary Wells Lawrence	2009 – William "Bill" Sharp
2000 – Patricia Martin	2010 – Roy Eaton
2001 – Katharine Graham	2011 – Earl G. Graves, Sr.
2008 – Andrea Alstrup	2012 – Jonathan A. Rodgers
2009 – Charlotte Beers	2013 – Byron Lewis
2010 – Geraldine B. Laybourne	2014 – Ed Lewis
2011 – Laurel Cutler	2015 – Spike Lee
2012 – Tere A. Zubizarreta (posthumously)	
2013 – Shelley Lazarus	
2014 – Jane Newman	
2015 – Linda Kaplan Thaler	
2015 – Catherine L. "Cathy" Hughes	

Source: American Advertising Federation, www.aaf.org.

Note
* Inducted 237 individuals between 1948 and 2015.

sources of information regarding environmental context. In addition, suitable secondary literature is reviewed to provide appropriate historical background concerning important major social shifts and events during the lifetimes of the subjects which impacted their career circumstances and choices. For the time period under study, important events include the U.S. Civil Rights Movement, the Women's Liberation Movement, the Black Power and Black Pride movements, corporate interest in black consumers, and the emergence of multiculturalism as a marketing orientation.

Biographical study involves the process of compelling storytelling with a consideration of the people involved, beyond mere recitation of facts (Savitt, 2011). This approach requires a cogent recreation of key events during the subjects' lives, an indication of the significance of these events, and analysis and explanation of the causes and consequences of those events. Historical biography helps researchers comprehend subjects' motivations and personalities and assists in explaining the conditions which influenced their ideas and behaviors including social, economic, and political environments (Jones, 2012). As such, historical biography is an appropriate method for analyzing the professional opportunities, behaviors, and contributions of the subjects for this study. This method is particularly suitable when the number of subjects is small, as in the study conducted here.

Research materials, sources, and implications

The data referenced in this study were obtained from a number of sources including archival and library materials; memories derived from personal interviews with available subjects, colleagues, and family members; articles from the trade and popular press; books and documents, audio and video recordings including content available online. These materials include:

1. Caroline Jones' personal and business papers and artifacts obtained from the National Museum of American History at the Smithsonian in Washington, D.C. and interviews and social media interactions with a family member and advertising industry colleagues.
2. Documents archived at the Chicago Historical Society's Research Center and interviews with former colleagues and a family member concerning Barbara Proctor. Although Proctor is retired and unavailable for personal interviews, there is sufficient evidence to produce a coherent biography from available print, video, and interview sources.
3. Personal interviews with Carol H. Williams, colleagues, and family members at her agency offices in Chicago during June 2014 and subsequent information obtained via telephone, email, social media, and the internet.
4. Interviews with Dr. Joel P. Martin, conducted during February 2015 via telephone and email.
5. Telephone interviews with Sarah Burroughs, Suzanne Stantley, and other African-American adwomen who served in important managerial roles in advertising.
6. Numerous articles, documents, audio and video recordings, and advertisements pertaining to all subjects from public sources including the Schomberg Center for Black Culture in New York City, trade publications, popular magazines, and newspapers in hard copy or downloaded from the internet.

The intent of this study is to tell the stories of African-American adwomen in their own voices such that their histories are preserved and available to future generations interested in understanding black women's experiences in the advertising profession. The circumstances of the subjects in this book serve as important barometers concerning career development and opportunities for black women in advertising – past, present, and future. The study of history helps individuals prepare for the future by understanding the past. Since few publications exist which address the distinctive challenges of black women in this profession, this study provides insights, information, and strategies – which are not otherwise readily available elsewhere – in a comprehensive source. Publication of this research complements other efforts which seek to understand the diversity problem in the advertising industry and issues related to systemic discrimination in the industry. As such, this research provides a bridge from the past to the future by addressing contemporary problems and offering valuable insights and information for scholars, practitioners, and others interested in understanding the advertising business, especially as it relates to women of color.

Layout of this book

In order to understand the significance of the careers and accomplishments of the pioneering African-American advertising women examined in this study, their experiences must first be presented in appropriate historical context. To that end, the organization of this book is as follows:

1 Chapter 1 provides a review of the literature concerning an historical overview of the evolution of the advertising industry in the United States from the 1800s into the early 2000s, followed by a detailed summary of the collective experiences of white women and African-Americans, respectively, in the advertising business from an historical perspective based on academic and trade sources. References to portrayals of women and African-Americans employed in the advertising industry in relevant pop culture settings are also included in order to provide perspectives on the advertising business.
2 Chapters 2 through 5 provide biographical profiles, respectively, of four African-American women who are the primary subjects of this research: Barbara Gardner Proctor, Caroline R. Jones, Joel P. Martin, and Carol H. Williams. They entered the advertising business during the 1960s, served in ground-breaking professional positions in general-market advertising firms *and* went on to establish advertising agencies bearing their own names. Regarded among the most successful black women in advertising, their opportunities, challenges, and accomplishments are presented and analyzed with respect to available personal, intellectual, professional, and environmental data, with emphasis on career-related events, activities, and experiences using a biographical narrative approach. Information concerning relevant social and economic conditions during their lives is included for appropriate context.
3 Chapter 6 draws on findings from the subjects' experiences to explain why their careers evolved as they did. In addition, information pertaining to other notable black adwomen is included to provide important context. These women had important experiences and made significant contributions to the field and therefore stand to be recognized as part of the historical record concerning professional black women in advertising. This analysis is grounded in the model of Structural Oppression, a theoretical construct which identifies a variety of discriminatory practices

commonly exercised in the workplace which impact the opportunities and choices of women and African-Americans in the advertising business, with unique implications for African-American women.

4 An Epilogue provides summary conclusions and insights concerning the subjects and other black women's experiences in the advertising business. Adland's ongoing struggle with diversity and inclusion is also discussed.

References

3% Conference (2015) Organization website. Available at: www.3percentconf.com (Accessed: June 2, 2015).

AAF.org (2015) 'Advertising Hall of Fame' [Online]. Available at: http://advertising-hall.org/history/index.html (Accessed: June 3, 2015).

Advertising Age (2012) 'The 100 Most Influential Women in Advertising,' September 24, Front Cover and p. 28.

Applegate, E. (1994) *The Ad Men and Women: A Biographical Dictionary of Advertising*. Westport, CT: Greenwood Press.

Arnberg, K. and Svanlund, J. (2016) 'Mad Women: Gendered Divisions in the Swedish Advertising Industry, 1930–2012,' *Business History*, 58 [Online]. Available at: www.tandfonline.com/doi/abs/10.1080/00076791.2016.1182158 (Accessed: May 25, 2016).

Batthany, J. (2015) 'The Tough Reality Facing an Advertising Mother of the Year,' *Advertising Age*, May 8 [Online]. Available at: http://adage.com/article/agency-viewpoint/tough-reality-facing-advertising-mother-year/298478 (Accessed: May 18, 2015).

Bendick, M. and Egan, M. (2009) 'Research Perspectives on Race and Employment in the Advertising Industry,' Washington, D.C. Bendick and Egan Economic Consultants [Online]. Available at: www.bendickegan.com/pdf/2009/Bendick%20Egan%20Advertising%20Industry%20Report%20Jan%2009.pdf (Accessed: February 20, 2015).

Black Enterprise (2012) 'B.E. Advertising Agencies,' June, p. 128.

Bruell, A. (2015) 'Interview: Matthew Weiner Takes on an Era, the Ad Industry and TV,' *Advertising Age*, May 4 [Online]. Available at: adage.com/article/agency-news/matthew-weiner-advertising/298377 (Accessed: May 4, 2015).

Bush, M. (2011) 'Sorry State of Diversity in Advertising is also a Culture Problem,' *Advertising Age*, January 31 [Online]. Available at: adage.com/print/14865 (Accessed: October 10, 2013).

Chambers, J. (2008) *Madison Avenue and the Color Line: African-Americans in the Advertising Industry*. Philadelphia, PA: University of Pennsylvania Press.

City of New York (1968) *Report: Affirmative Action Follow-up to Advertising and Broadcasting Hearing*. City of New York Commission on Human Rights, November.

Dates, J. and Barlow, W. (1990) *Split Image: African-Americans in the Mass Media*. Washington, D.C.: Howard University Press.

Davis, J. F. (2002) 'Enterprise Development under an Economic Detour? Black-Owned Advertising Agencies 1940–2000,' *Journal of Macromarketing*, 22(1), pp. 75–85.

Davis, J. F. (2003) 'Caroline Robinson Jones: Advertising Trailblazer, Entrepreneur and Tragic Heroine,' *Proceedings of the 11th Conference on Historical Analysis and Research in Marketing (CHARM)*, Eric Shaw, Ed., pp. 210–219.

Davis, J. F. (2007) 'Aunt Jemima is Alive and Cookin'? An Advertiser's Dilemma of Competing Collective Memories,' *Journal of Macromarketing*, 27(1), pp. 25–37.

Davis, J. F. (2013a) 'Beyond "Caste-typing"? Caroline Robinson Jones, Advertising Pioneer and Trailblazer,' *Journal of Historical Research in Marketing*, Special Issue: Remembering female contributors to marketing theory, thought and practice, 5(3), pp. 308–333.

Davis, J. F. (2013b) 'Realizing Marketplace Opportunity: How Research on the Black Consumer Market Influenced Mainstream Marketers, 1920–1970,' *Journal of Historical Research in Marketing*, 5(4), pp. 471–473.

Davis, T. (2015) 'Women in Advertising Creative Departments in South Africa: Restricting Factors and Empowerment.' A thesis presented to the Department of Journalism & Communications and the Robert D. Clark Honors College, June [Online]. Available at: https://scholarsbank.uoregon.edu/xmlui/bitstream/handle/1794/19067/Thesis%20 Final-Davis.pdf?sequence=1 (Accessed: November 29, 2015).

eMarketer (2014) 'Global Ad Spending Growth to Double This Year, 2012–2018,' July 9 [Online]. Available at: www.emarketer.com/Articles/Print.aspx?R=1010997 (Accessed: April 1, 2015).

Feehery, J. (1966) 'Negro has Precarious Foothold in Agency Field, 3: City Survey Shows,' *Advertising Age*, October 17, pp. 3, 44.

Fox, S. (1984) *The Mirror Makers: A History of American Advertising and its Creators*. New York: Morrow.

Hall, E. (2011) 'Only 5.3% of Actors in U.K. TV Commercials are Minorities, Study Finds,' August [Online]. Available at: http://adage.com/article/global-news/5-3-actors-u-k-tv-commercials-minorities/227134/ (Accessed: October 7, 2013).

Historymakers.com (2015) 'Cathy Hughes' [Online]. Available at: www.thehistorymakers.com/biography/cathy-hughes-39e] (Accessed: December 8, 2015).

Jones, B. D. G. (2012) *Pioneers in Marketing: A Collection of Biographical Essays*. New York: Routledge.

Knight, C. (2013) *Mad Women: A Herstory of Advertising*. Linkoping, Sweden: Olika Publishing House Ltd.

Liesse, J. (2013) 'Women in Advertising: The Agency Challenge,' *Advertising Age*, July 22, pp. 10–11.

Maclaran, P., Stevens, L., and Catterall, M. (1997) 'The "Glasshouse Effect": Women in Marketing Management,' *Marketing Intelligence and Planning*, 15(7) pp. 309–317.

Mad Men (2013) AMC-TV, 'To Have and To Hold,' April 1.

Mad Men (2014) AMC-TV, 'A Day's Work,' April 20.

Mad Men (2015) AMC-TV, 'Lost Horizon,' May 3.

Mallia, K. (2009) 'Rare Birds: Why So Few Women Become Ad Agency Creative Directors,' *Advertising and Society Review*, 10(3) [Online]. Available at: www.aef.com/on_campus/asr/contents (Accessed: February 12, 2012).

Newman, A. (2008) 'The Minority Report,' *Adweek*, December 1 [Online]. Available at: www.adweek.com/news/advertising-branding/minority-report-97659 (Accessed: May 15, 2015).

Patel, K. (2010) 'Cyrus Mehri Filing EEOC Charges Against Advertising Companies,' *Advertising Age*, February 10 [Online]. Available at: http://adage.com/article/news/advertising-industry-faces-eeoc-discrimination-charges/142038/ (Accessed: June 2, 2015).

Reagan, R. (1984) *Address before a Joint Session of the Congress on the State of the Union*, January 25 [Online]. Gerhard Peters and John T. Wooley, the American

Presidency Project. Available at: www.presidency.ucsb.edu/ws.?pid=40205 (Accessed: October 7, 2013).

Savitt, R. (2011) 'On Biography in Marketing,' *Journal of Historical Research in Marketing*, 3(4), pp. 486–506.

Sivulka, J. (2009) *Ad Women: How They Impact What We Need, Want, and Buy*. Amherst, NY: Prometheus Books.

Still, L. (1986) 'Women Managers in Advertising: An Exploratory Study,' *Media Information Australia*, 40(2), pp. 24–30.

Vega, T. (2012) 'With Diversity Still Lacking, Industry Focuses on Retention,' *New York Times*, September 3 [Online]. Available at: www.nytimes.com/2012/09/04/business/media/ (Accessed: October 7, 2013).

Walker, J. E. K. (1998) *The History of Black Business in America*. New York: Macmillan.

Winski, J. (1992) 'The Ad Industry's "Dirty Little Secret,"' *Advertising Age*, June 15, pp. 16–17.

1 Women and African-Americans in the advertising profession

An historical overview of the industry and people

Historical examination of opportunities for women and African-Americans in the advertising business is a study of slow improvement and persistent inequalities. In order to appreciate the history of African-American women in the advertising profession, it is useful to first understand how the advertising industry evolved and how cultures within advertising workplaces developed. This chapter summarizes an extensive body of existing literature to provide context which explains how white women, African-Americans, and African-American women, respectively, came to participate in the advertising profession, with emphasis on advertising agencies from the mid-1800s into the early 2000s. Numerous books and articles concerning the history of advertising, advertising agencies, and practitioners have been written by historians, marketing scholars, industry journalists, and biographers, although few have addressed African-American adwomen.

An industry evolves: a short history of American advertising agencies

Until about 1800, there were no advertising agencies in either Europe or America and most early institutions were established by white men. Before then, businesses – which were primarily local enterprises – dealt directly with newspapers to get advertisements published. But, as businesses began to expand their distribution of goods over wider geographic areas, entrepreneurs such as Volney B. Palmer of Philadelphia provided services on behalf of these businesses to get their ads in newspapers during the mid-1800s. This established the idea of an "agent" – a liaison between communications media and advertisers – providing a basic model which would endure into the future. Various sources point to Palmer's firm or N.W. Ayer & Son as the first advertising agency, when Nathan Wheeler Ayer and his son, Francis Wayland Ayer, took over the remains of Palmer's business in 1869. No women worked for Ayer during its first five years of existence and the first – Jennie Waterman – was briefly employed in 1874 in a clerical role (Hower, 1939, p. 536). Over time, the number of women employed at Ayer rose, but the positions were almost exclusively clerical through at least the 1930s. In 1938,

Ayer management developed a method which aided in the selection of candidates for future employment with the agency. Their goal was to identify prospects who had the appropriate ability, character, and ambition the agency wanted candidates to have before they completed school. This ensured a pipeline which included – and excluded – certain types of people. According to Hower (1939, p. 537) all prospects were men with European-sounding surnames.

The Industrial Revolution and the post-Civil War Reconstruction period brought sweeping change across America. Black slaves were freed, society became more urban, and people became more dependent on manufactured goods. Mass production and mass distribution – along with the development of chain stores and innovations in transportation and communications – led to mass marketing which promoted mass consumption. As such, in addition to Ayer, many of the largest and most venerable advertising agencies came into existence in the late 1800s to help manufacturers promote products to consumers. They included the Lord and Thomas agency (later Foote, Cone and Belding, or FCB) in 1871, the George Batten Company (later Batten Barton Durstine and Osborne, or BBD&O) in 1891, and the J. Walter Thompson agency founded by James Walter Thompson in 1878 in New York City. Thompson – or JWT – as it became known, was considered the first "modern" advertising agency, providing a full range of client services and becoming dominant in the industry. With offices across the world, it remains the oldest continuously operating global advertising agency. James Thompson introduced the phrase "it pays to advertise" and conceived the idea of a professional account executive to service clients (Mermigas, 2003, p. 1530). In 1908, Thompson hired Stanley Resor and his brother to open a branch office in Cincinnati, Ohio. Resor hired Helen Lansdowne, who had experience writing advertisements, as the office's sole copywriter. Yale-educated Resor, the first major agency chief with a college degree, advocated scientific approaches to advertising which produced predictable outcomes. Hence, JWT was the first agency to establish a research department, which became standard practice across the marketing industry. Resor had a relationship with the Procter & Gamble manufacturing company, also in Cincinnati, having previously worked at its in-house advertising department. In 1916, Resor bought out Thompson for $500,000 and became President of JWT. Resor and Helen Lansdowne married the following year and, together, they established a foundation which not only impacted the agency's culture and growth over the next 50 years, but also influenced the structure and practices of American advertising agencies. By the time the Resor retired in the early 1960s, the agency had grown to bill over $370 million annually and employed over 6,000 people in 55 offices worldwide (Applegate, 1994, p. 270). A discussion of Helen Resor's contributions to the advertising industry follows later in this chapter.

In addition to JWT, FCB, and BBD&O, other major American advertising agencies founded in the early to mid-1900s, or their derivatives, remained dominant into the twenty-first century including Darcy, Masius, Benton and Bowles (1906), Campbell Ewald (1911), Grey (1917), Young & Rubicam (1923), McCann Erickson (1930), Leo Burnett (1935), Bates (1940), Ogilvy & Mather (1948), and Doyle Dane Bernbach (1949). Historian Fox (1984) indicated that the identities, reputations, and cultures of advertising agencies were heavily influenced by the personalities and viewpoints of their founders and principals. An example was David Ogilvy, one of the most influential practitioners in advertising history, whose 1963 book *Confessions of an Advertising Man* is considered a classic in the study of advertising. Ogilvy believed in advertisements which told a sales story and gave consumers "reasons why" they should buy – seeking quantifiable results (Fox, 1984, p. 226; McDonough, 2003, p. 1157). Born in England, Ogilvy came to America to open a "British Agency" in the United States and started what became Ogilvy & Mather (O&M), one of the most successful advertising agencies of all time. Ogilvy wrote thousands of memos and policy papers to his staff reflecting his personal philosophies and was often a critic of advertising practice.

In the post-World War II period through the late 1950s, the advertising industry grew massively along with the bustling economy and ad spending more than doubled from about $5 billion to over $11 billion between 1949 and 1959. Media purchases were split among magazines, newspapers, radio, and later – television – as the proportion of households with TVs rose from 10 percent in 1950 to 90 percent by 1960, providing large audiences for advertisers. Advertising agencies grew in size and revenue along with this expansion and top advertisers included major brands such as GM, Ford Motor Company, Chrysler, Procter & Gamble, Colgate-Palmolive, Lever Brothers, Kraft General Foods, RCA, Westinghouse, and Seagram's Distillery. As such, advertising careers seemed very exciting, glamorous, and lucrative. Cracknell (2011, p. 16), an industry insider, observing professional ad men in the 1950s mused: "It was the best of times, it was the best of times. To be white, male and healthy in New York in the 1950s was to be blessed as any individual at any time in history."

Over the years, the fortunes of individual advertising agencies fluctuated with national events and economic cycles. Agencies, especially medium and small-sized firms, came and went. Agencies often faltered or lost their character when their founders departed and succession of leadership, even among family members, became problematic. Fox (1984, p. 80) observed: "finding the next generation of leaders remains a recurrent dilemma of agency management." In addition, many agencies earned reputations as male-centric white, Anglo-Saxon Protestant (WASP) enclaves where relationships predicated business opportunities. Careers in advertising became known as stressful, subject to the whims of clients and outside pressures. Moreover, as an unregulated service business, the long hours and alcohol consumption often associated with agency work took their toll, especially on agency account personnel charged with servicing clients. Cracknell (2011, p. 20) recalled a mid-1950s industry study which showed that advertising men died on average at age 57.9, about ten years sooner than the national average. Thus, in efforts to keep up workplace morale, many agencies tolerated workplace hijinks, sexual innuendo, and similar activities because they contributed to an enjoyable work environment and, thus, work satisfaction and attendance (Cracknell, 2011, p. 194).

New phenomena occurred which affected the advertising business starting in the 1960s. Demands stemming from Civil Rights and Women's Movement proponents concerning job opportunities for women and people of color exerted pressure on the industry to examine and alter its employment practices. In a major development – where virtually no agencies were publicly held in 1960 – over the next 20 years the industry witnessed the emergence of publicly held agencies, agency mergers, acquisitions, and consolidations on a large scale. By the early 1980s, many large agencies founded in earlier periods were acquired by major holding companies. In the 2000s, four holding companies dominated the global advertising scene: London-based WPP Group; New York-based Omnicom Group; New York-based Interpublic Group of Companies (IPG); and Paris-based Publicis Groupe. In addition, two other smaller holding companies – France-based Havas and Tokyo-based Dentsu – rounded out the top six. Therefore, in the new millennium, the ad industry had transformed from an industry mostly characterized by entrepreneurial, independent firms led by personable leaders, into an oligopoly of huge holding company conglomerates with responsibilities to stockholders and other stakeholders. Reflecting on the industry's past, journalist Joe Cappo (2003, p. 13) noted: "The advertising business was more personal then. The entrepreneurial head of an agency often had close personal ties, even friendships, with the entrepreneurial head of a major client." By the early 2000s, 56 of the 100 largest U.S. agencies were owned by publicly traded holding companies and represented 82 percent of the billings among the top 100 agencies (Chura and Cuneo, 2001). On the client side, mainstream companies were also involved in numerous merger, acquisition, and consolidation activities. Therefore, a shift toward the corporatization of marketing had a major impact on advertising agencies, their cultures, and professional opportunities in advertising.

Women advertising pioneers and entrepreneurs

Background concerning women's careers in advertising indicates that women historically had limited choices concerning career paths and advancement opportunities, like those illustrated by the female characters in the *Mad Men* television series. *Mad Men*'s popularity inspired real-life practitioners like Andrew Cracknell (2011) and Jane Maas (2012) to publish firsthand accounts of their observations on the advertising industry. Maas, one of a small number of adwomen who served in executive and entrepreneurial positions during the 1960s to 1980s, provided eye-opening accounts concerning industry practices. Academic scholars found that women in advertising often faced career barriers, using terms like "glass ceiling," "Glasshouse Effect," and similar terms to describe women's experiences (Alvesson, 1998; Maclaran, Stephens, and Catterall, 1997; Mallia, 2009; Still, 1986). Historians published histories of women's involvements in the industry and biographies of important advertising women; and a few pioneering adwomen wrote autobiographies. These materials provide excellent insights into the evolution of women's roles in the advertising profession.

The 1880s to 1920s: trailblazing advertising women

Some of the earliest white adwomen entered the profession and served in non-clerical or entrepreneurial roles which served to uplift other women. Women's early participation in the ad business was small and the industry had yet to organize itself into "men's jobs" and "women's jobs." For example, Mathilde Weil opened the M.C. Weil Agency in 1880 in New York and was the first woman to start an advertising agency (Sivulka, 2009, p. 25). Widowed and suddenly needing to support herself, she discovered that brokering advertising space was more lucrative than writing stories for the same publications. At the time, an unmarried white woman's capacity to earn a living was socially acceptable and black women routinely worked outside of the home. Weil's agency promoted nostrums – potions and cure-alls intended for a variety of health-related issues – which were the backbone of many advertising agencies of the period, since such products were not regulated as medicinal brands are today. Weil ran the company for nearly 20 years and another woman, Mary Morrow Craig, inherited the business and ran it herself, over her husband's objections (Sivulka, 2009, p. 49).

By the late 1800s and early 1900s, social norms were shifting and women increasingly sought educational and employment opportunities. While there were only 10,000 female office workers in 1870, by 1920 there were about two million (Sivulka, 2009, p. 59). However, between the late 1800s and late 1920s, historians noted a backlash against women working in offices and other settings outside of the home (Sivulka, 2009, p. 58). Office work in American businesses was becoming highly separated among gender lines, with men assuming higher-paying and managerial roles and women clustering in lower-paying clerical and personnel jobs. In the meantime, advertising was promoted as a career choice for women and an alternative to traditional professions such as teaching. The Women's Christian Temperance Union published a book called *Occupations for Women* in 1897 which included a chapter on "Women in Advertising"; and the Women's Educational and Industrial Union of Boston published "Advertising as a Vocation for Women" in 1911 (Sivulka, 2009, pp. 47, 110). These guides encouraged women to enter the advertising business as writers, as researchers discovering the needs of consumers, or as stenographers. Talented stenographers could move up to manage promotion programs for companies. Under these circumstances, a small number of women were able to move into office manager positions in advertising firms and those with some artistic ability could find opportunities in printing, lithography, illustration, photography, and other aspects of creative work. However, women often found themselves barred from educational institutions, licensing programs, trade associations, clubs, and dining facilities which were conduits to professional career development and relationships. For example, until the 1960s, women were not allowed to eat in the executive dining room of the BBD&O advertising agency (Cracknell, 2011, p. 198). Schools which had advertising as part of their curricula – including Harvard, New York University, Boston University, Northwestern, and the University of Missouri – often excluded women from their programs, and Columbia University, which launched its full-time business program in 1913, only admitted men; women were limited to a one-year clerical track (Sivulka, 2009, p. 109).

Despite obstacles, resourceful women garnered professional advertising skills through a variety of avenues and leveraged other opportunities. Fed up with the exclusion from trade groups like the Advertising Men's League of New York, around 1912 women started forming their own clubs, including the League of Advertising Women, a precursor to the respected Advertising Women of New York association (Sivulka, 2009, p. 108). Inspired, women in other major cities established similar organizations. These women's advertising clubs promoted advertising as a profession and provided needed support and mentorship. When World War I created a labor shortage among men in the mid-1910s, some women maintained low-level managerial positions in advertising agencies. For example Helen Woodward became the first woman account executive at a major agency – the Frank Presby Agency – in the early 1900s and was among the highest-paid women of the era (Sivulka, 2009, p. 119). Woodward retired in 1924 and wrote books offering harsh critiques of unsavory practices within the advertising business (Sivulka, 2009, p. 123). Nedda McGrath was the first woman hired as an Art Director when she went to work for Blackman in 1926 (Fox, 1984, p. 287). Women of means were able to attend excellent liberal arts colleges such as Vassar, Smith, Bryn Mawr, Barnard, Wellesley, and Radcliff and a few went on to work in advertising and related occupations. While there are some inconsistencies in the literature regarding the nature of women's participation in advertising jobs in the mid-1920s, the vast majority worked in clerical positions and under 10 percent worked in non-clerical roles, often as copywriters (Maxwell, 2003, p. 1655; Sivulka, 2009, p. 111). Seeing copywriting as a viable career path, some women honed their skills working as copy or publicity writers for retailers and later joined advertising agencies with relevant experience, able to earn better pay.

With the recognition that female consumers made the majority of household purchasing decisions, women could position themselves in the advertising world as authorities on the "woman's point of view," a stance that was very appealing to marketers. Many advertising women capitalized on this aspect as a catalyst for their careers. For example, Erma Perham Proetz won major awards for effective illustrations in advertising aimed at women during the 1920s, which often featured recipes (Sivulka, 2009, p. 112). Proetz spent many years with Gardner Advertising of St. Louis, Missouri as a successful copywriter, account executive, Director, Creative Vice President, and Executive Vice President. President of the Women's Advertising Club of St. Louis, in 1935 *Fortune* magazine named Proetz one of 16 outstanding women in American business; and in 1952, she was the first woman inducted into the Advertising Hall of Fame.

Helen Lansdowne Resor

At the JWT agency, Helen Lansdowne Resor, wife of agency President Stanley Resor, had a major impact on the overwhelmingly male advertising profession and the advancement of women within it. A feminist and suffragette, she possessed keen marketing insight and creative aptitude. Called the greatest copywriter of her generation, her copy for Woodbury Soap – "a skin you love to touch" – increased sales of the brand by 1,000 percent in the early 1900s (Egolf, 2003b). Raised by her mother, a divorcee, young Helen was taught a strong work ethic so that she would never lack self-sufficiency (Fox, 1984, p. 94). Charismatic and resourceful, she graduated as valedictorian of her high school class and went to work immediately at a series of jobs including JWT. In 1911, JWT promoted and moved her to the agency's New York office, where she worked on the introduction of a new Procter & Gamble brand – Crisco shortening. Unheard of at the time, she made several presentations about the brand to Procter & Gamble's board, becoming the first woman to address a Procter & Gamble board meeting. According to Tungate (2007, p. 26), Stanley Resor's administrative skills coupled with Helen's "creative genius" took the agency to staggering heights. JWT was the first major agency to handle accounts for Procter & Gamble and was the first agency to bill in excess of $100 million.

Helen Resor's prowess in creative endeavors and her proximity to the head of the agency – where she and Stanley routinely collaborated on decisions – provided vital opportunities. Aware that many of the agency's clients produced brands which were purchased by women, by the early 1920s Helen Resor established and led her own team of female copywriters – known as JWT's Women's Editorial Department. Aware of the norms and practices in the industry which limited women's potential, she was fully engaged in the hiring and mentoring of these women and believed that women were more apt to achieve in their own rights if they were separated from the men. Ruth Waldo, a protégé who later became JWT's first female Vice President, explained Helen Resor's rationale for separation of the genders (Sutton, 2009, p. 32):

> "When a woman works for a man or in a men's group, she become less important, her opinion is worth less, her progress and advancement less rapid.

> Then she does not have the excitement and incentive to work as hard as she can, nor, in a men's group, does she get the full credit for what she does ... But with the knowledge and confidence of Mrs. Resor's support, a woman at Thompson could advance in her own group without having to compete with men for recognition of her ability. She has greater independence and freedom; a woman's ideas could be judged on their value alone. It was one less handicap."

Helen Resor lacked a college degree, but hired smart women who attended some of the best schools and were instrumental to JWT's success. Through family, college, political, and social connections, these women were often from the same upper-class socioeconomic circles as the men at the agency. According to Sutton (2009, p. 23), "Women that reflected the class and race of those already working at the agency were the ones most likely to be hired" and employment practices "helped perpetuate homogeneity among the managerial and copywriting staff." In this environment, ethnic diversity among the JWT women was nearly non-existent and whiteness was promoted as an ideal (Sutton, 2009, p. 69). There was one woman of color in the Women's Editorial Department: Aminta Casseres, a Columbian raised in Jamaica who spoke English and Spanish. However, Sutton (2009, p. 34) indicates that Casseres was highly assimilated with an upper-class background and therefore fit in with JWT colleagues. Some JWT women were involved in feminist activities and political organizations such as the Suffrage League, the League of Women Voters, and the National Women's Party. They participated with Resor, who organized JWT staffers to march in suffragette parades in New York during the mid-1910s (Applegate, 1994, p. 268) and joined celebrations when the 19th Amendment to the U.S. Constitution was ratified in 1920, giving women the right to vote. The Women's Editorial Department was highly successful, accounting for 58 percent of the agency's total revenues in 1918 (Sutton, 2009, p. 22). Under Helen Resor's leadership, JWT was the first major agency to put women in high-level professional positions and Sivulka (2009, p. 131) notes that these women earned about a third more than the average working woman of the period. Overall, the women's department was a major contributor to the agency's dominant position in the industry and Helen Resor was a major influence on the agency's culture for more than 40 years. In 1967, Stanley and Helen Resor were inducted posthumously into the Advertising Hall of Fame.

The 1930s to 1945: adwomen during the Great Depression and World War II

The Great Depression ushered in by the stock market crash of October 1929 decimated the American economy over the next decade including the advertising industry. Every economic indicator showed dramatic contraction and the annual volume of advertising expenditures fell from \$3.4 billion in 1929 to \$1.3 billion in 1933 (Fox, 1984, p. 119). Most surviving agencies cut staff and reduced salaries, although a few brave souls, like William Esty and Leo Burnett, launched agencies in the 1930s. Under conditions of scarce resources, marketers were admonished to offer "cheap, honest, durable products" and dubious or frivolous advertising practices were shunned (Fox, 1984, p. 120). Yet, by adhering to high professional standards and focus on consumers' needs, agency President Raymond Rubicam navigated the Young & Rubicam (Y&R) agency through the economic storm, rising "from nowhere" to trail only JWT in annual billings by the mid-1930s (Fox, 1984, p. 127). Y&R remained a dominant agency into the future.

Pay and opportunities for women, including those in advertising agencies, were significantly reduced during the Great Depression. According to the American Women's Association, pay rates for stenographers were cut from about $40 per week in 1929 to about $15 per week in 1933 (Sivulka, 2009, p. 159) and gender discrimination proliferated. Companies often fired or refused to hire married or older women and jobs once held by two women were often consolidated and given to one man. In addition, under the government's New Deal work programs, labor policies favored one member of a household, who was often the male head of a family. Moreover, between the late 1920s and 1950s, major advertising agencies including Ayer, BBD&O, Y&R, and McCann Erickson had earned reputations as "WASP preserves" led by men (Fox, 1984, p. 273). There were a few spotty examples of significant progress for adwomen during the Depression, including Ruth Waldo, copy head over the Women's Editorial Department at JWT; Dorothy Dignam, a copywriter at Ayer who developed a 1936 campaign for Ford's V-8 automobile aimed at women; and Louise Taylor Davis, the first woman copy supervisor and Vice President at Y&R (Fox, 1984, p. 291; Sivulka, 2009, pp. 161, 189). Other adwomen found opportunities outside of agencies, such as managing advertising in the retail sector or writing radio soap operas as advertising vehicles. Discontent with Depression-era opportunities was expressed among agency women who did not see prospects for advancement. One ad agency stenographer complained (Fox, 1984, p. 291): "All you get out of years in the business world is a terrific bitterness for things as they are. How many girls I know who have let burning ambition become cynical indifference."

It is important to note that Depression-era adwomen had various opinions regarding the feminist viewpoint and women's advancement in the profession. Feminist Dorothy Dignam actively mentored and promoted women's advancement in advertising and thought their participation in women's ad clubs was important. She believed: "Going to conventions, mingling, making speeches, seeing new cities [and] meeting new people did a great deal for the development of advertising women" (Wills, 2015, p. 231). But some adwomen opposed the feminist stance and believed that certain roles were not suitable for women. Advertising writer Dorothy Barstow, who eventually married McCann Erickson's Harry McCann, said in 1934 (Fox, 1984, p. 291):

> "The jobs that women hold are held because they are better fitted to hold them. There aren't very many women executives in advertising agencies, because there is not very much need for women executives in advertising agencies."

Another adwoman expressed a similar opinion (Fox, 1984, p. 291):

> "There are still functions in advertising to which women are entirely unsuited. They cannot, for instance, go out and drink themselves under the table angling for accounts."

Dissention over the appropriate role of women in advertising abated as the United States shifted into another reality and entered World War II in late 1941. As with the Great Depression, the war had a profound impact on Americans' daily lives (Blum, 1976). Staples like food and gasoline were rationed and manufacturers ceased making durable items like cars and refrigerators to engage in defense production. Thus, lifestyles oriented around scarcity and thrift continued. Millions of women supported the war in a variety of ways, including going to work in factories to do the work vacated by men who went to serve in the military. Helen Resor worked for the Advertising War Council, which produced the iconic "Rosie the Riveter" figure and the theme "Soldiers without guns" which promoted the war effort by encouraging women to work outside of the home. Toward the end of the war, two adwomen made significant advancements and were the first to become vice presidents in their respective agencies: Ruth Waldo at JWT in 1944 and Jean Wade Rindlaub at BBD&O in 1946. Regarded an expert on advertising to women, Rindlaub was elected to the Advertising Hall of Fame in 1989.

1946–1970s: the rise of women advertising executives and entrepreneurs

The end of World War II in 1945 signaled the beginning of a new boom time for the American economy, the births of many babies, and a bounce back in opportunities for women in advertising. Women were accepted in creative and research jobs and their value was often linked to their presumed expertise regarding the woman's perspective. Demand from businesses prompted the number of agencies to triple between 1939 and 1948, supporting an overall increase in advertising jobs (Sivulka, 2009, p. 236). The 1950 U.S. Census indicated that about one-third of the jobs in advertising were held by women. In agencies, three identifiable paths to women's advancement emerged: moving up from agency secretary; writing for a woman's magazine; or writing in-house copy for retail stores. Starting in the late 1940s, some agencies followed the lead of JWT and BBD&O and promoted one or more women to the level of vice president including: Ayer; Dancer-Fitzgerald-Sample; D'Arcy; Doyle Dane Bernbach (DDB); FCB; Grey;

McCann Erickson, O&M; and a few smaller agencies (Fox, 1984, p. 293). By 1960, in addition to JWT – which had seven female vice presidents among 132 at the company – McCann Erickson emerged as a relatively progressive place for women, with six women among its 100 vice presidents, the highest proportion among major agencies at the time (Fox, 1984, p. 294; Sivulka, 2009, p. 243).

With few exceptions, women executives in advertising held leadership roles in the creative sphere, usually with responsibilities concerning "women's products." For example, one of the most celebrated adwomen was Shirley Polykoff, who rose through the ranks starting as a secretary at *Harper's Bazaar* magazine. Hired at FCB in 1955 as the only female copywriter, she wrote the famous line: "Does she or doesn't she?" for Clairol hair coloring in the late 1950s. The controversial campaign was successful at convincing "respectable" middle-class suburban women that it was socially acceptable for them to dye their hair – and if they used the Clairol brand, no one would know. Polykoff understood the power of appearance and believed that women could "acquire all of the accoutrements of the established affluent class, which included a certain breeding and a certain kind of look" (Sivulka, 2009, p. 263). Within six years, the campaign increased sales of Clairol by 413 percent and more than half the women in America were dyeing their hair (Egolf, 2003a). Highly respected, Polykoff was named Advertising Woman of the Year in 1967 and was inducted into the Advertising Hall of Fame in 1980 – the first living adwoman to do so. FCB promoted Polykoff to Senior Vice President and Creative Director and she was the first woman to sit on FCB's Board of Directors. After retirement from FCB, she launched an agency in 1973 – Shirley Polykoff & Betuel – with a male business partner and handled the Miss Clairol account and other women's brands. Ironically, Polykoff was nothing like the suburban housewives that were portrayed in her advertisements. Career-focused, she used her maiden name for professional purposes and was called "a very flamboyant, very domineering type who had brilliantly succeeded in a man's world" (Sivulka, 2009, p. 263).

Unlike many adwomen, Phyllis Robinson, who became the first female copy chief at a U.S. agency when she was hired by the fledgling DDB agency in New York in 1949, was never limited to "women's accounts." DDB, led by Ned Doyle, Mac Dane, and Bill Bernbach, set out to challenge the status quo set forth by the major agencies of the period and was a major force in the 1960s "Creative Revolution" in advertising. Bernbach was an outspoken advocate urging advertising to become "bolder, wittier and more stylish" (*Advertising Age*, 2002). Robinson, promoted to Vice President at DDB in 1956, was involved with innovative concepts such as the irreverent "Lemon" campaign for the Volkswagen Beetle automobile and the famous "We're Number Two" slogan for Avis rental cars. A Barnard graduate with experience as an editor, copywriter, and sales promotion specialist, she was also involved with the Levy's Jewish rye bread account, known for the phrase: "You don't have to be Jewish to love Levy's." The campaign was an early multicultural effort by a major general-market firm and a nod to DDB's heritage as a Jewish agency. The campaign linked several minorities to one – Jewish people – in a memorable series of ads featuring people of various ethnicities. Robinson stepped down and assumed a part-time work schedule when her daughter was born in 1962, an arrangement she maintained at DDB for 20 years (Sivulka, 2009, p. 289). Under Robinson's leadership, DDB nurtured and promoted many women including future agency entrepreneurs Paula Green and Mary Wells. The culture at DDB was markedly different from many traditional agencies. Women outnumbered men in its copy department and Robinson claimed: "I've never encountered any difficulty" as a woman in advertising (Fox, 1984, p. 295). Mary Wells elaborated on Robinson's comments about DDB, explaining: "Everyone cared only about how effective an ad was. No one drank. No one did anything but work" (Applegate, 1994, p. 215).

Despite the accomplishments of adwoman like Shirley Polykoff, Phyllis Robinson, and Mary Wells, a 1960 trade publication dismissed praise concerning the "progress" of women in advertising agencies as a sham (Sivulka, 2009, p. 243). The article acknowledged that the great majority of advertising women were still concentrated in clerical positions, were segregated into women's only departments, and were paid less than men. It further indicated that women were routinely subjected to men's biases and that the small number of women who held top posts were "unusual." Cracknell (2011, p. 199) concurred, commenting on adwomen's opportunities for advancement to upper-level agency positions: "as for promotion to senior executive level – apart from copywriting or research – the glass ceiling was so obvious it might as well have been iron."

These conclusions were consistent with the observations of another high-achieving adwoman, Jane Maas, who published a book in 2012 titled *Madwomen: The Other side of Life on Madison Avenue in the '60s and Beyond*, based on observations from women in advertising. Maas, named by *Advertising Age* (2012) as one of the 100 most influential women in advertising and an Advertising Woman of the Year, started as a copywriter at O&M in 1964. She rose to become its Creative Director and Vice President in 1967 – the second woman to do so – behind Reva Korda, another O&M pioneer. She was President of Muller Jordan Weiss and briefly ran her own agency in the early 1980s. She observed that most agency jobs for women were as secretaries or copywriters and the overwhelming majority had male bosses. Women copywriters were assigned to "female" accounts – fashion, cosmetics, baby, food, and cleaning products associated with domestic responsibilities – and ads often depicted women in subservient and stereotypical roles. Although some agencies had "junior copywriter" groups, many were essentially typing pools, she claimed. Male executives were slow to accept women in non-clerical positions or on certain types of accounts. Mistaken for a secretary at a client meeting with American Express, Maas was asked: "Did you forget your steno pad, dear? I heard that a hotshot new copywriter from Ogilvy was just assigned to our business – which one is he?" (Maas, 2012, p. 63). According to Maas, the most difficult aspect was the power structure in agencies since "the boss was in control of your salary, your raise, your career advancement ... your life" (Maas, 2012, p. 29). This structure influenced the workplace culture in myriad ways. For example, there was an unwritten dress code for women, prohibiting them from wearing pants, since they allegedly revealed women's figures. However, women still had to cope with unwanted sexual advances and other undesirable behaviors. Extensive drinking, smoking, and adulterous sex were commonplace in the New York ad scene and account men were expected to secure prostitutes for clients. At the time, there were no sexual harassment policies in place and women had to think creatively in order to avoid unwelcome sexual situations. But, sometimes women who wanted to advance in the agencies were the ones doing the seducing – and women who complained were ostracized. Maas noted (2012, p. 29):

> "If [the boss] wanted to go to bed with you, you had to ask yourself what mattered more: your self-respect or your career? The best way to get promoted from secretary to copywriter was for your boss to make it happen."

Interestingly, Maas (2012, p. 33) contends that JWT was an exception to the sexually permissive cultures in many agencies. Among the important ad firms, it had the reputation of being the most conservative of the big agencies. Sex was limited at JWT because most offices had no doors. Reportedly, this was due to the influence of Helen Resor, who was aware of the sexual escapades which occurred in agencies and sought to curb such behaviors.

Maas and others remember advertising workplaces which were inhospitable to working mothers, provided unequal pay for women, and limited advancement opportunities. Agencies often asked pregnant women to leave when they started to show and "there was no maternity leave, paid or unpaid" at the time (Maas, 2012, p. 80). Women who left to have babies often did not return since there were no day care facilities or employer assistance. The tiny number of executive adwomen, like Maas, often had to secure live-in help to manage family responsibilities. With respect to compensation, women copywriters earned "pittances" in the area of $35–50 per week, about half the salary of male copywriters in the 1950s and 1960s (Maas, 2012, p. 52). Women with credentials in research, including Ph.D. degrees, were hired for as little as $18,000 per year (Maas, 2012, p. 55). Married men made more than single women in similar jobs, since – management reasoned – they had families to support. In fact, a man merely engaged to be married could anticipate a raise of several thousand dollars for doing the same work. Although Maas was hired at O&M in 1964 making $10,000 and left in 1976 making $40,000 – considered a meteoric pay raise – she acknowledges that her pay barely budged the first few years. Maas (2012, p. 55) explained,

> "Of course we didn't make the same salary as a man with the same title, even if we knew we were doing a better job. We didn't even have equal space – the guys got offices with windows; we got cubicles. The problem is that we simply submitted to the situation."

Women's advancement opportunities outside of creative areas were often limited and difficult. Cracknell asserted that account executive positions, which typically led to senior-level responsibilities, were unappealing to women given the hard drinking and sexually oriented entertainment associated with servicing clients. This being the case, another path to advancement pursued by a few women was the establishment of their own agencies. On this topic, Cracknell (2011, p. 199) observed: "No agency was led by a woman unless it was started by her."

The entrepreneurs

Whether they were seeking to circumvent the career barriers established in many advertising firms, or were motivated by other personal factors, some enterprising women chose the entrepreneurship path and launched their own agencies between the late 1940s and 1970s. In addition to Polykoff and Maas, white women including Jacqueline Brandwynne, Janet Marie Carlson, Jo Foxworth, Paula Green, Adrienne Hall, Margaret Hockaday, Joan Levine, Jane Trahey, and Mary Wells established agencies during this era. Several became among the most prominent women in the advertising business – running successful companies, authoring books and trade articles, and maintaining high profiles in the industry. Most were advocates for women's advancement in business and a few were feminist supporters of the Women's Movement.

Among these entrepreneurs was Vassar-educated Margaret Hockaday who opened Hockaday and Associates in 1949 in New York City. Hockaday's small agency produced work described as "offbeat, whimsical and saucy" for such brands as Capezio footwear, Dunbar furniture, and Jantzen swimwear (Applegate, 1994, p. 186; Sivulka, 2009, p. 243). The agency made headlines in 1959 when it beat out large agencies BBD&O and McCann Erickson for the Jantzen account (Applegate, 1994, p. 190). In the male-dominated ad business, Hockaday believed that clients who would not work with women missed out on women's tendencies to find the "extra plus that makes the ordinary extraordinary in advertising" (Applegate, 1994, p. 192).

Jane Trahey Associates (a.k.a. Trahey/Caldwell and Trahey/Wolf) started in 1958 and was best known for campaigns for fashion and cosmetic brands like Bill Blass, Calvin Klein, and Elizabeth Arden. Among her agency's most recognized work was for Blackglama minks with the phrase: "What becomes a legend most?" featuring high-profile celebrities such as Barbra Streisand, *Vogue* editor Diana Vreeland, opera singers Maria Callas and Leontyne Price, and others. Holding a Master's degree in Fine Arts from Columbia, Trahey authored over 16 books, plays, and screenplays and was a columnist for

Advertising Age and other publications. She credited male mentors with nurturing her business skills and deflected criticism that her accounts were too heavily oriented toward female brands – pointing out that she was often not invited to participate in pitches for other types of products. An ardent feminist, Trahey advocated for educational attainment and pay equity for women. She belonged to NOW – the National Organization of Women – and actively supported the Equal Rights Amendment, a proposed amendment to the U.S. Constitution. Never married, Trahey credited her widowed mother for instilling in her a strong sense of independence and self-sufficiency. Acknowledging the difficulties and sacrifices that high-achieving advertising women face when attempting to manage career and family responsibilities, she told *Advertising Age* (Freeman, 2003b, p. 1568):

> "To get to the top in the advertising business, a woman has to have almost a neurotic devotion to her career, and this almost excludes marriage. Sooner or later, the adwoman who is married and has children is going to have to make a decision in favor of home, and this decision, even if it is the right one, will hurt her career."

Before launching her own agency, Jo Foxworth was known as an advocate for women's careers and advancement within the corporate environment. A mentee of the IPG's Mr. Marion Harper, she served in executive roles at several Interpublic agencies until the launch of the Jo Foxworth Agency in 1968 which handled accounts including J.C. Penney, Shiseido cosmetics, and Chiquita Banana (Applegate, 1994). Her work as an advertising agency executive, owner, author, columnist, and lecturer gained national attention and her 1978 book, *Boss Lady*, became a cult classic on college campuses and in corporate suites. Between 1967 and 1978, she was named Advertising Woman of the Year five times and was elected to the Advertising Hall of Fame in 1996. Denouncing gendered roles in jobs, Foxworth urged women to be ambitious, supportive of one another, and to stop favoring male subordinates (Fox, 1984, p. 297).

Paula Green, a protégé of DDB's Phyllis Robinson, launched her agency in the late 1960s. Unlike Trahey and Foxworth, she maintained a low profile with respect to feminist issues. Starting as a secretary for a publishing concern in the 1940s, she moved on to Grey advertising agency as a copywriter, but interrupted her career when her son was born. Eventually she returned to work out of necessity when her husband returned to college full-time. Given little childcare assistance for working mothers in the early 1950s, she arranged a support system of neighbors, her husband, and an African-American sitter who became her son's "surrogate mother" (Applegate, 1994, p. 167). Sensing no room for advancement at DDB, she launched Green Dolmatch (later Paula Green, Inc.) in 1969. Her agency did innovative work for a number of clients including the popular song "Look for the Union Label" for the International Ladies Garment Workers Union and a successful campaign for the

Goya Hispanic food company aimed at mainstream consumers (Applegate, 1994, p. 169). A personal scare with breast cancer led her to do a breakthrough commercial for the American Cancer Society in the early 1970s encouraging regular breast self-examinations – a first for TV advertising. Crediting her success to her upbringing and a supportive husband, she acknowledged problems and opportunities concerning women in the advertising business, stating (Applegate, 1994, p. 171):

> "As long as business is run mainly by men, I think it's much harder for women. Businessmen don't mingle with women. I think younger men have learned to some degree to look at women as not just as women, but as people to do business with – as people of stature, of substance, who have good ideas, who operate well."

Mary Wells Lawrence

Among the most accomplished businesswomen of the 1960s, Mary Wells (a.k.a. Mary Wells Lawrence) was recognized as "the most famous, most successful and highest paid woman in the history of advertising" (Maas, 2012, p. 69). Known for her captivating looks, style, and presence, throughout her career she focused on account strategy, selling, and financing. Not limited to women's products, Wells worked on traditionally male-dominated accounts such as razor blades, pharmaceutical products, liquor, cigarettes (Benson and Hedges), airlines (Braniff, TWA, Continental, Pam Am), and automobiles (Volkswagen, American Motors Corporation, Ford) in addition to soft drinks, packaged household goods, the New York State Lottery, and the iconic "I Love New York" tourism campaign. She was hired at DDB in 1957 by Phyllis Robinson, despite a mediocre interview (Lawrence, 2002, p. 5). By age 35 Wells was promoted to DDB copy chief and was a Vice President making $40,000 – considered an astronomical sum at the time, since the average man made $10,000 (Applegate, 1994, p. 215). In 1964, she was recruited by Mr. Marion Harper of the IPG to work for Jack Tinker & Partners, an elite think tank within Interpublic's holdings. Harper wanted to create a new age agency which would set a new standard in the industry and promised Wells it would be her dream agency. The Tinker agency hired top candidates including prominent researcher Dr. Herta Herzog and did breakthrough work. For example, it transformed the image and positioning of Alka-Seltzer antacid and created the popular "Plop plop, fizz fizz" campaign. Tinker flourished under Wells' leadership of the creative team, taking advantage of her theatrical background and philosophy about creativity which pushed the work in new directions. Wells explained (Lawrence, 2002, p. 71):

> "Great advertising, the kind that works, almost always comes out of the product you are going to advertise or the product's world. You need to have an open mind, the nosiness of a detective, and assimilate all the information you can from every imaginable source when you start to create advertising. It is knowledge that stimulates great advertising ideas and your own intuition."

In 1965, her repositioning of the lackluster Braniff airlines brand catapulted Wells' reputation as a brilliant creative thinker who got results. She persuaded Harding Lawrence, the President of Braniff to support her ideas, which included the catchphrase: "The end of the plain plane," and had the company paint its planes in seven different, eye-catching, colors – including shimmering turquoise – upholster the seats with Herman Miller fabric, and dress the flight attendants in Pucci designer outfits, resulting in a memorable passenger experience no other airline offered. The rebranding effort was accompanied by a campaign featuring a controversial TV commercial titled "Air Strip" which featured airline stewardesses taking off their traditional uniforms in flight – layer by layer – in a sexy striptease manner to reveal their designer duds (*Come Fly With Us Magazine*, 2014). The international press went wild over the campaign and the extensive media coverage recast Braniff as the "fun, sexy, modern approach to air travel" (Applegate, 1994, p. 216). Bookings on the airline increased dramatically and the campaign fundamentally changed how airlines were advertised and marketed across the industry.

Wells was very sensitive to the power of relationships – with colleagues and clients – in moving forward in advertising careers. When Jack Tinker, head of the agency fell ill of a heart attack, Wells expected to be named president of the agency. However, Marion Harper refused, saying: "It is not my fault, Mary, the world is not ready for women presidents" (Lawrence, 2002, p. 44). Incensed, Wells resigned and formed her own agency in April 1966, taking two Tinker associates – Dick Rich and Stewart Greene – and the Braniff account with her. The new Wells, Rich, Greene (WRG) agency grew quickly and enjoyed spectacular financial success. In 1971, WRG went public and Wells was distinguished as the first woman CEO to have her company listed on the New York Stock Exchange. By 1972, WRG was billing $115 million and heading toward $150 million (Lawrence, 2002, p. 94). Wells was paid a salary of $300,000, not including stock value, making her the highest paid woman in advertising (*Advertising Age*, 2002). Years later, in 1990, after a phenomenally successful career, Wells retired and sold her share of WRG to BDDP, a Paris-based advertising concern, for $160 million (*Advertising Age*, 2002, p. 16). About ten years later, Mary Wells Lawrence was inducted into the Advertising Hall of Fame and subsequently published her autobiography. Interestingly, *Advertising Age* (2002, p. 16) reported that after Mary Wells left the agency, Wells BDDP faltered. Through the 1990s, the agency changed ownership and names several times, lost major clients and hundreds of millions of dollars. In 1998, the agency closed permanently.

Despite Mary Wells' meteoric rise in the industry, she had a controversial reputation and fans as well as detractors. Jane Maas, who was a WRG executive for several years, marveled at Wells' self-discipline, indicating that she worked 12–14 hour days and never looked tired. Maas (2012, p. 67) recalled:

> "Everybody at WRG belonged to the cult of Mary, and I was no exception. I worshipped her, was in awe of her, and was a bit afraid of her at the same time. She was always elegant, perfectly dressed, coiffed and made up. Despite endless client lunches and dinners, she never gained an ounce."

Wells' ethics were questioned along with her lukewarm embracement of feminist issues. For example, although she helped turn around the struggling Braniff airline, she married its CEO Harding Lawrence in 1967. Their marriage created an obvious conflict of interests, since Mary Wells Lawrence was spending millions per year of a public company's money headed by her husband (Bird, 1976, p. 181). Thus, WRG resigned the Braniff account, but caused a stir when it accepted the TWA airline account shortly thereafter. Some feminists criticized Wells for capitalizing on her looks in business and not providing enthusiastic support for the Women's Movement. Wells acknowledged that she was not in concurrence with some of the more strident voices of the Women's Movement and carried herself as such. For example, as a working wife, Wells would fly to Texas every weekend to be with her husband rather than have him travel to New York where her office was located. However, she believed that her record in business spoke for itself in terms of what a woman could accomplish. Reflecting on how she achieved success in a male-dominated industry, Wells explained (Lawrence, 2002, p. 165):

> "Well, advertising was and still is a man's world if there ever was one, and a sexy female chief executive officer of an advertising agency would be viewed as a horror show – a nuisance, an embarrassment and even a danger to men interested in powerful business careers. My highly publicized marriage and my low gender awareness were two of the reasons I was trusted by the CEOs who controlled America's most important advertising accounts and was able to build a large, international agency. They saw me as one of their own."

While Wells did not consider herself a feminist, she recognized that major success in business could be achieved, but acknowledged the sacrifices in doing so. She explained: "I pretty well eliminated a social life except with my clients. My life was simply my family, Wells Rich Greene and my clients" (Maas, 2012, p. 68). She further suggested that she did not expect women to emulate her, but rather than seeking power, that women mainly wanted *choices* in life. She told *Advertising Age* (2002, pp. 20–22):

> "Maybe what it takes to build a company is so consuming that it cuts off so many interests that women have. Maybe women don't want to [run agencies] because it cuts off so much of their life. It may be that women are smart enough to say, 'Why should I do that? What's so terrific about that? What's so wonderful about that?'"

The 1980s and beyond: "superwomen" at the top

Proponents of equality and economic advancement for women had a tremendous impact on women's progress in society and the professions including advertising. Moreover, research released by JWT in 1980 showed that adult women in the labor force – for the first time – accounted for more than 52 percent of the female population (Bartos, 1982). Therefore, advertisers wanted to reach this New Woman effectively. Entrepreneur Lois Geraci Ernst took the idea of female empowerment to a new level and opened an agency named Advertising to Women. With a largely female staff, the agency's work was based on the old philosophy that it takes a woman to sell to a woman – but took notice of women's shifting roles in society. Its accounts included Charles of the Ritz fragrances, Gillette personal care products, and RJR Foods, helping to bring total billings to $50 million in 1980 (Sivulka, 2009, p. 305). Claiming to have special insights regarding the new "middle-American" woman, the agency developed a number of notable campaigns. One such example was a famous television commercial for Charles of the Ritz Enjoli brand perfume, promoted with the song ("Enjoli," 2011):

> I can bring home the bacon!
> [Chorus] Enjoli
> Fry it up in a pan!
> [Chorus] Enjoli!
> And never, ever, let you forget you're a man!

Marketing approaches like this sparked new controversy: advertising now promoted a "Superwoman" ideal where women could "have it all" – a lucrative career, home, family, and a sexually fulfilling marriage. This prompted a backlash among those who believed the imagery was unrealistic and made women feel overwhelmed by the expectations. While debates ensued about women's liberation and their roles in society, new coping tools emerged in the marketplace to help working women juggle multiple responsibilities, such as the widespread emergence of daycare programs, proliferation of convenience products and services, advancements in time-saving technology, and lifestyle concepts like "multitasking." But at the same time, a pro-family movement – sometimes viewed as anti-feminist – emerged and the proposed Equal Rights Amendment, supported by feminists, was defeated in 1982.

For women willing to make the personal sacrifices necessary to reach the highest levels in business, the success of Mary Wells and other female leaders of previous eras represented a turning point in the advertising industry. Joined with the influence of the Women's Movement, the ideal of female empowerment significantly impacted adwomen who participated in the industry from the 1980s forward. Thus, entrepreneurs like Olivia Trager and Marcella Rosen, and Pat Martin and Joan Lipton partnered to launch agencies. Linda Kaplan Thaler, who had worked at WRG, started an agency in 1997 which went on to bill in excess of a billion dollars, handling such brands as Aflac insurance and Clairol. The firm eventually joined the Publicis network and was renamed Publicis Kaplan Thaler. Later, Linda Kaplan Thaler was inducted into the Advertising Hall of Fame in 2015.

During the 1990s, women moved into senior management positions in advertising agencies in noticeable numbers, backed by substantial educational credentials and work experience. At large agencies, Charlotte Beers and Shelly Lazarus rose to positions that adwomen of the previous decades could not have dreamed of. Beers – referred to as "the woman who broke the glass ceiling" (Bennington, 2012) – is the only person in history to serve as the Chairman of two top ten global advertising agencies – O&M from 1992–1997 and JWT from 1999–2001. With math and physics degrees from Baylor University, Beers started her advertising career on the client side in marketing research and brand management for the Uncle Ben's brand. A divorcee with one daughter, her rise in the corporate world was so significant that colleges including Harvard introduced courses dedicated to the study of her career and business practices (Bennington, 2012; Freeman, 2003a). Credited with modifying O&M's corporate culture, Beers expressed commitment to "changing women from the inside out so they can go change their cultures" (Bennington, 2012).

Shelly Lazarus succeeded Beers as Chairman of O&M in 1997 after more than 25 years at the company, the first time a major agency had a succession of two women chairmen. Joining O&M as an account executive in 1971, Lazarus rose through the account management ranks. By then, women with the right credentials could enter agencies in account management positions, so she earned an MBA from Columbia so she wouldn't be expected to type (*Encyclopedia of World Biographies*, n.d.). A wife and mother of three, Lazarus advocated for employee work–life balance and described the O&M culture during her tenure as a meritocracy (*Encyclopedia of World Biographies*, n.d.), signaling a major change for women compared with previous eras. Lazarus believed that successful women must have a passion for their work as they sought to maintain family and job responsibilities concurrently. Noting the progress of women, she stated: "I think we're coming to the day when noting the gender of a powerful person in business will be a thing of the past" (*Encyclopedia of World Biographies*, n.d.). Beers and Lazarus were inducted into the Advertising Hall of Fame in 2009 and 2013, respectively. From the 1990s forward, in addition to O&M, other major agencies placed women in prominent executive positions including Ayer, BBD&O, Chiat/Day, Deutsch, Grey, Leo Burnett, McCannErickson, and Wieden & Kennedy (Sivulka, 2009, pp. 367–368). While white women made major advances in the advertising industry, African-Americans also entered the business and made significant contributions to the profession.

African-American advertising pioneers and entrepreneurs

Compared with the participation of white women, African-American involvement in the advertising business lagged behind by 40 years or more. The earliest black advertising professionals handled ad placements for newspapers, like Claude Barnett's advertising company in the 1910s and 1920s which worked on behalf of local and black businesses that wanted to reach black consumers (Chambers, 2008, p. 23). Social norms restricted black participation to the fringes of the ad industry until at least the 1940s (Chambers, 2008; Davis, 2002). Meanwhile, jobs for African-Americans in white advertising firms were essentially unheard of until about 1950, and, even then, opportunities were sparse and mostly limited to clerical positions. Recognizing the difficulties associated with entering the advertising business for African-Americans, Bill Sharp – one of a tiny number of black advertising professionals – self-published a book in 1969 titled *How to be Black and Get a Job in the Advertising Agency Business Anyway*. Intended to spur black participation in the business, the 61-page primer provided a short history and description of jobs in the advertising business, described how to prepare for work in the industry and gave advice for succeeding in advertising interviews and jobs. Downplaying racial issues and offering encouragement to future advertising professionals, Sharp (1969, p. 2) optimistically advised: "in the advertising agency business, success lies in the talents you have to offer; how well you express them and how they are perceived by others. It's not how you look. It's what you can do."

Art imitates life? Pop culture portrayals of black advertising professionals

Sharp's book acknowledged long-standing negative perceptions concerning African-Americans and the advertising business, some of which were addressed in fictional works like the *Mad Men* television series. With the exception of the 1992 movie *Boomerang*, which features positive portrayals of professional African-American men and women in a black advertising agency, pop culture works often portrayed the black experience in advertising in undesirable terms. For example, a fiction novel *Mad Man* by Glover (2010) illustrates the despair of a black creative executive in a general-market agency who complains about stolen ideas, exclusion, and other ill-treatment, but is dismissed as an ungrateful whiner when he protests (Miller, 2011). An early example was the 1969 movie *Putney Swope*, a satire which underscores the absurdity of blacks running advertising firms. Swope's character is the token black man on the executive board of a large, mostly white Madison Avenue advertising agency when the chairman dies suddenly. Having to choose a successor, but due to a company rule which prohibits members from voting for themselves, the board votes for Swope – the least likely candidate – who wins by a landslide. Swope immediately uses this opportunity to address past grievances, replace nearly all the staff with blacks, and renames the agency "Truth and Soul, Inc." – which will no longer take accounts for tobacco, liquor, or war toys. Truth and Soul produces unorthodox ads which are wildly successful at selling clients' products. But under a new company policy, the agency only accepts client payments up front and in cash – which are placed in a

Plexiglas vault at the agency. Gullible clients line up to give the agency millions of dollars. However, the agency's unconventional practices are regarded as subversive by federal authorities and the agency is viewed a threat to national security. Consequently, Swope – challenged by the government and dissidents within the agency – abandons the company dressed in Castro garb, carrying a bag of money. As he flees, an insurgent throws a Molotov cocktail into the vault containing the agency's cash and Truth and Soul's assets literally go up in smoke. Mocking the advertising industry, the film insinuates that African-Americans are unsuited to managerial positions and promotes a cynical view of advertising practice and people. At one point in the movie, an earnest reporter asks Swope whether he thinks his role will encourage young people to pursue careers in advertising. Swope replies sarcastically "I hope not" (*Putney Swope*, 1969).

Another pop culture program – *Black-ish* – a contemporary television comedy, illustrates the circumscribed reality for many black advertising professionals. In the September 2014 debut episode, the lead character, "Andre Johnson," excitedly anticipates a big promotion at the general-market advertising agency where he works. His advancement would make him the first African-American Senior Vice President at the firm, and he refers to himself as "breaking down barriers" (*Black-ish*, 2014). He acknowledges that since there are so few African-Americans at the agency, that when one does well, it is as if they all do. However, upon hearing the announcement of his new position at a company-wide meeting, Johnson is disappointed to learn that he has been named Senior Vice President of the agency's newly created Urban Division. Given that the term "urban" is often a code word for "black," Johnson, dismayed, asks himself: "Wait – did they just put me in charge of black stuff?" (*Black-ish*, 2014). Later, at a family celebration dinner, Johnson laments that he had hoped to become the first senior executive at the agency who happened to be black, rather than an African-American in charge of "urban" marketing. Despite Johnson's disillusionment that upper management fails to see beyond his skin color and presumed expertise, in future episodes the character appears resigned to his fate as the person responsible for the black perspective in his professional work role.

African-Americans in general-market advertising firms

The experience of the fictional Andre Johnson, who finds himself pigeonholed as an expert on black consumers in his professional role, is a familiar circumstance for many real-life African-American marketing practitioners, whether the year was 1945 or 2015. Historically, African-American marketing professionals found acceptance as specialists regarding black consumers.

The challenging economics of the Great Depression and World War II prompted mainstream marketers to seek new customers to compensate for reduced spending among their traditional consumers. As such, interest slowly developed among white firms who recognized black consumers as a feasible market and turned to black media and marketing professionals for help reaching them (Davis, 2013). Thus, by the 1930s, major brands like Camel cigarettes, Seagram's liquor, and Pepsi-Cola soft drinks joined others who advertised in media aimed at black consumers (Chambers, 2008, p. 31). Pepsi-Cola, particularly aggressive in this regard, maintained a dedicated national "Negro Sales" team from 1947–1951 which traveled nationwide promoting the Pepsi brand to black consumers and providing insights on effective advertising appeals (Capparell, 2007). This strategy proved successful and Pepsi achieved a 40 percent market share among black cola drinkers by the late 1940s (Hirschhorn, 1949). Recognizing the attractiveness of the black consumer market, other brands such as Pabst, Coca-Cola, Royal Crown Cola, Ford Motor Company, Buick, American Sugar, Best Foods, and Safeway supermarkets pursued black consumers in the 1940s (Weems, 1998, p. 36). However, although the economic value of black consumers was becoming increasingly apparent to corporate marketers, their limited knowledge about how to address them effectively was problematic. Given societal practices which often segregated blacks and portrayed them negatively, many mainstream marketers did not understand how to appeal to black consumers. This lack of understanding put their marketing efforts at risk, especially when it was revealed that African-Americans – *as consumers* – were repelled by stereotypical, servile, and demeaning black advertising images (Edwards, 1932, p. 234). Such images were prevalent in marketing materials prior to the mid-1900s, like the ad for Aunt Jemima flour shown in Figure 1.1.

Large mainstream corporations needed help understanding the perceptions, attitudes, and motivations of black consumers so that effective marketing messages could be crafted. Addressing this need, African-American men like David Sullivan, John H. Johnson, Moss Kendrix, John Benjamin Harris, Leonard Evans, Clarence Holte, and others positioned themselves as authorities on relating successfully to black consumers, just as early advertising women claimed special insights into selling to women. Cortese (2008, p. 92) argued that African-Americans are regarded as cultural producers in the eyes of mainstream marketers, capable of producing "culturally authentic" messages which in turn helped companies sell products to black consumers. Therefore, white corporations found it acceptable to utilize black marketing professionals for guidance, which in turn provided opportunities for African-Americans to participate in corporate advertising and marketing activities. To improve their efforts, men like Kendrix, Walter Davis, H. Naylor Fitzhugh, Sam Whitman, Herbert Wright, and other black sales and marketing practitioners established the National Association of Market Developers (NAMD) in 1953 (Kendrix, 2011a; Kendrix, 2011b). The NAMD was the leading support and networking organization for blacks in the commercial communications fields during the 1950s and 1960s and its members specialized in "Negro Market" sales and promotion work for major brands including Pepsi-Cola, Royal Crown Cola, Esso Standard Oil, Phillip Morris, Greyhound, Anheuser-Busch, and Marriott (Chambers, 2008, p. 63; Weems, 1998, p. 53). Harris, possessing an MBA, was an important

14
THE SATURDAY EVENING POST
April 10, 1920
"lawzee!"
mekkin' pancakes is th' mos' impawtines thing ah does, than which dere aint no better, effen ah does say so! Jes mah flour and water, on de griddle and —— whuf! dey's done honey. Grab em!
AUNT JEMIMA
PANCAKE FLOUR

Figure 1.1 Early advertisements often portrayed blacks in stereotypical and servile roles, which black people found demeaning. Increased sensitivity to the views of black consumers and the participation of African-American marketing professionals helped to diminish such images (*Saturday Evening Post*, April 10, 1920).

Source: www.library.illinois.edu/adexhibit/racism.htm.

"Negro market" consultant to corporate brands like Kodak and Pillsbury in the 1950s and 1960s (Davis, 2013). Similarly, at general-market advertising agencies, two African-American men were hired around 1950 to help companies capitalize on black consumers. Leonard Evans was hired in 1949 by Arthur Meyerhoff & Company in Chicago (Chambers, 2008, p. 85), and Clarence Holte was hired in 1952 by BBD&O in New York City (*Tide*, 1952). Holte, the best known of the two, was the first black person hired in a significant executive position at a leading New York agency where he was brought in to head the "Negro Markets" division (Chambers, 2008, pp. 88–89). Holte, who became an officer with the NAMD, added 450 black families to BBD&O's national consumer research panel and quickly became a high-profile, respected, and sought-after expert on black consumers from the 1950s into the 1970s (Chambers, 2008, pp. 91–92).

Knowing that black consumers sought positive acknowledgment in the marketplace, these men had direct influence on marketing decisions in major corporations, often proposing marketing themes which underscored black pride and inclusion. They understood that black consumers would willfully support brands which regarded their patronage with respect. Their participation in planning marketing executions fundamentally changed the way that African-Americans were addressed – and portrayed – in advertising messages. At the same time, these pioneers were careful to provide sound business rationales which supported the profit-seeking motives of the marketers they counseled (Davis, 2013). Their efforts, coupled with good quality research, established black consumers as an important and lucrative market for corporate advertisers.

Black employment in mainstream advertising agencies

While African-American marketing professionals were accepted by mainstream corporations as experts on black consumers, prior to the early 1960s, employment in mainstream advertising agencies on general-market business was exceedingly difficult. Most agencies did not hire blacks, except for low-level positions or as specialists like Evans and Holte. However, there were a couple of rare exceptions of the period in terms of mainstream agency hiring and promoting black men to managerial roles: Roy Eaton, hired at Y&R in 1955; and Georg Olden, hired by BBD&O in 1960. They possessed exemplary credentials which made them outstanding candidates, regardless of race (Chambers, 2008 pp. 95–106). Eaton had four degrees, was trained in classical music, and spoke several languages; Olden was a highly skilled graphic artist and designer, so their talents did not limit them to black consumers and products. Both men assumed prestigious managerial positions in general-market advertising agencies.

Despite the advancement of black men like Holte and Eaton in mainstream agencies, over the next 40 years issues concerning prejudice against African-Americans and other people of color prompted regular protests by stakeholders and activist groups against the advertising industry. An African-American man, one of a few working in a general-market agency management position in the 1990s, observed deliberate efforts to block his professional advancement, prompting him to eventually leave the firm. He explained to *Black Enterprise* (Ayers-Williams, 1998, p. 154):

> "Advertising is a relationship business. Many whites don't like you being buddies with their clients, their friends. They often resent black participation in the business. There's also a prevailing sense of denial that blacks ever create anything of value. Instead, whites may put our work down, ignore it or co-opt it."

Employment issues lingered well into the 2000s and people of color often expressed dissatisfaction with prospects for advertising jobs, especially in general-market firms. A 2006 survey by the AAF showed that only 15 percent of advertising companies were successful in recruiting and retaining minority talent (Harris, 2007, p. 162). Claiming entrenched discrimination against African-Americans in the advertising industry, the NAACP and the civil rights law firm Mehri & Skalet launched the Madison Avenue Project in 2009, providing research which illustrated bias in hiring, promotion, and compensation practices in advertising agencies with respect to African-Americans (Bendick and Egan, 2009).

The development of black-owned advertising agencies

Given the difficulties obtaining positions and advancing in general-market advertising agencies, black advertising practitioners often pursued entrepreneurship as means of participating in the industry. Davis (2002) examined the origins and development of black-owned advertising firms from 1940 through 2000, suggesting that they were forced to follow an Economic Detour model of enterprise development, which meant that their business activities were largely limited to services concerning the black consumer market, given prevailing societal norms and customs. This conclusion was consistent with the development of black-owned firms in other industries examined by scholars including Stuart (1940), Pierce (1947), and Butler (1991). In contrast, Chambers (2008, p. 255) argued that the black consumer orientation among black advertising entrepreneurs was simply a means for these professionals to establish a foothold in the industry. Beyond these points of view, to understand how black-owned advertising firms developed over time, it is also important to understand how three socioeconomic paradigms – racial segregation, desegregation, and multiculturalism – impacted opportunities for black advertising entrepreneurs.

The 1940s to 1950s: pioneering black agencies in the era of segregation

A few black-owned advertising firms existed in the 1940s. David Sullivan set up an agency in New York in 1943; and Fusche, Young, and Powell established an agency in Detroit the same year (Fox, 1984, p. 278). William B.

Graham – who dramatically increased distribution of Pabst beer to black communities in the late 1930s – launched an agency with Henry Parks in 1944 with Pabst as its main client (Chambers, 2008, p. 79). Edward Brandford opened a small modeling and advertising agency in New York in 1946 (Chambers, 2008, p. 75). With the exceptions of Brandford and Sullivan, little is known about the specific business activities of the 1940s-era agencies, which are now defunct, but it is generally acknowledged that they were mainly involved in promoting black-oriented products to black consumers through black-oriented media – a practice labeled the "special markets" approach (Fox, 1984, p. 278). Sullivan, with a background in sales and advertising for the black press, was the most recognized expert on black consumers during the World War II era, writing for trade and academic publications and speaking at professional conferences (Chambers, 2008, p. 73). In a 1943 *Sales Management* article, he warned advertisers against portrayals which were offensive to blacks and gave examples of art and copy appeals to avoid. Sullivan's standing was boosted significantly among corporate marketers when the executive editor of *Sales Management* endorsed his recommendations exclaiming: "Why this article is important!" (Sullivan, 1943). In other trade articles, he cited income data and spending patterns among African-Americans (Sullivan, 1944; Sullivan, 1945), providing valuable insights for marketers looking to cultivate domestic markets during World War II. Unfortunately for Sullivan, his agency – the "Negro Market Organization" – run mainly as a consultancy since he was unable to maintain a sufficient client base among white advertisers – was closed for financial reasons in 1949 (Chambers, 2008, p. 74). Overall, the practices of early black agencies were consistent with the common racial segregation and overt discrimination of the era which often restricted blacks from opportunities in the broader business sphere. Sullivan, for example, after closing his agency – despite his influence and good reputation – was unable to secure a position in a general-marketing advertising company, although he sent out 1,200 résumés over the next 15 years (Fox, 1984, pp. 278).

World War II and its aftermath had a significant impact on the marketplace. The war increased blacks' awareness of the disparity between America's democratic rhetoric and its unequal treatment of them at home and it also heightened consumer expectations among blacks and other "ethnics" (Blum, 1976). Some marketers capitalized on these rising expectations, like Lever Brothers Corporation – whose president was a member of President Truman's Commission on Civil Rights – which announced a major advertising campaign in the black press in the late 1940s (Walker, 1998, p. 350). By the 1950s, compelling factors fueled interest in black consumers by corporate marketers, such as census data indicating that the black population had increased significantly in size and urban concentration (Weems, 1998), evidence of a growing and economically viable black middle class (Frazier, 1962), successful salesmanship by disk jockeys on "Negro-appeal" radio (Williams, 1998, p. 12), and the landmark 1954 Supreme Court decision in *Brown* vs.

Board of Education, which outlawed segregated facilities in public education. While many desegregation efforts were met with tumultuous public resistance, signs indicated that a more integrated society was approaching. Mainstream marketers and advertising agencies, interested in exploiting this trend, sought help in courting black consumers. Vincent Cullers launched Vince Cullers Advertising, Inc. in Chicago in 1956, America's first black-owned full-service advertising agency. Cullers, a war veteran who studied business and art direction, sought work in mainstream advertising agencies, but due to racial discrimination could not get hired (Chambers, 2008, p. 82). Observing poor-quality and unrealistic advertising executions aimed at black consumers, Cullers launched his agency committed to the idea that "selling Black" involved "thinking Black" (Kern-Foxworth, 2003, p. 426). During the 1950s and 1960s, most of the work done by Culler's agency was for small, local, black businesses. However, some white companies did utilize Cullers – covertly – for help crafting ads for black consumers. Interestingly, Cullers lost a project when a client canceled the job after discovering that he was black, illustrating the overt racial prejudice of the period (Chambers, 2008, p. 82). Yet, Culler's agency would become sustainable over the next decades and its philosophical grounding would propel the agency into the limelight in the 1970s, when the fruits of Civil Rights efforts manifested.

The 1960s: civil rights and "special markets"

The 1960s ushered in a bewildering array of social ideals and controversial issues and the Civil Rights Movement became more strident. Prominent Civil Rights leaders were major proponents of racial desegregation, espousing the benefits of an equal and inclusive society. Passage of the Civil Rights Act of 1964, which outlawed discrimination in public accommodations and employment, dramatically increased opportunities for people of color. The Black Power Movement also emerged during this period, seeking to improve the status of African-Americans through more militant approaches. Overall, socioeconomic gains created new, affluent black consumers on a large scale, who now had unprecedented access to educational, employment, and consumption venues (Davis, 2013). Earning greater incomes, Weems (1998) demonstrates that the monies of black consumers became increasingly infused into the general economy as never before.

Some civil rights efforts focused directly on the advertising industry in the 1960s. Investigations by the Urban League and the NYCCHR indicated discriminatory hiring practices at the major advertising agencies which prompted hearings and picketing in the early 1960s (Fox, 1984, p. 279; Winski, 1992). In 1963, the NAACP and CORE – the Congress for Racial Equality – citing social responsibility, formally lobbied the American Association of Advertising Agencies (4 A's) and the Association of National Advertisers, the industry's leading trade groups, requesting greater employment opportunities and expanded portrayals of black models in ads (Boyenton, 1965, pp. 229–230;

Fox, 1984, pp. 279–280). While the number of blacks in advertisements did improve, agencies largely dismissed the social responsibility argument, claiming that their hiring decisions could not be justified on social and moral grounds, but only in light of marketing objectives and advertiser concerns (Boyenton, 1965). In 1967, figures reported by the NYCCHR showed that blacks held only 3.5 percent of jobs in 35 leading New York City advertising agencies, with a concentration of them in clerical positions (City of New York, 1968, p. 4). The small number of blacks who were hired into professional advertising positions often found themselves assigned to the "special markets" area catering to black consumers. The investigation also showed several blacks had jobs in the media, creative, or research areas within their respective agencies; but only 11 worked in the Account/Client services area and only four held administrative or management jobs. (It is likely that Clarence Holte, Roy Eaton, and George Olden accounted for several of these management positions.) Recommending that advertising agencies adopt affirmative action programs, the NYCCHR did a follow-up study one year later in 1968. It found that the number of blacks at ad agencies had increased to 5.1 percent, but that most of the new jobs were low-level positions in accounting, secretarial, or traffic positions (City of New York, 1968, p. 5). Between 1967 and 1968, the number of blacks doing Account/Client service work only increased by three and the number in administrative jobs remained the same – four. Thus, the NYCCHR concluded that the industry engaged in an "unacceptable pattern of exclusion" (City of New York, 1968, p. 7). White personnel directors blamed the lack of black advertising professionals on poor quality prospects and small numbers of applicants, arguing: "the problem is that the Negroes do not tend to move into the advertising business" (Fox, 1984, p. 279). But a black personnel specialist countered their explanations claiming: "There's discrimination under every rock. Agencies shy away from hiring Negroes because they're afraid an account in the South might object" (Fox, 1984, p. 279). Therefore, while America was preoccupied with issues of race and opportunity in the 1960s, the advertising industry, in general, seemed dismissive of the problems.

Perspectives on "special markets"

While debates over the impact of Civil Rights policies ensued, mainstream interest in black consumers continued to grow along with questions about how to appeal to these consumers. D. Parke Gibson, a black marketing consultant whose influential text – *The $30 Billion Negro* – appeared in 1969, forcefully advanced the idea of a sizeable and lucrative black consumer market and advocated treating this market as distinct, arguing "Customer-oriented programs aimed at Negro consumers are not segregation in reverse, but simply provide the Negro with what he wants – recognition" (Gibson, 1969, p. 12). Gibson's book complemented the efforts of businessman John H. Johnson, publisher of *Ebony* magazine, the era's most financially successful black-owned publication, which launched in 1945 with no support from mainstream advertisers (Dingle, 1999, p. 7). Johnson spent much of the 1960s educating corporate executives on the value of black consumers, running trade ads in *Advertising Age* and the *New York Times* (*Business Week*, 1968). Like Gibson, Johnson encouraged majority firms to treat the black consumer market as separate and unique, and to use black models in ads, arguing that blacks had a psychological need for "self-identification" (Berkman, 1963). These efforts helped to promote the idea of treating minority consumers as distinctive "special markets" and significantly advanced the practice of using ethnic models in advertisements.

Societal desegregation and increased corporate interest in courting black consumers intensified by the late 1960s, establishing the foundation for significant black entrepreneurship in advertising. Joining Vince Cullers, several African-Americans including Junius Edwards, Howard Sanders, John Small, Ray League, and Joan Murray launched advertising agencies between 1965 and 1969. Some were expatriates from mainstream corporations and agencies – among the few who could get hired – but found difficulty advancing in those firms. Others sought to benefit from the new socioeconomic climate, believing the time was right for African-American professionals to attract significant assignments from government and mainstream corporate advertisers.

The 1970s: the golden age of black-owned advertising agencies

Black-owned advertising were agencies opened at a fast pace: by 1972, there were 25 in the United States and more opened later in the decade (Lloyd and Hayes, 1995; Mitchell, 1979). In addition to Vince Cullers Advertising, several of these firms would become the most prominent among black-owned agencies, including: Uniworld in New York City, founded in 1969; Proctor & Gardner (discussed in Chapter 2) founded in 1970, and Burrell McBain (later Burrell Communications) founded in 1971, both in Chicago; and Mingo-Jones-Guilemenot (discussed in Chapter 3) in New York City in 1977. Each of these firms produced significant work and was led by individuals who received substantial recognition within the industry. Uniworld, founded by Byron E. Lewis, was noted for its inventiveness and cultivation of a "blue chip" corporate client roster such as Avon, AT&T, and Gulf Oil. Although Lewis' agency experience was limited, his entrepreneurial leanings prompted the agency to develop noteworthy advertising, promotional, and entertainment work. For example, Uniworld's "Sounds of the City" radio program sustained the agency during lean times and its business interests eventually expanded to include South Africa and the Caribbean (Crain, 2013; Savage, 1999b, p. 361). Tom Burrell, who coined the phrase "Black people are not dark-skinned white people" was credited with developing an advertising method called "positive realism" – showing black models using consumer products in ways realistic and relevant to black consumers, contrary to many of the demeaning images and omissions of the past (Burrell, 2010, p. xi;

Davis, 2003, p. 240; Kern-Foxworth, 1994). Unlike most other black advertising professionals, Burrell prepared for a career in advertising based on a high school aptitude test. Burrell gained experience in the industry for more than ten years at general-market Chicago agencies including Wade Advertising, Leo Burnett, and Needham, Harper & Steers and worked in FCB's London office after his college graduation. At Roosevelt University, where he majored in English and minored in Advertising, Burrell's instructors discouraged him from pursuing a career in advertising warning him that "agencies did not seem to welcome African-Americans on their staffs" (Applegate, 1994, p. 87). But his preparation led to successful leadership of the firm and Burrell's agency garnered a list of major accounts including Procter & Gamble, Ford Motor Company, Coca-Cola, McDonald's, and other national brands. Work for Coca-Cola and McDonald's won Clio awards in the late 1970s, elevating the agency's reputation. Mingo-Jones-Guilemenot, led by Frank Mingo, was the first agency established by a team of black professionals with significant general-market agency management experience; it quickly rose to the top among black-owned agencies. When their advertising careers concluded, Vince Cullers, Byron Lewis, Tom Burrell, and Frank Mingo were all inducted into the Advertising Hall of Fame.

In the 1970s, there were several signals that black agencies had arrived. Agency leaders formed the Afro-American Association of Advertising Agencies in 1973 with Howard Sanders as president and early members including Vince Cullers, Ray League, Byron Lewis, Emmet McBain, Barbara Proctor, and John Small, with a mission to support growth and professionalism among black agencies (*Jet*, 1973). *Black Enterprise*, a magazine concerning black businesses and professionals, began covering the industry and published its first listing of black-owned advertising agencies in 1973. The publication said these agencies did well by acting as "translators" between corporate boardrooms and black communities (Mitchell, 1979). Often, black agencies were involved in adapting national advertising campaigns – initially intended for white audiences – to fit the cultural nuances of the black consumer market. Many also engaged in corporate public relations projects relative to the social uneasiness of the period. While some of these agencies aspired to service general-market accounts, others believed their most viable opportunities were centered on specializing in the black consumer market. Cullers, for example, embraced the black market orientation wholeheartedly, explaining: "Black separation is a fact and we deal with it in a positive way" (*Black Enterprise*, 1973, p. 74). Inspired by the Black Power and Black Pride movements, work produced by Cullers' agency in the 1970s was boldly and unapologetically black – featuring black cultural signs, African-inspired fashion like dashikis, and African language – such as the classic "wantu wazuri" (Swahili for "beautiful people") campaign for the Afro Sheen hair product brand (Kern-Foxworth, 2003, p. 427). Culler's agency also serviced mainstream corporate accounts including Johnson Products, Bristol-Myers, Kellogg's, and Sears aimed at the black consumer market.

Now that targeting black consumers was in vogue, from 1978 through 1991 there was an annual program in New York called the CEBA (Communications Excellence for Black Audiences) Awards, which honored exemplary work in advertising and marketing communications. Where the Clio awards were seen as equivalent to the Oscars for advertising work, the CEBA Awards were earned by black and white advertising firms and professionals for outstanding work aimed at black consumers. Each year, the awards program was co-chaired by two agency or media company CEOs – one black and one white – who served as ambassadors for the program. It also produced an exhibit journal (see Figure 1.2) showcasing hundreds of pages of advertising and marketing materials, research

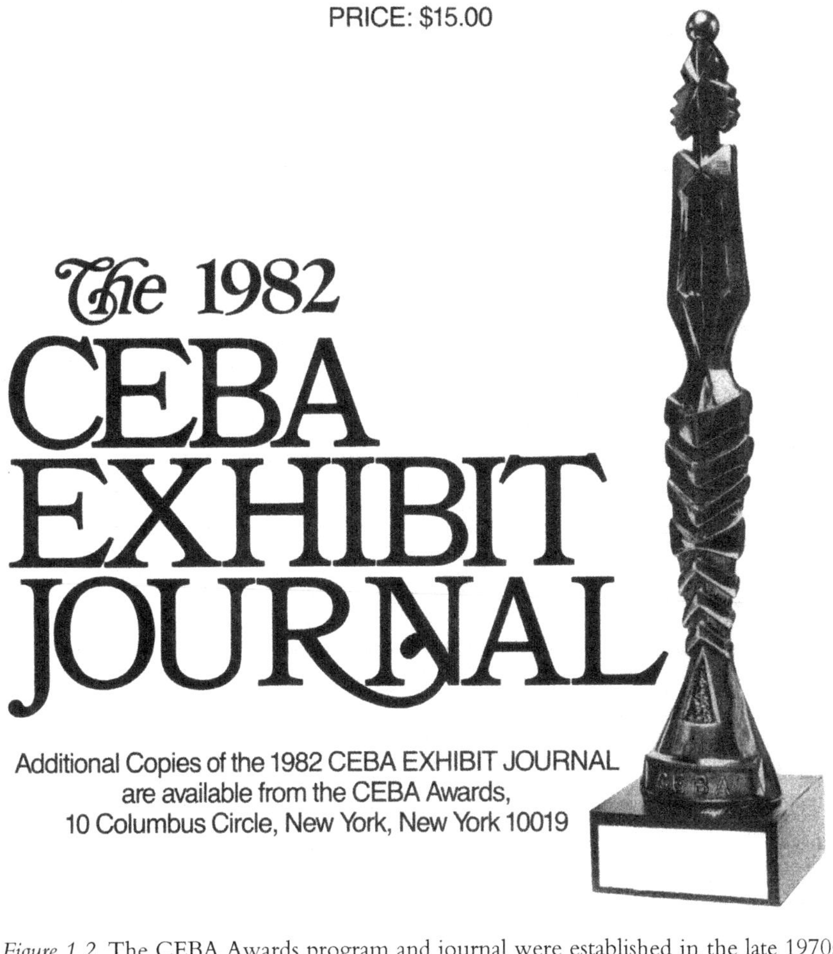

PRICE: $15.00
The 1982
CEBA
EXHIBIT
JOURNAL
Additional Copies of the 1982 CEBA EXHIBIT JOURNAL
are available from the CEBA Awards,
10 Columbus Circle, New York, New York 10019

Figure 1.2 The CEBA Awards program and journal were established in the late 1970s to recognize excellence in marketing communications toward black consumers. The CEBA statuette design symbolized traditional and contemporary influences concerning African and American culture.

Source: *CEBA Exhibit Journal* 1982, inside cover. © World Institute for Black Communications.

on black consumers, and directories of advertising agencies and suppliers. Since the CEBA Awards showcased work targeting black consumers, by default it showcased a lot of black agencies' work and was an important point of pride for black advertising professionals.

Black agencies and black media

By now, corporate leaders generally agreed that using black-oriented media, along with work from black advertising agencies, was an effective strategy for reaching the black consumer market (Weems, 1998, p. 96). In addition to publisher John Johnson's *Ebony* and *Jet* magazines, along with black radio, the early 1970s witnessed a proliferation of new black-oriented magazines: *Essence*, aimed at black women; and *Black Enterprise*, aimed at black professionals, offering advertisers greater access to a national black consumer market in glossy full color (Dates and Barlow, 1990, p. 375). Ads for Afro Sheen created by Vince Culler's agency were key sponsors of the popular *Soul Train* dance program of the 1970s. Thus, black-owned advertising agencies developed a dependency on black-owned media and these entities enjoyed a healthy symbiotic relationship. However, black media had difficulties attracting a "fair share" of advertising dollars, especially for upscale products and services (Graves, 1997, p. 23). When an important agency study suggested that black media were more expensive, on a cost-per-thousand basis, compared with comparable white publications, John Johnson, by now the unofficial spokesperson on black media issues, challenged this conclusion and spent the rest of the decade re-convincing the advertisers of the appropriateness of black media (*Advertising Age*, 1972; Johnson, 1972; Johnson, 1979).

Fallout

The golden age for black advertising firms was short-lived and a number of agencies did not survive the period. Some, like Junius Edwards and John Small, had anticipated a receptive business climate for black advertising entrepreneurs and therefore positioned their agencies to handle mainstream accounts not directed exclusively at black consumers. However, they found it difficult to attract and maintain sufficient general-market business. For example, Small thought he scored a coup in 1970 when he signed a $1 million general-market account with the Singer Corporation's home products division, however, in 1971, Singer started phasing out that division (Chambers, 2008, p. 216). Their aspirations notwithstanding, Small's and Edwards' clients were mainly interested in using them to target black consumers. Another entrepreneur, Howard Sanders, focused heavily on public relations campaigns for corporations, but ran into difficulty as budgets for that type of work diminished when the economy worsened. Some critics complained that corporations were using black agencies only in a token fashion to shore up their images among black consumers (*Black Enterprise*, 1973). An economic recession which began in the mid-1970s had a detrimental impact on the advertising business overall and clients emphasized cost controls and sales results, rather than creative awards and public relations campaigns (Sivulka, 1998, p. 338). By the late 1970s many black-owned agencies fell victim to the bad economy, poor managerial practices, heavy debt loads, and reduced advertiser commitments, culling their ranks from 25 to 13 by 1979 (Johnstone, 1976; Mitchell, 1979).

Black agencies faced a variety of problems by the end of the 1970s. A major issue was that too many agencies were seeking the same small slice of the advertising pie and vying for the same accounts. In 1977, it was estimated that total billings by black-owned agencies accounted for only one-half of 1 percent of the advertising industry's $35 billion total, that only about 20 corporations were targeting black consumers on a consistent basis, and that advertising budgets for the black consumer market were disproportionately small (Dougherty, 1981; Mitchell, 1979). Some critics called the work of black agencies into question, suggesting that they relied too heavily on black slang and stereotypes (Cruz, 2015). Therefore, in order to promote the viability of black-owned agencies, two major solutions were entertained: that the leading black firms merge in order to leverage combined resources; and that agencies do more "crossover" work – i.e., produce more ads designed primarily for black audiences, but which were also extraordinarily appealing to general audiences. However, by the end of the decade, no consolidation among black-owned agencies materialized and substantial crossover assignments were difficult to attract and sustain. There was also talk of black-owned agencies pursuing non-ethnic general-market assignments; however, in the fall of 1979, *Black Enterprise* concluded (Mitchell, 1979):

> "Although their expertise in selling to blacks is usually unquestioned, an opportunity to pitch ads to the general population has been virtually out of the question. It is the advertising industry's equivalent of separate but equal. Black agencies start out aspiring to general-market business, but, with few exceptions, they are forced to limit their sights to the black specialty market – a fact which restricts them to smaller budgets and even smaller profits."

The 1980s: crossing over and the new "urban" appeal

The black-owned agencies which survived the 1970s had achieved a respectable degree of business success. For example, Burrell scored a coup in 1983 when Procter & Gamble hired it to do an African-American-targeted campaign for Crest toothpaste, the first time Procter & Gamble had gone outside of its usual roster of agencies (Dates and Barlow, 1990, p. 439). This assignment significantly raised Burrell's profile within the advertising community and was believed to be tied to the agency's success in future years (Fawcett, 1996). Both the Burrell and Mingo-Jones agencies produced popular campaigns which held crossover appeal, for Martell cognac and Kentucky Fried Chicken, respectively (Smikle, 1985). However, dissension continued over the limited availability of crossover work and the viability of continuing to specialize in the black consumer market amidst growing competition from white agencies. Doug Alligood, an African-American and head of BBD&O's Special Markets division, argued that white-owned agencies were equally capable of targeting black consumers effectively (Mabry, 1989, p. 36). In the mid-1980s, seeking to assist black agencies, long-time Illinois Congresswoman Cardiss Collins proposed legislation to have the U.S. Defense Department set aside 10 percent of its advertising budget for minority agencies (Congress.gov, 2016a); and called for an elimination of tax deductions for advertisers which discriminated against minority agencies (Congress.gov, 2016b; Ellis and Arnold, 1996). However, neither proposal received sufficient support by lawmakers. In the meantime, competition for crossover and general-market assignments intensified among black agencies and it was suggested that the performance of these firms had earned them the right to pursue more lucrative, general-market contracts (Smikle, 1985).

Other critical issues emerged for black agencies. In the 1980s, African-Americans became the "in" group with respect to social cultural cues regarding fashion, language, sports, and entertainment. Around this time, the term "urban" emerged and was largely associated with black trendsetters, who often lived in cities and urban environments. However, this term not only connoted a lifestyle associated with African-American opinion leaders, but expanded to influence marketing directed at youth and other demographic groups situated in urban settings. This prompted general-market advertising agencies to pursue "urban" consumers and their followers with greater intensity, creating more competition for black-owned agencies. For example, in 1987 the general-market agency Backer Spielvogel Bates backed a venture led by two black co-CEOs, Dr. Charles Jamison and Kathryn Leary, for help catering to black consumers based on a psychosocial understanding of the market (King and Reid-Dove, 1988). Former executives with the Bates agency, Jamison, who held a Ph.D. in psychology, and Leary, who had an MBA from Stanford, owned 51 percent of the Jamison & Leary agency while the parent company Bates owned 49 percent. For several years, the agency successfully handled accounts including tourism for the island of Martinique, Gazelle skin care products, General Foods, PepsiCo, the Alvin Ailey Dance Theater, and M&M Mars – winning a CEBA award in its second year (Jamison, 1994). However, the agency lost its footing when a corporate merger abruptly changed its relationship with its parent company and disagreements over operation of the company emerged (Jamison, 1994). In the midst of a severe recession and five years after its inception, Jamison & Leary closed forever and the partners moved on to other lines of work.

The 1990s: new industry configurations and the rise of multicultural marketing

The brutal economic recession of the late 1980s to early 1990s hit the advertising industry particularly hard. *Business Week* magazine asked "What Happened to Advertising?" (Landler, 1991) citing widespread reductions in corporate spending on advertising and dynamic changes within the industry, including new compensation models and the growing influence of an integrated marketing communications orientation whereby promotional activities were no longer limited to advertising (Jones, 1999). In addition, as indicated early in this chapter, a major change in the industry was the transformation of independent advertising agencies into publicly held entities held wholly or partly by holding companies, in efforts to establish scale economies and to protect agency incomes from large fluctuations (Jones, 1999, p. 9). Now, advertising agencies were managed separately and operated in competition with one another under the same corporate umbrella. In the meantime, old and new problems faced black-owned agencies, which largely remained independent. Trade reports indicated that the practice of using minority-owned agencies to produce minority-oriented campaigns was entrenched in the industry, yet, general-market assignments were largely unavailable (*Advertising Age*, 1997). Robert Dale, CEO of R.J. Dale Advertising in Chicago, bluntly observed: "[Black agencies] often specialize in African-American markets because we are forced to. We are not allowed to compete for and service advertisers on a general-market basis" (*Knight-Ridder/Tribune Business News*, 1995). Moreover, by this time, a similar business model had replicated itself among other minority advertising entrepreneurs – Hispanics and Asians – who had mostly entered the industry after 1980 to cater to "multicultural" consumers (*Advertising Age*, 2001). *Advertising Age* began grouping these firms in a separate "multicultural" listing on a regular basis, indicating industry-wide normalizing of the practice. Jo Muse, head of Muse Codero Chen, a multicultural agency, lamented (Winski, 1992, p. 17):

> "The biggest tragedy that I confront every day is this 'ghettoization' of the business. In the ad business, we're still set up so that if you happen to have a brown skin or if you happen to have a black skin, you have got to create your own league to play in.... If you want to be successful, entrepreneurial, you've got to have a Negro league or you've got to have an Hispanic league. Do you know how outrageous that sounds?"

Given the conditions in the industry, industry expert John Jones (1999, p. 12) indicated that despite fundamental changes within the industry, the largest advertising agencies at the end of the 1990s were essentially the same as 30 years prior. Data reported in trade publications supported Jones' conclusions. Davis' (2002) study compared the top ranked black- and white-owned advertising agencies in 1972 with those in 2000, based on U.S. billings data reported in *Black Enterprise* and *Advertising Age* (see Table 1.1). Among the white-owned agencies, 11 of the 15 largest agencies (or their derivatives) in 1972 were also among the 15 largest in the year 2000. In contrast, only two of the black-owned agencies identified by *Black Enterprise* among the top 15 in 1972 – Uniworld and Burrell – appeared on the list in 2000. In the meantime, industry data showed an increase in the total number of U.S. advertising

Table 1.1 Top 15 black- and white-owned advertising agencies, 1972 and 2000 (ranked by U.S. billings, in $000,000s)

1972 data			*2000 data*		
Rank	*Agency*	*Billings*	*Agency*	*Billings*	*Holding company affiliation*
	Black-owned agencies:				
1	John F. Small, Inc.	7.0	Don Coleman/GlobalHue	270.0	Interpublic
2	Zebra Associates	4.7	Uniworld Group, Inc.*	245.8	WPP Group
3	Junius Edwards, Inc.	3.5	Burrell Comm. Group*	179.4	Publicis
4	Uniworld Group	3.5	Chisholm-Mingo Group	104.6	None
5	Vince Cullers Adv., Inc.	2.5	Carol H. Williams Adv.	91.0	None
6	Burrell McBain	2.0	Muse Creative Holdings	76.0	None
7	Proctor and Gardner	1.8	The Wimbley Group	32.3	None
8	PHAT Advertising Cons.	1.2	E. Morris Comm.	31.5	None
9	Howard Sanders Adv.	1.2	Spike/DDB	30.0	Omnicom
10	Eden Advertising	1.0	R. J. Dale Adv. & PR	28.0	None
11	Vanguard Associates	1.0	Matlock Adv. & PR	25.0	None
12	Tom Cleveland & Assoc.	0.850	Sykes Communications	22.7	None
13	Communicon, Inc.	0.500	Washington Daniel Adv.	20.0	None
14	Wright, Edelen Adv., Inc.	0.500	Anderson Communications	17.5	None
15	Few, Hunter & Wilson	0.200	Caroline Jones, Inc.	15.2	None

	White-owned agencies:				
1	J. Walter Thompson	393.0	McCann-Erickson WW*	6,564.4	Interpublic
2	Young & Rubicam	357.7	Young & Rubicam*	6,194.7	WPP Group
3	BBD&O	323.2	FCB Worldwide*	5,712.1	Interpublic
4	Leo Burnett	313.4	BBDO Worldwide*	4,599.3	Omnicom
5	DDB	259.1	DDB Worldwide*	4,252.8	Omnicom
6	Ted Bates & Co.	252.8	Grey Worldwide*	4,068.7	Grey Global Group
7	Grey Advertising	247.0	J. Walter Thompson*	4,032.5	WPP Group
8	McCann-Erickson	207.7	Ogilvy & Mather WW*	3,972.5	WPP Group
9	Ogilvy & Mather	200.0	Euro RSCG Worldwide	3,324.7	Havas
10	FCB	194.3	Leo Burnett Worldwide*	3,140.0	Bcom3 Group
11	Darcy, McManus & Masius	181.0	Darcy, Masius, Benton & Bowles *	2,991.6	Bcom3 Group
12	Dancer-Fitzgerald-Sample	178.0	Saatchi & Saatchi	2,676.8	Publicis
13	Needham, Harper & Steers	171.5	Campbell-Ewald	1,936.3	Interpublic
14	William Esty & Co.	165.0	TBWA Worldwide	1,877.4	Omnicom
15	N.W. Ayer & Sons	160.2	Bates USA*	1,594.5	Cordiant

Sources: *Advertising Age* Agency Report, February 26, 1973, p. 30; *Advertising Age* Agency Report, April 23, 2001, p. s-2; *Advertising Age*'s Advertising Organization Family Trees, April 23, 2001; *Black Enterprise*, Advertising Agencies, June 1973, p. 67; *Black Enterprise*, B.E. Advertising Agencies, June 2001, p. 195.

Note

* These agencies appear on both the 1972 and the 2000 listings of the top 15 advertising firms.

agencies billing at least $1 million annually, according to listings in the *Standard Directory of Advertising Agencies* (1996). Burrell boosted its size by acquiring DFA Communications, a general-market and direct marketing agency in the mid-1990s, thereby expanding its presence and billings over the $100 million mark (Davis, 2003, p. 240; Savage, 1999a, p. 99). Yet, the Table 1.1 data also underscore the relatively small size of the leading black-owned agencies compared with the leading white-owned agencies. In 2000, total billings for the top 15 black agencies accounted for about $1.2 billion, which was about half of 1 percent of the industry's $214 billion U.S. total, consistent with black agencies' reported 1970s-era share of the advertising market. In contrast, the top 15 white agencies in the same year collectively billed nearly $57 billion, equivalent to about 27 percent of the industry's total. These findings indicated quantitatively that a business model which often restricted black agencies to the black and "urban" consumer segments constrained their abilities to grow their firms significantly over time. Therefore, for the most part, black agencies – compared with white agencies – started out and remained as relatively small enterprises.

Multicultural focus

Urban marketing was soon followed by another marketing trend – multiculturalism – in the 1990s (Teinowitz, 1998; Webster, 1997). Multiculturalism emerged as a potent new socioeconomic orientation, prompted by shifting population demographics indicating the "browning" of America. Agencies owned by people of color faced a new formidable threat: their traditional niches were being pursued – this time by competitor agencies seeking expansion into the newly popular "multicultural" markets. In this environment, some black-owned agencies gained new stature: in a landmark moment in March 1998 trade publication *Adweek* named Burrell and Uniworld on its list of the top 100 advertising agencies for the first time (Ayers-Williams, 1998, p. 153). Pleased with the listing, Tom Burrell commented that the recognition "confirms our creativity and also that we are a solid business enterprise" (Ayers-Williams, 1998, p. 156). That same year, *Black Enterprise* resumed its annual report on the advertising business after a 25-year hiatus (Ayers-Williams, 1998, p. 153). Agencies with expertise in multicultural markets became hot properties and by 2000, 136 agencies were listed in the "Special Markets" section of the *Standard Directory of Advertising Agencies* (2000), with 32, 30, and 74 indicated as specializing in the African-American, Asian, and Hispanic market segments, respectively. A few agencies were listed across multiple ethnic categories. By 1998, a number of major general-market agencies formed ethnic boutiques including JWT, BBD&O, Leo Burnett, Saatchi & Saatchi, and DDB Needham – a merger of the DDB agency with Needham, Harper, and Steers (Hayes, 1998, p. 170). In partnership with the famous African-American filmmaker Spike Lee, DDB Needham formed Spike DDB in 1997, with 51 percent ownership by Lee, to specialize in multicultural urban marketing. An industry insider predicted that all major agencies would eventually have multicultural divisions (Linnett, 2001). Ethnic divisions and partnerships were often supported by generous resources available from their parent companies, and some hired away the most talented employees from existing minority-owned agencies, creating consternation among advertising professionals of color (Hayes, 2000b). Once again, established black agencies pondered survival strategies, which included adding more integrated marketing services to their offerings, delving into internet-based marketing, and merging to form a black superagency. Noting that since the late 1980s, only about one-third of the advertising dollars aimed at black consumers was channeled through black-owned agencies (Hayes, 1999), an industry insider concluded (Ayers-Williams, 1998 p. 154):

> "In a sense, the black agency has been the victim of its own success. It sold white advertisers on the potential of the black consumer market, and now these companies are turning to their white agencies to help deliver the goods. Black agencies are fighting for the very market they helped create."

By the 1990s, new black-owned agencies appeared, receiving significant press attention and causing concern among the more senior black agencies. Uniworld's Lewis commented, "It's ironic that we, the pioneers, must compete with upstarts for our survival" (Ayers-Williams, 1998, p. 154). Chief among these new players was Don Coleman, who established an agency in Michigan in 1988 and later renamed it GlobalHue to reflect its multicultural orientation; and the Carol H. Williams Advertising (CHWA) agency, launched in 1986 by an African-American woman (discussed in Chapter 5). Unlike early black agencies, Coleman purposefully avoided pursuing general-market accounts in favor of multicultural business, asking: "Why would I jump into that shark tank when I'm dealing with the fastest growing ethnic segments that my general-market competition knows nothing about?" (Hayes, 1998, p. 170). Coleman's agency avoided reliance on so-called "ghetto" portrayals often presented in urban multicultural advertising, instead using a blend of sophistication and hipness; it also declined assignments from cigarette companies, citing deaths from lung cancer (Hayes, 1998, p. 168). By 2001, Coleman, a former Burrell employee, surpassed all black-owned agencies in billings and remained in the top position for well over a decade, beginning in 2001. Coleman's firm is the only black-owned agency in history named three times by *Black Enterprise* as "Agency of the Year" – in 1998, 2003, and 2010 (Alleyne, 2010; Hayes, 1998; Hughes, 2003). Moreover, in 2009, trade publication *Adweek* recognized GlobalHue as "Multicultural Agency of the Decade" (Aditham, 2009). Starting out focused on African-American consumers, Coleman's long-term strategy was to capitalize on the national multicultural marketing trend by also catering to Hispanic and Asian consumers and offering a wide range of marketing communication services. To execute his vision, Coleman acquired several other agencies which specialized in

Asian and Hispanic consumer segments and renamed the agency GlobalHue in 2001. Eventually the agency split into four divisions – GlobalHue Africanic, GlobalHue Latino, GlobalHue Asian, and GlobalHue Next – which targeted the influential youth market (Alleyne, 2010, p. 164). GlobalHue's positioning catapulted the agency's billings above other top black-owned agencies – often by millions of dollars (see Table 1.2). GlobalHue's client roster included Chrysler, Verizon, Federal Express, Subway, the U.S. Navy, the U.S. Census, Wal-Mart, and the Bermuda tourism account. In the late 1990s, an industry insider noted: "Only five or six [black] companies are really doing any serious business out there today – particularly Uniworld, Burrell and Don Coleman. Nearly everybody else is struggling, at best" (Ayers-Williams, 1998, p. 154). Indeed, in 1999, *Black Enterprise* data indicated that the leading three black agencies, Don Coleman, Uniworld, and Burrell, accounted for 53 percent of all billings, and 50 percent of all employment, among all black agencies listed (*Black Enterprise*, 1999).

The 49 percent solution

Given the emphasis on urban and multicultural consumers, mainstream firms were keenly interested in acquiring black advertising agencies (*Detroit Free Press*, 1999). The major prospects were Burrell, Uniworld, and Don Coleman Advertising/GlobalHue, since they were the largest black-owned agencies and billed in excess of $100 million (*Black Enterprise*, 1999; Hayes, 1999; Snyder, 1999). Like GlobalHue, Uniworld also added Hispanic marketing to its repertoire of services to better compete in the multicultural marketing sphere. Highly sensitive to their positions within the black business community, the leadership of these agencies appeared interested in developing alliances which would enhance their survival and growth, but also allowed them to maintain management control over their enterprises. Heide Gardner, then Vice President of diversity programs at the AAF, noted (Hayes, 1999, p. 173):

> "Black agencies have been the last holdouts. [They are] classic entrepreneurs with dreams and visions. It's important that their companies still retain the vision and they have some control. If they were in it for the money, they would have sold a long time ago."

Around the turn of the new millennium, the three largest black-owned agencies each formed a strategic alliance with a large holding company or partner, selling a 49 percent stake in their firms (Alexander, 2000; Chura, 1999; Dreazen, 1999). Burrell partnered with Publicis; Uniworld with WPP Group; and GlobalHue with True North Communications, which named Don Coleman as CEO of its New America Strategies Group, a multicultural unit comprising various ethnic specialty marketers (Hughes, 2003, p. 194). However, True North was subsequently acquired by holding company

Interpublic, so GlobalHue became a part of that large network. Coleman defended his company's partnership arguing (Moss, 2001, p. 190):

> "In general, the advertising business is going to consolidate more. I think we are going to end up with four major holding companies, when it's all said and done. The acquisition could only help us. I'm a believer, that if you are not on one of the major teams, you are not going to be able to play in the big league. I think the day of the big viable independent [agency] is rapidly coming to a close. You're probably going to have to be a part of a major agency network to get at some of these big clients."

Similarly, mainstream conglomerates also sought ownership of black-oriented media outlets (McCoy, 1998; Pine, 2001). BET Holdings, parent company of the Black Entertainment Television cable channel, was acquired by Viacom in 2000. BET founder, Bob Johnson, responding to critics of the sale, called the agreement "strategically sound" (Ernst, 2000; Smith, 2000). Later, conglomerate Time Inc. acquired *Essence* magazine and JP Morgan Chase purchased a substantial stake in Johnson Publishing, parent company of popular *Ebony* and *Jet* magazines (Marek, 2015). In an interview, Bob Johnson argued: "the days of 100 percent black-owned business are dead … because major enterprises are coming after our market" (Hocker, 2001).

Black agencies in the new millennium: multiculturalism goes mainstream

As in previous decades, the American economy fluctuated significantly during the first ten years of the 2000s, impacting the fortunes of advertising agencies. Significant events of the decade included the 2008 election of Barack Obama as America's first African-American President and the Great Recession which started that same year. By now, America's population was more diverse and multiculturalism became the new normal. While interest by large marketers in multicultural consumers intensified, articles in trade publications reflected dissention over the meaning of multiculturalism and its effect on practices within the advertising industry. One issue was whether multiculturalism increased business opportunities for agencies owned by people of color. Responding to this issue during an Advertising Educational Foundation (2001) internet chat, agency chief Jo Muse said:

> "More business for minority-owned agencies *can* be a result of diversity. But if a general-market firm is a great one and also diversifies, it could be bad for firms like mine. The point is, minority shops compete with bigger, stronger general shops who can also diversify."

Acknowledging the practice of establishing multicultural departments within mainstream agencies, often staffed by minorities, critics argued that such arrangements limited the professional development of people of color and

Table 1.2 Top ten black-owned advertising agencies, in U.S. billings (000,000), 1998–2010 (even years)

Rank	*1998*	*2000*	*2002*	*2004*	*2006*	*2008*	*2010*
1	Burrell Comm. $168.0 Staff: 162 Thomas Burrell	Uniworld $230.0 Staff: 138 Byron Lewis	GlobalHue $330.0 Staff: 182 Don Coleman	GlobalHue $325.0 Staff: 180 Don Coleman	GlobalHue $470.0 Staff: 205 Don Coleman	GlobalHue $720.0 Staff: 300 Don Coleman	GlobalHue $483.5 Staff: 183 Don Coleman
2	Uniworld $162.0 Staff: 135 Byron Lewis	Don Coleman/ GlobalHue $202.0 Staff: 141 Don Coleman	Uniworld $258.5 Staff: 154 Byron Lewis	CHWA $300.0 Staff: 135 Carol Williams	CHWA $367.5 Staff: 173 Carol Williams	CHWA $345.0 Staff: 155 Carol Williams	CHWA $280.0 Staff: 101 Carol Williams
3	Don Coleman $111.0 Staff: 101 Don Coleman	Burrell Comm. $175.2 Staff: 125 Thomas Burrell	Burrell Comm. $181.6 Staff: 135 Thomas Burrell	Burrell Comm. $190.0 Staff: 129 Thomas Burrell	Uniworld $200.2 Staff: 130 Byron Lewis	Uniworld $242.7 Staff: 146 Byron Lewis	Uniworld $202.0 Staff: 110 Byron Lewis
4	Chisholm-Mingo $173.7 Staff: 43 Sam Chisholm	Chisholm-Mingo $100.5 Staff: 65 Sam Chisholm	Chisholm- Mingo $100.0 Staff: 68 Sam Chisholm	Uniworld $183.6 Staff: 127 Byron Lewis	Burrell Comm. $200.0 Staff: 135 Fay Ferguson/ McGhee Osse	Burrell Comm. $205.0 Staff: 135 Fay Ferguson/ McGhee Osse	Burrell $180.0 Staff: 116 Fay Ferguson/ McGhee Osse
5	Muse-Codero- Chen $50.0 Staff: 47 J. Melvin Muse	Muse Creative Holdings $73.7 Staff: 45 J. Melvin Muse	Muse Creative Holdings $73.0 Staff: 45 J. Melvin Muse	Compas, Inc. $140.0 Staff: 55 Stan Woodland	Compas, Inc. $200.0 Staff: 53 Stan Woodland	Sanders/Wingo $89.6 Staff: 72 Robert Wingo	Sanders/Wingo $130.0 Staff: 115 Robert Wingo

6	CHWA $48.5 Staff: 24 Carol Williams	CHWA $61.0 Staff: 35 Carol Williams	CHWA $72.0 Staff: 38 Carol Williams	Muse-Codero-Chen Partners $80.0 Staff: 43 J. Melvin Muse	Muse Comm. $75.0 Staff: 45 J. Melvin Muse	IMAGES USA $72.4 Staff: 45 Robert McNeil	IMAGES USA $86.5 Staff: 55 Robert McNeil
7	Sykes Comm. $24.0 Staff: 22 Ray Sykes III	Wimbley Grp. $50.30 Staff: 25 Chas. Wimbley	Equals 3 Comm. $68.0 Staff: 80 Eugene Faison	Equals 3 Comm. $70.0 Staff: 70 Eugene Faison	Matlock Adv. & PR $63.1 Staff: 38 Kent Matlock	Prime Access $71.4 Staff: 44 Howard Buford	o2ideas Inc. $77.4 Staff: 65 Shelley Stewart
8	Wimbley Group $23.0 Staff: 18 Charles Wimbley	E. Morris Com. $27.1 Staff: 30 Eugene Morris	E. Morris Com. $32.1 Staff: 43 Eugene Morris	Spike/DDB $45.0 Staff: 45 Spike Lee	Sanders/Wingo $56.5 Staff: 42 Robert Wingo	Muse Comm. $71.2 Staff: 45 J. Melvin Muse	Prime Access $73.1 Staff: 61 Howard Buford
9	RJ Dale Adv. $22.7 Staff: 19 Robert Dale	Sykes Comm. $25.0 Staff: 30 Ray Sykes III	RJ Dale Adv. $26.6 Staff: 15 Robert Dale	Anderson Comm. $40.0 Staff: 18 Virgil Scott	E. Morris Com. $54.7 Staff: 43 Eugene Morris	Matlock Adv. & PR $56.7 Staff: 35 Kent Matlock	FUSE $65.1 Staff: 20 Clifford Franklin
10	Spike/DDB $22.5 Staff: 15 Spike Lee	RJ Dale Adv. $24.7 Staff: 22 Robert Dale	Matlock Adv. $25.0 Staff: 30 Kent Matlock Spike/DDB $25.0 Staff: 10	Matlock Adv. $38.0 Staff: 30 Kent Matlock	FUSE $52.0 Staff: 24 Clifford Franklin	FUSE $55.5 Staff: 23 Clifford Franklin	Walton Isaacson $25.0 Staff: 45 Aaron Walton/ Cory Isaacson

Sources: *Black Enterprise*, BE 100s Annual Advertising Agency listings, June issues, 1998–2010.

continued to breed ethnic and racial separation within the advertising profession, similar to character Andre Johnson's dilemma on the *Black-ish* television program. A creative director wrote to *Advertising Age* (Hall, 2001, p. 20):

> "The creation of such departments, as does the creation of companies that supposedly specialize in urban youth and multicultural marketing, also relieves whites of their responsibility to learn about other cultures and their responsibility to include us in advertising. While I'm sure the intentions by most industry leaders are honorable, the language, strategies and practices by many seem to be leading us in the wrong direction, and continue to breed a segregated workplace that creates segregated communications."

But the issue became moot as the industry increasingly established ethnic cells within mainstream firms. A 2004 industry survey showed that nearly 60 percent of advertising professionals favored maintaining dedicated multicultural departments within general-market agencies (Wentz, 2004). They believed that this arrangement would give them competitive advantages in addressing lucrative segments while remaining sensitive to the cultural nuances of African-American, Hispanic, Asian, and other "specialty" consumer markets. Some also believed that merely fusing multicultural efforts together with general-market advertising strategies would dilute messages aimed at multicultural segments such that the efforts would be ineffective. Therefore, the business model of maintaining separate multicultural units in mainstream firms gained considerable acceptance.

There was also discord concerning alliances between minority agencies and major holding companies. Proponents argued that such relationships were reflective of industry trends and were essential to firms' survival. For example, Uniworld's Byron Lewis was pleased with his agency's relationship with WPP Group, but, by 2003, Coleman's relationship with Interpublic appeared strained and *Advertising Age* reported that Coleman desired to buy back GlobalHue's shares and return to independence (Halliday and Sanders, 2003). Several minority agency chiefs predicted fewer black-owned advertising firms in the future due to increased consolidations and failures among independent agencies. Critics disparaged the motivations behind holding company partnerships, citing opportunism and a lack of commitment to the equitable sharing of wealth among minority business partners (Jackson, 1999; Leo, 1999). One advertising executive complained in *Advertising Age* (Leo, 1999, p. 54):

> "Marketers are merely trying to keep pace with the changing face of consumers. The degree to which a marketer can meaningfully appeal to a cultural script is the degree to which multicultural advertising will be effective. Multicultural agencies have further mystified the discipline by blurring the distinction between marketing and social/political correctness. These agencies, for the most part, are driven by high profile and strong personalities within the various [ethnic] communities. Once they cash out, what will be left of the business? What are mainstream agencies buying? More business? Expertise? Conflict shops?"

In the meantime, much of the emphasis on multicultural marketing shifted toward Latino consumers – since data from the 2000 U.S. Census showed Hispanics as the largest ethnic minority group. Therefore, given the language aspect, mainstream marketers turned to Latino professionals for help in courting the Hispanic market, just as they turned to African-American professionals in the past for help courting black consumers (Hayes, 2002). As such, marketing dollars increasingly flowed toward Hispanic campaigns, often at the expense of budgets previously allocated toward the black consumer market. For example, GlobalHue derived 52 percent of its billings from Hispanic-oriented marketing in 2006 (*Black Enterprise*, 2006, p. 166). Concurrently, the popularity of urban, hip-hop, and Latino cultures expanded and many young whites, Asians, suburban-dwellers, and others embraced these lifestyle trends. Mindful of the influences on consumer tastes, general-market agencies continued to emphasize their own departments oriented toward urban and multicultural marketing.

Still seeking equality

Along with new competitive pressures, the old equality issue for black advertising professionals was still problematic and the relevance of black agencies in the new millennium was questioned (Smiley, 2014). Concerns over contract awards and media purchasing practices ensued, with activists claiming black companies were not receiving their fair share of advertising budgets. A trade report showed that only 1 percent of total advertising spending was allocated toward "minority" agencies and of that small percentage, black agencies received about 30 percent (Hayes, 2003, p. 178). In addition, investigations by the Federal Communications Commission (FCC) revealed documentation of "no urban dictates" – warnings not to buy advertising time on radio stations with predominantly minority audiences – leading the FCC to conclude that minority-owned agencies and media were underutilized and underpaid, even when audience demographics were comparable to white consumers (Hayes, 1999, p. 174; Ofori, 1999). Calling for greater enforcement of existing policies, David Honig, President of the Minority Media and Telecommunications Council, complained to the FCC (*Target Market News*, 2009): "This travesty has gone on for decades ... although the practice most often occurs under the cover of whispered oral instructions." Seeking to improve conditions for black agencies and media, diversity and inclusion efforts were advocated by federal legislators, civil rights organizations, trade groups, and educational institutions (American Advertising Federation, 1999; Hayes, 1999; Teinowitz, 2000). President Bill Clinton signed an executive order mandating that the federal government offer more procurement opportunities to minority contractors, with special language pertaining to advertising (*Advertising Age*, 2000). However, in the mid-2000s, the NYCCHR – as it had in the 1960s – again probed the advertising industry, alleging bias in hiring and media buying practices and holding a demonstration in front of a major New York advertising agency (Sanders, 2004).

New industry realities

In the new millennium, the modern advertising industry was highly consolidated, corporatized, and cost-conscious. Alcohol-soaked client lunches, lavish entertainment, and copious gift-giving were things of the past. In addition, technological advancements including internet-based marketing, social media, and mobile devices grew dramatically and impacted how consumers connected with media, marketers, and each other. Spending on digital marketing increased significantly while some media platforms, especially traditional print and radio, lost revenues. Entrepreneurs and firms possessing high-tech skills became very valuable to marketers, yet new concerns arose regarding tech issues such as audience measurement accuracy, ad avoidance behaviors, and consumer privacy. At the same time, the industry increasingly embraced an integrated marketing communications orientation, which promoted a synergistic approach to marketing using a variety of new and digital marketing tools. Overall, the advertising business had become very complex, forcing professionals and agencies – black or white – to embrace new skill sets and business models in order to remain competitive.

Introducing pioneering African-American adwomen

As the background in this chapter indicates, women and – much later – African-Americans served in significant professional roles in the advertising industry from the late 1800s forward. Such participation also included African-American women who have often been overlooked by advertising historians. Retired adwoman Jane Maas recalled when O&M hired its first African-American copywriter, a woman named Betty – her last name was not recalled – in 1968 who was assigned to Maas' group. Maas (2012, p. 131), explained:

> "The day before Betty arrived, the copy chief of the agency took me aside and told me quite seriously that if I became aware of any 'anti-Negro comments or gestures,' I had full power to fire the perpetrator on the spot. Nobody said a word. Betty came quietly, stayed with us for about a year, wrote some effective ads, and moved on to a better job at another agency. She helped us take a big step forward."

Maas does not discuss whether Betty was hired in response to political pressures of the day, such as the well-known 1960s-era investigations of New York advertising agencies, but the historical record suggests this is a plausible explanation for Betty's employment. In fact, a number of "Bettys" worked in American advertising firms starting in the 1960s, including those who later served in significant executive and entrepreneurial roles. This research recognizes the presence and contributions of these women, although all their names may not be known or reflected in the historical record. In the context of this research, there are only four African-American advertising women – Barbara Gardner Proctor, Caroline R. Jones, Joel P. Martin, and Carol H.

Williams – whose biographical data were available *and* who met the criteria for inclusion given the parameters of this study. This research focuses on pioneering African-American women who served in significant managerial positions in mainstream advertising agencies *and* founded prominent advertising firms bearing their own names.

There is another African-American woman – G. Joyce Hamer – who also ran an agency bearing her own name, in the late 1970s through mid-1980s. Although she was unavailable for full examination in this study, there is limited information about her business activities from other sources. She was a partner in the black-owned Lockhart, Pettus, and Hamer agency which launched in 1977, but left about a year later to start her own agency to focus on the "lucrative women's market" (Brooks and Walls, 1982). Located at 157 West 57th Street in New York City, Hamer Advertising and Marketing Concepts first appeared in the 1979 *CEBA Exhibit Journal* and featured public service advertising and ads for several local political candidates. In the early 1980s, her agency did assignments for black hair care products including Johnson Products' Stay-Sof-Fro and Carson's Little Miss Honey & Spice brand. Sensitive to the climate concerning black women in high-level advertising positions, Hamer often sent a white male to initial client meetings so that the men could "tell the boys' jokes and get it out of the way" (Fox, 1984, p. 323). By 1981 the agency had developed a magazine as a single advertiser vehicle for the Seagram's Distillers Company aimed at black readers. Called "Seagram's Guide to Taking Care of Business," the magazine concerned career advice, economic development, and cultural enrichment for black consumers. Explaining the purpose of the vehicle, Hamer told a newspaper "Our readers are an untapped market growing in sophistication and income" (*Afro-American*, 1985, p. 6). While Hamer's firm enjoyed recognition through the mid-1980s, after 1985 her work no longer appeared in the CEBA publications and no further information about the agency is available. In addition, Hamer's main client – Seagram's – went out of business in the mid-2000s and the demise of the distiller was widely reported in the press.

Oddly, Hamer is the only black adwoman referenced in Fox's *The Mirror Makers*, one of the most oft-cited sources on the history of advertising and its people. However, by the time Fox's book was published in 1984, pioneers Barbara Proctor, Caroline Jones, Joel Martin, and Carol Williams already had distinguished advertising careers. Therefore it is curious that they were left out of his book. But, in the next four chapters, the experiences and contributions of these four prominent African-American adwomen executive/entrepreneurs are examined in detail. Subsequently, their roles are analyzed and conclusions about their experiences are drawn. Other African-American adwomen who served in significant executive roles are acknowledged in the Epilogue of this book and the future for African-American women in advertising is discussed.

References

Aditham, K. (2009) 'GlobalHue's Kelli Coleman Reacts to *Adweek* Nod,' *Adweek*, December 14 [Online]. Available at: www.adweek.com/agencyspy/globalhues-kelli-coleman-reacts-to-adweek-nod/6190. (Accessed: December 22, 2015).

Advertising Age (1972) 'Black Media Less Efficient, Y & R Says,' April 3, p. 1.

Advertising Age (1997) 'Where the 100 LNA Go for Help,' November 17, pp. s-14.

Advertising Age (2000) 'Minority Ad Shops Win Support from President,' October 9, pp. 1–2.

Advertising Age (2001) 'Top 25 Multicultural Shops,' April 23, p. s-22.

Advertising Age (2002) 'There's Something about Mary,' April 15, pp. 15–22.

Advertising Age (2003) 'Women to Watch,' June 2, pp. s-1–s-16.

Advertising Age (2012) '100 Most Influential Women in Advertising,' September 24, pp. 18–44.

Advertising Educational Foundation (2001) Internet Chat with Jo Muse, CEO, Muse Codero Chen, Inc. Available at: www.aef.com (Accessed: February 7, 2001).

Afro-American (1985) 'Ad Agency Takes Over Magazine for Black Men,' September 14, p. 6.

Alexander, G. (2000) 'Matter of Survival,' *Black Enterprise*, September, p. 23.

Alleyne, S. (2010) 'Making Cultural Connections,' *Black Enterprise*, June, pp. 162–167.

Alvesson, M. (1998) 'Gender Relations and Identity at Work: A Case Study of Masculinities and Femininities in an Advertising Agency,' *Human Relations*, 51(8), pp. 969–1005.

American Advertising Federation (1999) 'Procter & Gamble, True North and Chisholm-Mingo Executives to Head AAF Committee on Multicultural Advertising Practices' [Online]. Available at: www.aaf.org/news/pr-multiculturalcomm.htm (Accessed: September 1, 2000).

Applegate, E. (1994) *The Ad Men and Women: A Biographical Dictionary of Advertising*. Westport, CT: Greenwood Press.

Ayers-Williams, R. (1998) 'A Battle for Billings,' *Black Enterprise*, June, pp. 153–160.

Bartos, R. (1982) *Moving Target: What Every Marketer Should Know About Women*. New York: Free Press.

Bendick, M. and Egan, M. (2009) *Research Perspectives on Race and Employment in the Advertising Industry*. Washington, D.C.: Bendick and Egan Economic Consultants, Inc.

Bennington, E. (2012) 'Charlotte Beers: It's "Tough" at the Top and Women Need to Be Ready,' *Forbes*, September 12 [Online]. Available at: www.forbes.com/sites/emilybennington/2012/09/28/charlotte-beers-its-tough-at-the-top-and-women-need-to-be-ready/ (Accessed: September 28, 2012).

Berkman, D. (1963) 'Advertising in Ebony and Life: Negro Aspirations vs. Reality,' *Journalism Quarterly*, 40(1), pp. 57–58.

Bird, C. (1976) *Enterprising Women*. New York: Mentor.

Black Enterprise (1973) 'Advertising Agencies,' June, pp. 67, 74, 132.

Black Enterprise (1999) 'B.E. Advertising Agencies,' June, p. 177.

Black Enterprise (2006) 'Advertising Agencies,' June, pp. 164–166.

Black-ish (2014) ABC-TV, 'Pilot,' September 24.

Blum, J. M. (1976) *V was for Victory: Politics and American Culture during World War II*. New York: Harcourt Brace Jovanovich.

Boyenton, W. H. (1965) 'The Negro Turns to Advertising,' *Journalism Quarterly*, 42(Spring), pp. 228–229.

Brooks, D. and Walls, L. (1982) 'Advertising in the Black,' *Dollars and Sense*, February/March, pp. 16–28.

Burrell, T. (2010) *Brainwashed: Challenging the Myth of Black Inferiority*. New York: Smiley Books.

Business Week (1968) 'Uncle Tom Magazine takes off the Kid Gloves,' March 23, pp. 70–76.

Butler, J. S. (1991) *Entrepreneurship and Self-help Among Black Americans: A reconsideration of Race and Economics*. Albany, NY: State University of New York.

Capparell, S. (2007) *The Real Pepsi Challenge*. New York: Wall Street Journal Press.

Cappo, J. (2003) *The Future of Advertising: New Media, New Clients, New Consumers in the Post-television Age*. Chicago, IL: Crain Communications/McGraw Hill.

Chambers, J. (2008) *Madison Avenue and the Color Line: African-Americans in the Advertising Industry*. Philadelphia, PA: University of Pennsylvania Press.

Chura, H. (1999) 'True North takes Multicultural Lead,' *Advertising Age*, September 6, p. 6.

Chura, H. and Cuneo, A. (2001) 'Public Lives of Agencies,' *Advertising Age*, April 23, p. 3.

City of New York (1968) *Report: Affirmative Action Follow-up to Advertising and Broadcasting Hearing*. NYCCHR, November.

Come Fly With Us Magazine (2014) 'Braniff Airline Hostess,' commercial, YouTube [Online]. Available at: www.youtube.com/watch?v=2ZwnDdTw-n8 (Accessed: January 26, 2016).

Congress.gov (2016a) 'H.Amdt.1148 to H.R.4428, 99th Congress (1985–1986)' [Online]. Available at: www.congress.gov/amendment/99th-congress/house-amendment/ (Accessed: June 10, 2016).

Congress.gov (2016b) 'H.R.5373: Non-Discrimination in Advertising Act of 1986, 99th Congress (1985–1986)' [Online]. Available at: www.congress.gov/bill/99th-congress/house-bill (Accessed: June 10, 2016).

Cortese, A. J. (2008) *Provocateur: Images of Women and Minorities in Advertising*. New York: Rowman & Littlefield.

Cracknell, A. (2011). *The Real Madmen: The Renegades of Madison Avenue and the Golden Age of Advertising*. Philadelphia, PA: Running Press.

Crain, R. (2013) 'Byron Lewis on Advertising: It's Always been about Storytelling,' *Advertising Age*, September 2, p. 23.

Cruz, L. (2015) '"Dinnertimin" and "No Tipping": How Advertisers Targeted Black Consumers in the 1970s,' *The Atlantic*, June 7 [Online]. Available at: www.theatlantic.com/entertainment/archive/2015/06/casual-racism-and-greater-diversity-in-70s-advertising/394958 (Accessed: September 12, 2015).

Dates, J. and Barlow, W. (1990) *Split Image: African-Americans in the Mass Media*. Washington, D.C.: Howard University Press.

Davis, J. F. (2002) 'Enterprise Development under an Economic Detour? Black-Owned Advertising Agencies, 1940–2000,' *Journal of Macromarketing*, 22(1), pp. 75–85.

Davis, J. F. (2003) 'Burrell Communications Group, Inc.,' in J. McDonough and K. Egolf (eds.) *The Advertising Age Encyclopedia of Advertising*. New York: Fitzroy, vol. 1, pp. 239–241.

Davis, J. F. (2013) 'Realizing Marketplace Opportunity: How Research on the Black Consumer Market Influenced Mainstream Marketers, 1920–1970,' *Journal of Historical Research in Marketing*, 5(4), pp. 471–473.

Detroit Free Press (1999) 'Black Ad Agencies are Hot Commodities,' October 16, B-1.
Dingle, D. T. (1999) *Black Enterprise Titans of the B.E. 100s: Black CEOs who Redefined and Conquered American Business*. New York: John Wiley.
Dougherty, P. H. (1981) 'Advertising; Ethnic Ad Budgets Holding Up,' *New York Times*, December 17 [Online]. Available at: www.nytimes.com/1981/12/17/business/advertising-ethnic-ad-budgets-holding-up.html (Accessed: May 17, 2014).
Dreazen, Y. (1999) 'France's Publicis Buys 49% Stake in Minority-Owned Burrell Agency,' *Wall Street Journal*, June 3, B-12.
Edwards, P. K. (1932) *The Southern Urban Negro as a Consumer*. New York: Prentice-Hall. John W. Hartman Rare Book, Manuscript, and Special Collections Library, Duke University.
Egolf, K. (2003a) 'Polykoff, Shirley 1908–1998,' in J. McDonough and K. Egolf (eds.) *The Advertising Age Encyclopedia of Advertising*. New York: Fitzroy Dearborn, vol. 3, pp. 1252–1254.
Egolf, K. (2003b) 'Resor, Helen Lansdown 1886–1964,' in J. McDonough and K. Egolf (eds.) *The Advertising Age Encyclopedia of Advertising*. New York: Fitzroy Dearborn, vol. 3, pp. 1350–1352.
Ellis, W. and Arnold, E. (1996) 'A History of African-American Owned Advertising Agencies,' *AAF Foundation's Salute to African-American Advertising Agencies*, Chicago, IL, February 29.
Encyclopedia of World Biographies (n.d.) 'Shelly Lazarus Biography' [Online]. Available at: www.notablebiographies.com/supp/Supplement-Ka-M/Lazarus-Shelly.html (Accessed: September 1, 2015).
"Enjoli" (2011) 'Classic '80s Commercial,' YouTube [Online]. Available at: www.youtube.com/watch?v=_Q0P94wyBYk (Accessed: January 26, 2016).
Ernst, S. (2000) 'Viacom Buys BET for $3 Billion,' *Diversity, Inc.* November 3 [Online]. Available at: www.DiversityInc.com (Accessed: December 3, 2000).
Fawcett, A. (1996) 'Perseverance Pays Dividend at $128 Million Burrell Shop,' *Advertising Age*, June 3, pp. c-2–c-8.
Fox, S. (1984) *The Mirror Makers: A History of American Advertising and Its Creators*. New York: William Morrow.
Frazier, E. F. (1962) *Black Bourgeoisie*. New York: Collier Books.
Freeman, L. (2003a) 'Beers, Charlotte 1935–,' in J. McDonough and K. Egolf (eds.) *The Advertising Age Encyclopedia of Advertising*. New York: Fitzroy, vol. 1, pp. 158–160.
Freeman, L. (2003b) 'Trahey, Jane 1923–2000,' in J. McDonough and K. Egolf (eds.) *The Advertising Age Encyclopedia of Advertising*. New York: Fitzroy, vol. 3, pp. 1567–1568.
Gibson, D. P. (1969) *The $30 Billion Negro*. Toronto: Macmillan.
Glover, J. (2010) *Mad Man*. Bloomington, IN: AuthorHouse.
Graves, E. G. (1997) *How to Succeed in Business Without being White*. New York: Harper Collins.
Hall, C. (2001) 'The New Segregation' (a letter to the editor), *Advertising Age*, May 7, p. 20.
Halliday, J. and Sanders, L. (2003) 'GlobalHue, IPG mull Divorce,' *Advertising Age*, January 6, pp. 1, 19.
Harris, W. (2007) 'Battling to Bounce Back,' *Black Enterprise*, June, pp. 157–162.
Hayes, C. (1998) 'A Creative Point of View,' *Black Enterprise*, June, pp. 164–170.
Hayes, C. (1999) 'Dogfight on Madison Avenue,' *Black Enterprise*, June, pp. 171–176.

Hayes, C. (2000a) 'Changing Culture,' *Black Enterprise*, June, pp. 188–195.
Hayes, C. (2000b) 'Media Meltdown: Buy Now!' *Black Enterprise*, June, pp. 179–185.
Hayes, C. (2002) 'Crossing the Color Line,' *Black Enterprise*, June, pp. 199–204.
Hayes, C. (2003) 'Massacre on Madison Avenue,' *Black Enterprise*, June, pp. 177–182.
Hirschhorn, A. (1949) 'Pepsi-Cola's Campaign to the Negro Market,' *Printers' Ink*, September 9, pp. 38–40.
Hocker, C. (2001) 'Are 100% Black-Owned Businesses Dead?' *Upscale*, August, pp. 60–62.
Hower, R. (1939) *The History of an Advertising Agency: N.W. Ayer & Son at Work 1869–1939*. Cambridge, MA: Harvard University Press.
Hughes, A. (2003) 'United Colors of GlobalHue,' *Black Enterprise*, June, pp. 186–194.
Jackson, J. (1999) 'Rainbow Imperative,' *Advertising Age Special Issue: the Next Century*, pp. 56, 75.
Jamison, C. (1994) 'Why my Business Failed,' *Black Enterprise*, June, pp. 236–242.
Jet (1973) 'Top 11 Black Ad Agencies form National Association,' March 22, p. 28.
Johnson, J. H. (1972) 'Our Longevity Shows We've been Efficient,' *Advertising Age*, May 29, p. 50.
Johnson, J. H. (1979) 'Black Media Fill Needs not Recognized Elsewhere,' *Advertising Age*, April 15, p. s-25.
Johnstone, L. (1976) 'Black Agencies: Their Quiet Demise,' *ANNY Newsletter*, June 18, p. 16.
Jones, J. P. (1999) *The Advertising Business: Operations, Creativity, Media Planning, Integrated Communications*. Thousand Oaks, CA: Sage.
Kendrix, M. (2011a) 'About Moss Kendrix,' *Moss H. Kendrix: A Retrospective, the Museum of Public Relations*. Available at: www.prmuseum.com/kendrix/life (Accessed: August 24, 2011).
Kendrix, M. (2011b) 'The Coca-Cola Years,' *Moss H. Kendrix: A Retrospective, the Museum of Public Relations*. Available at: www.prmuseum.com/kendrix/coke (Accessed: August 24, 2011).
Kern-Foxworth, M. (1994) *Aunt Jemima, Uncle Ben and Rastus: Blacks in Advertising Today, Yesterday and Tomorrow*. Westport, CT: Praeger.
Kern-Foxworth, M. (2003) 'Vince Cullers Advertising, Inc.,' in J. McDonough and K. Egolf (eds.) *The Advertising Age Encyclopedia of Advertising*. New York: Fitzroy Dearborn, vol. 1, pp. 425–428.
King, M. and Reid-Dove, A. (1988) 'Fast-Lane Professionals,' *Black Enterprise*, May, pp. 77–82.
Knight-Ridder/Tribune Business News (1995) 'Black Ad Agencies Sought as Advertisers pursue African-American Market,' Columbia, SC, no. 01104428.
Landler, M. (1991) 'What Happened to Advertising? *Business Week*, September 23, pp. 66–72.
Lawrence, M. W. (2002) *A Big Life in Advertising*. New York: Alfred A. Knopf.
Leo, D. (1999) 'After Gobbling Minority Shops, Indigestion Next?' *Advertising Age*, September 27, p. 54.
Linnett, R. (2001) 'BBD&O Crafts Minority Ad Alliance,' *Advertising Age*, April 23, pp. 1, 39.
Lloyd, F. M. and Hayes, C. (1995) 'Twenty-five Years of Blacks in Advertising,' *Black Enterprise*, January, pp. 92–93.
Maas, J. (2012) *Madwomen: The Other side of Life on Madison Avenue in the '60s and Beyond*. New York: Thomas Dunne Books.

Mabry, M. (1989) 'A Long Way from Aunt Jemima,' *Newsweek*, August 14, pp. 35–36.
Maclaran, P., Stevens, L., and Catterall, M. (1997) 'The "Glasshouse Effect": Women in Marketing Management,' *Marketing Intelligence and Planning*, 7, pp. 309–317.
McCoy, Q. (1998) 'The Stand-alones,' *Industry@large*, November 30 [Online]. Available at: www.gavin.com/industry (Accessed: September 1, 2000).
McDonough, J. (2003) 'Ogilvy, David 1911–1999,' in J. McDonough and K. Egolf (eds.) *The Advertising Age Encyclopedia of Advertising*. New York: Fitzroy Dearborn, vol. 1, pp. 1157–1158.
Mallia, K. (2009) 'Rare Birds: Why So Few Women Become Ad Agency Creative Directors,' *Advertising and Society Review*, 10(3) [Online]. Available at: www.aef.com/on_campus/asr/contents (Accessed: February 12, 2012).
Marek, L. (2015) 'Publisher of *Ebony* Shrinks in Search of Growth,' *Crain's Chicago Business*, February 7 [Online]. Available at: www.chicagobusiness.com/article/20150207/ISSUE01/302079987/publisher-of-ebony-shrinks-in-search-of-growth (Accessed: June 10, 2015).
Maxwell, A. (2003) 'Women: Careers in Advertising,' in J. McDonough and K. Egolf (eds.) *The Advertising Age Encyclopedia of Advertising*. New York: Fitzroy Dearborn, vol. 3, pp. 1655–1660.
Mermigas, D. (2003) 'J. Walter Thompson Company,' in J. McDonough and K. Egolf (eds.) *The Advertising Age Encyclopedia of Advertising*. New York: Fitzroy Dearborn, vol. 3, pp. 1530–1537.
Miller, P. (2011) 'Mad Ave Racism Pushes Creative to Extremes in "Mad Man,"' *Advertising Age*, July 7 [Online]. Available at: http://adage.com/article/the-big-tent/jim-glover-s-mad-man-basis-sad-reality/228588/ (Accessed: January 14, 2015).
Mitchell, G. (1979) 'And Then There Were 13,' *Black Enterprise*, September, pp. 43–49.
Moss, M. (2001) 'The Battle for Urban Markets: Black Agencies Surrender Partial Ownership to Compete for their Ethnic Share,' *Black Enterprise*, June, pp. 187–192.
Ofori, K. A. (1999) *When Being No. 1 is Not Enough*. Washington, D.C.: Federal Communications Commission.
Pierce, J. A. (1947) *Negro Business and Business Education*. New York: Harper & Bros.
Pine, J. (2001) 'Black Media is Going Mainstream, But is it Losing its Voice?' *Diversity Inc.*, March [Online]. Available at: www.DiversityInc.com (Accessed: March 27, 2001).
Putney Swope (1969) Internet Movie Database.com. Available at: www.imdb.com/title/tt0064855/ (Accessed: September 10, 2015).
Sanders, L. (2004) 'Black Radio Targets Ogilvy in Protest Aimed at Agencies,' *Advertising Age*, June 7, p. 58.
Savage, T. (1999a) 'Burrell, Thomas J.,' in J. E. K. Walker (ed.) *Encyclopedia of African American Business History*. Westport, CT: Greenwood Press, pp. 98–99.
Savage, T. (1999b) 'Lewis, Byron Eugene,' in J. E. K. Walker (ed.) *Encyclopedia of African American Business History*. Westport, CT: Greenwood Press, pp. 360–361.
Sharp, B. (1969) *How to be Black and Get a Job in the Advertising Agency Business Anyway*. Bethesda, MD: Sharp Publishing.
Sivulka, J. (1998) *Soap, Sex and Cigarettes: A Cultural History of American Advertising*. London: Wadsworth.
Sivulka, J. (2009) *Ad Women: How They Impact What We Need, Want, and Buy*. Amherst, NY: Prometheus Books.

Smikle, K. (1985) 'The Image Makers,' *Black Enterprise*, December, pp. 44–52.
Smiley, T. (2014) 'RIP Black Ad Agencies: The Decline of Black Ad Shops,' *Tavis Smiley Show*, Series no. 11898, June 9 [Online]. Available at: www.tavissmiley radio.com/panel-discussion-the-decline-of-black-owned-advertising-agencies/ (Accessed: June 30, 2014).
Smith, M. (2000) 'BET: Sellout or Success Story?' Available at: www.Africana.com (Accessed: November 29, 2000).
Snyder, B. (1999) 'Top Two Black Ad Agencies Up for Sale,' *Advertising Age*, February 1, p. 1.
Standard Directory of Advertising Agencies (1996) Skokie, IL: National Register Publishing.
Standard Directory of Advertising Agencies (2000) Skokie, IL: National Register Publishing.
Still, L. (1986) 'Women Managers in Advertising: An Exploratory Study,' *Media Information Australia*, 40(2), pp. 24–30.
Stuart, M. S. (1940) *An Economic Detour: A History of Insurance in the Lives of American Negroes*. New York: Wendell Malliet & Company.
Sullivan, D. J. (1943) 'Don't Do This: If You Want to Sell Your Products to Negroes!' *Sales Management*, March 1, pp. 46–50.
Sullivan, D. J. (1944) 'The American Negro: An "Export" Market at Home!' *Printer's Ink*, July 21, pp. 90–94.
Sullivan, D. J. (1945) 'How Negroes Spent their Incomes, 1920–1943,' *Sales Management*, June 15, p. 106.
Sutton, D. (2009) *Globalizing Ideal Beauty: How Female Copywriters of the J. Walter Thompson Advertising Agency Redefined Beauty for the Twentieth Century*. New York: Palgrave Macmillan.
Target Market News (2009) 'NABOB Wants to Meet with BMW to Discuss "No Urban Dictate" Media Buy Email,' *Target Market News*, August 17 [Online]. Available at: www.targetmarketnews.com/storyid08170902.htm (Accessed: October 12, 2015).
Teinowitz, I. (1998) 'Multicultural Marketing,' *Advertising Age*, November 16, p. s-1.
Teinowitz, I. (2000) 'AAF asks Clinton to Lend Support on New Ad Code,' *Advertising Age*, August 28, p. 3.
Tide (1952) 'Negro Market: As Customers and Citizens, Its People are Still Making Significant Progress,' July 25, p. 44.
Tungate, M. (2007) *AdLand: A Global History of Advertising*. London: Kogan Page.
Walker, J. E. K. (1998) *The History of Black Business in America*. New York: Macmillan.
Webster, N. C. (1997) 'Multicultural,' *Advertising Age*, November 17, pp. s-1–s-2.
Weems, R. E. (1998) *Desegregating the Dollar*. New York: New York University Press.
Wentz, L. (2004) 'Multicultural Issues Divides Ad Industry,' *Advertising Age*, August 23, p. 10.
Williams, G. A. (1998) *Legendary Pioneers of Black Radio*. Westport, CT: Praeger.
Wills, J. (2015) 'Marketer and Mentor: Dorothy Dignam's Support for Careers for Women in Advertising: 1920–1950,' *Proceedings of the 17th Conference on Historical Analysis and Research in Marketing*, Hawkins, R. A. (ed.) Long Beach, CA, May 28–31, CHARM Association.
Winski, J. (1992) 'The Ad Industry's "Dirty Little Secret,"' *Advertising Age*, June 15, pp. 16–17.

2 Barbara Gardner Proctor

Unconventional advertising pioneer

Figure 2.1 Barbara Gardner Proctor.

Source: courtesy of Morgan Proctor.

Calling small business entrepreneurs like Barbara Gardner Proctor "heroes for the eighties," U.S. President Ronald Reagan presented the businesswoman to a national audience in late January 1984 during his State of the Union address (Reagan, 1984). "The spirit of enterprise is sparked by the sunrise industries of high-tech and by small business people with big ideas – people like Barbara Proctor, who rose from a ghetto to build a multi-million dollar advertising agency in Chicago," Reagan proudly declared. A few weeks earlier, Proctor was featured on the popular CBS-TV network news program *60 Minutes*, interviewed by correspondent Harry Reasoner, who described her as a modern "rags-to-riches heroine" (*60 Minutes*, 1984). With these telecasts, Barbara Proctor's story began to unfold in front of millions. People wondered – who is this polished and intriguing woman? Reasoner continued:

> "That's Barbara Proctor, in her chauffeured car, riding along Chicago's Lake Shore Drive – a long way, in every way, from the shack where she was brought up by her grandmother. How did she get there? By winning big in advertising. Her agency is now the second largest in the country aiming at the black consumer market."

Proctor, who was already well known in Chicago's business and advertising circles, had strategized to do something no other black woman had done before – launched Proctor & Gardner Advertising in 1970, becoming the first African-American woman to start an advertising agency.

Humble beginnings

Proctor's roots in rural North Carolina belie her eventual success in advertising. In those days "the only thing you could train for if you were a black girl in the South – rural, poor – was a teacher, a hairdresser or a nurse," Proctor (1989) recalls. Born in November 1932 in Asheville, North Carolina to unwed parents – William Gardner and 16-year-old Bernice Baxter – infant Barbara was sent to live as a boarder with a family in Asheville when her mother moved to Washington, D.C. to attend secretarial school (Ingham and Feldman, 1994; Krisman, 2005). Baxter, one of seven siblings, was expected to find work – but, in the Great Depression-era economy where black unemployment hovered around 50 percent (PBS.org, 2012), many Americans of all backgrounds were desperate for jobs and made great sacrifices merely to survive. Eventually, Baxter became employed at the newly built Pentagon building doing clerical work, married a man named Alexander, and sent money to help support her daughter, but Barbara Proctor never lived with her (Rich-McCoy, 1978). Although her mother provided financial help, the relationship between Proctor and her mother was emotionally distant and she recalls that her mother "never shared herself ... she just never liked to share herself a lot" (Rich-McCoy, 1978, p. 210).

Black Mountain, North Carolina

Proctor was about four years old when her grandmother, Mrs. Coralee Baxter, discovered the existence of her young granddaughter and sent for her to come live with her in Black Mountain, North Carolina, a small town deep in the country about 20 miles east of Asheville. In that area, mostly everyone – black and white – lived in extreme poverty. But Proctor insists that since everyone was poor, they didn't feel deprived and it was "like an extended family ... a really wonderful, warm place to be" (Blake, 1984). Proctor (1989) remembers that famous evangelist Billy Graham spent time in the area before establishing his ministry. At home in Black Mountain, Proctor's house – made out of clapboards and set up on bricks – was described as a "dirt-poor" shot-gun shack with four rooms, no electricity, and no indoor plumbing. "We went down the path for the outhouse and out to the well for water," Proctor (1989) reminisced. Proctor's segregated elementary school was similarly described as a "three-room shanty" and she recalls racial segregation and discrimination growing up there (Blake, 1984). Most black people in the close-knit community lived in crowded, run-down dwellings without lights or running water and performed menial jobs to sustain themselves and their families.

Despite the impoverished circumstances, Proctor described her grandmother as very loving, affectionate, strong-willed, and courageous and remembered her as a woman of dignity, pride, and inner-direction (Kimbro and Hill, 1991, p. 141). "I thought she was just the most beautiful thing in the world," Proctor commented wistfully (Rich-McCoy, 1978, p. 211). A proud and deeply religious woman, Coralee Baxter worked hard as a domestic, serving as a cook at a local college and a maid for white families and cleaning cottages for wealthy summer vacationers who came to the area (Rich-McCoy, 1978). Earning about two dollars a day, her grandmother gave young Barbara 25 cents on days she came to work with her (Rich-McCoy, 1978). Given the circumstances in Black Mountain, Proctor had no sense of the lack of material items or modern amenities until she returned to Asheville to attend Stephens-Lee High school and realized that there was another way to live (Blake, 1984; Proctor, 1989). Growing up, she also had limited male influences in her life, since her father was not involved and the whereabouts of her grandmother's husband were not disclosed. Her uncles – her mother's brothers – and other male family members had mostly gone off to serve in the military by the time Barbara was old enough to notice. Therefore, she looked up to female role models, especially the beautiful African-American entertainer Lena Horne, whom Proctor regarded as the essence of dignity and style; and her grandmother (Harrison, 1986; Krisman, 2005). Throughout her life, Proctor held unabated affection and respect for Coralee Baxter who raised seven children alone – and "none of them went to jail and all of them finished school," she recalled with pride (Proctor, 1989).

"Not cute – but right smart"

Coralee Baxter's guidance and instruction had a profound effect on her granddaughter's life and outlook, and Proctor credits her as central to the development of her character and moral grounding (Proctor, 1989). Strong, but realistic, she taught Proctor to "accept whatever your circumstances are, but first admit that *is* the circumstance. Because it is only when you admit it, that you can deal with it," Proctor recalls (Rich-McCoy, 1978, p. 211). When Proctor was growing up in Black Mountain, it was customary for white women to pat black children on their heads and compliment them about how cute they were – sometimes asking them to sing or perform (Blake, 1984). When this happened to young Barbara, Coralee Baxter would rebuff such comments by looking at her granddaughter and saying: "Oh no. She ain't cute, but she's right smart. And she's going to amount to something someday" (Rich-McCoy, 1978, p. 211). Believing outward appearances to be fleeting, Coralee Baxter taught Proctor to cultivate internal qualities such as intelligence and high principles. "She said it is important to put something inside you, some courage, knowledge or a skill – things that no one can take away," Proctor explained (Sellingpower.com, n.d., p. 1). Her grandmother's philosophy was: "You have to trade with your mind, your personality or you have to develop something that will stay with you long after your beauty is gone," Proctor continued (Rich-McCoy, 1978, p. 212). Proctor internalized her grandmother's words regarding her intelligence and looks: she excelled in academics, but believed that she was unattractive. "I was about five or six and ugly as sin," she recalled (Rich-McCoy, 1978, p. 212). Proctor continued, reminiscing about her life from elementary through high school, where she played drums in the band, worked on the student newspaper and yearbook, and was a cheerleader (Rich-McCoy, 1978, p. 212):

> "Seriously. [I was] a bad-news kid. And it occurred to me ... that I could get friends if I do their homework. And so that meant that I had to study everything. It's not a complaint when I say I was an ugly kid. I *was* an ugly kid ... but it never stopped me from doing anything. Skinny as a rail – I didn't have much going for me. I still got what I wanted."

Upon high school graduation in 1950, what Proctor really wanted was to marry a young man named Johnny Welles, whom she described as a "black John Wayne" – tall and gorgeous – and live "happily ever after" (Rich-McCoy, 1978, p. 212). But her mother and grandmother had other ideas. Reflecting on her own failed relationship with Proctor's father, Bernice Baxter "swooped down from Washington to knock some sense into me," Proctor recounted (Rich-McCoy, 1978, p. 212). Determined that Proctor was going to attend college, Bernice Baxter filled out three college applications for Proctor, who was accepted at all three schools and received scholarship money. Still, Proctor was adamant about marrying Johnny and not attending college. However, Welles – not wanting Proctor to lose out on her tremendous opportunities – broke off their relationship.

Heartbroken over the breakup with Welles, Proctor accepted a scholarship and enrolled in Talladega College in Alabama (Rich-McCoy, 1978, p. 212). Known as the "Garden Spot of the South," the most beautiful black women in the country attended the school according to local lore (Proctor, 1989). Insecure about her looks, Proctor was grateful that the year she applied, the school discontinued its practice of having women applicants provide a photograph of themselves. As in high school, Proctor excelled academically at Talladega, regarding herself as "not the prettiest, but the smartest girl at Talledega" (Proctor, 1989). The confident, articulate, young woman majored in Education and minored in English, completing her degree requirements in three years. She stayed an additional year to complete another degree, majoring in Psychology and minoring in Sociology. Since scholarship money did not cover all of Proctor's expenses, she worked part-time and Bernice Baxter provided supplemental financial support until Proctor's graduation with two degrees in 1954. During Proctor's final year in college, she won the Armstrong Creative Writing Award and planned to return home to North Carolina the following fall to begin a teaching career (Ingham and Feldman, 1994; Krisman, 2005).

Proctor's pre-advertising career

Many people are unaware of Barbara Proctor's prominent professional career *before* she entered advertising. The summer after college graduation, Proctor worked as a counselor at the Circle Pine Camp in Kalamazoo, Michigan, located on the western side of the state near a major highway which led to Chicago, Illinois. On her way back to North Carolina, she stopped in Chicago to purchase a wardrobe for her teaching job. However, she spent too much and could not afford the bus fare for a trip back to North Carolina. Forced to stay in Chicago, a local beauty shop owner had a place with a small room and let Proctor stay for a while so she could save money (Proctor, 1989). She used this opportunity to search for work in Chicago's thriving black business community, so that she could earn travel money back to North Carolina. She volunteered – or so she thought – at the Chicago Urban League office, doing social work in order to make job contacts. However, after two weeks, the Urban League issued her a paycheck (Proctor, 1989). Realizing she had a paying job and having second thoughts about a teaching career, she decided to stay in Chicago. After a while, she resigned from the social work position when she found it difficult to maintain her objectivity and disliked the "depressing" nature of the work (Ingham and Feldman, 1994, p. 564). She found another job as an office manager with the Oscar C. Brown Real Estate Company, owned by a prominent African-American businessman and civic leader, where she remained for six years. This job was fairly undemanding and gave Proctor the opportunity to pursue other interests – writing and music.

Music critic and record company executive

In her spare time after work, Proctor enjoyed listening to music and especially loved a radio broadcast hosted by jazz disk jockey Sid McCoy. His show, popular during the 1950s through mid-1960s, was broadcast from midnight to 5 a.m. on WCFL in Chicago (*Jet*, 1967). "He had the most magnificent voice in the world – it was so sexy – and I listened from twelve midnight until four in the morning. This was the most magnificent thing since Johnny [Welles]," Proctor remembered (Rich-McCoy, 1978, p. 213). McCoy's family owned a record store in Chicago and a friendship developed after Proctor volunteered to organize and catalog the store's 10,000 item record collection during her free time (Rich-McCoy, 1978). Sid McCoy also worked in the artist development area of the Vee-Jay Record Company, and helped Proctor get a position there writing descriptive comments on album covers and liners. Vee-Jay, founded in 1953 by African-American entrepreneurs Vivian Carter and her husband James Bracken, was a major R&B (rhythm and blues) recording label in the 1950s through the mid-1960s, considered by some as the most successful black-run recording label prior to Motown (Wickman, 2013). Through Vee-Jay, Proctor met some of the great jazz artists and performers of the time such as Cannonball Adderly, Nancy Wilson, Ray Charles, Miles Davis, and John Coltrane. Proctor began writing artist profiles and other articles on a freelance basis for *Downbeat* magazine, a well-respected jazz publication which published her articles. When *Downbeat* needed a full-time jazz writer, they approached Proctor, who became a contributing editor and a respected jazz music critic (Krisman, 2005; Rich-McCoy, 1978). In time, Proctor contributed to seven books on jazz, authored several TV specials, and wrote a music column for a South Side Chicago newspaper (Ingham and Feldman, 1994). Proctor adored being involved in the music business and writing about it, noting: "There were no black persons involved in the creative process of selling and marketing the black talent. They gave me the opportunity and I loved it" (Proctor, 1989).

Proctor's work with Vee-Jay Records and reputation in the jazz community served as a springboard for positions of greater responsibility within the company including public relations work. Around 1960, she was elevated to the position of Director of the International Division (Ingham and Feldman, 1994). This position allowed Proctor to travel to 17 European countries about four times each year, looking for new acts to sign and talent to trade – a high-profile and exhilarating job. There were also many wonderful perks associated with the position: a company car, an apartment, an expense account, plus a $17,000 salary (Rich-McCoy, 1978, p. 214). At this point, Coralee Baxter's steadfast predictions regarding her granddaughter's future had manifested. When Proctor traveled back to Black Mountain in 1961 for Coralee Baxter's funeral, she was content with the knowledge that she had fulfilled her grandmother's vision.

The British invasion

Proctor scored a career coup in December 1962, when she brought the Beatles to the United States as part of her job as International Director with Vee-Jay Records (Ingham and Feldman, 1994; Krisman, 2005; Proctor, 1989). Popular in the United Kingdom, the Beatles were unknown in the United States and the arrangement was part of an exchange with the Four Seasons, a white group on the Vee-Jay label (Proctor, 1989; Wickman, 2013). Before the legendary group became famous worldwide and created an entertainment sensation in the 1960s referred to as the "British Invasion," 30 sides of Beatles' music were recorded at Vee-Jay Records (Proctor, 1989). The Beatles' first U.S. album was produced by Vee-Jay Records (see Figure 2.2). But the first release, "Please, Please Me" in early 1963 on the Vee-Jay label only sold 5,650 copies (Wickman, 2013). After more disappointing releases, an executive with another record company said the Beatles were "stone-cold dead in the U.S. marketplace" (Wickman, 2013). However, the Beatles appeared on the Jack Paar show in February 1963 and Vee-Jay executives sensed they were going to be big. However, the Beatles were on a short-term contract with Vee-Jay and moved on to another record company. In December 1963, the Beatles released "I Want to Hold Your Hand" which became a top-selling record in the United States and worldwide, the first of a string of major hits for the group. The Beatles and their music were a phenomenon which helped to define the 1960s.

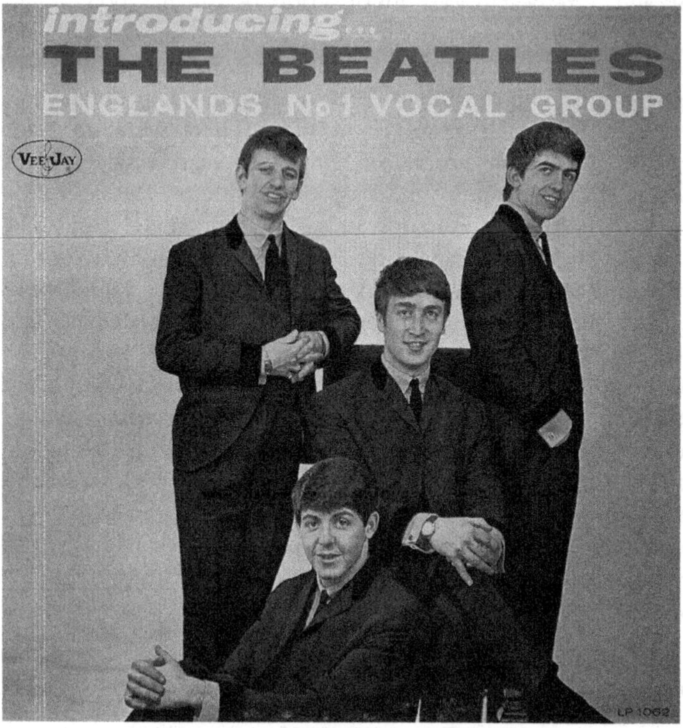

Figure 2.2 The Beatles' first U.S. album, on the Vee-Jay label, 1963. Barbara Gardner brought the Beatles to America in her position as International Director for Vee-Jay Records.

Source: Getty Images/Michael Ochs Archives.

Believing that "music is the best reflection of the spirit of a people," Proctor appreciated the impact that the Beatles' music had on society and its role in unifying people, commenting (Proctor, 1989):

> "The Beatles, along with Elvis, are those who began breaking down the barriers between people. The fact that they were not American white artists made a difference because they were not bringing American baggage. They expressed tremendous respect for black music; they were not ashamed or threatened by it. That made it OK for a whole generation of other people to do that. Once you have people recreating together, enjoying together, sharing common experiences together, they cannot again hate in the same way as they can when they are ignorant of each other. Knowledge reduces the level of hatred tremendously."

Unfortunately, neither Proctor – then known as Barbara Gardner – nor Vee-Jay Records profited from the growing widespread popularity of the Beatles, as they moved on to Capitol Records which released the major Beatles hits (Wickman, 2013). As the group's appeal soared, the Vee-Jay company was, in Proctor's words, "becoming unhinged" (Proctor, 1989). There were rumors that the company's chief manager used company funds to pay personal gambling debts, creating a serious cash flow problem and forcing Vee-Jay to temporarily cease operations in the second half of 1963 (Pruter, 1997). However, those allegations were dismissed by some as speculative (Callahan, 2006). Whatever the source of the problems, in 1963 the company had difficulty distributing recordings in sufficiently large quantities to keep up with demand for acts including the Beatles and Four Seasons; and paying fees, royalties, and other expenses. Unfortunately, as the Beatles' popularity skyrocketed, Vee-Jay's problems escalated. On August 3, 1963 a leading trade publication reported the departure of several key executives at Vee-Jay, including its President Ewart Abner and public relations and International Director Barbara Gardner, describing the shake-up as "having the force of an explosion" (*Billboard*, 1963, p. 8). A downward spiral ensued and several business interests filed lawsuits against the company, prompting Vee-Jay Records to declare bankruptcy in August 1966 (*Billboard*, 1966). Later, Vee-Jay records was revived to some extent, but it never regained the prominence it enjoyed in the 1950s through early 1960s (Callahan, 2006). Most of its assets, including its music catalog were eventually acquired by other entities.

Marriage and motherhood

As a well-known jazz critic, Barbara Gardner traveled to music events on a regular basis. It was at one of these events – the Newport Jazz Festival – in the late 1950s that she met her future husband, Carl Proctor, who was the road manager for jazz singer Sarah Vaughan, a friend of Barbara's. Of West Indian descent, she described Carl Proctor as a "life-of-the-party type" with a "fiery, exciting" kind of personality (Rich-McCoy, 1978, p. 214). Claiming she married out of boredom, they wed in the summer of 1961. The following year their son, Morgan, was born July 1, 1962. But the young marriage was troubled from the start. It was hard for Barbara Proctor – nearly 30 – to adjust to married life as she found it difficult to be accountable to someone and missed the flexibility of a single person's life (Rich-McCoy, 1978). Her position in the music world also created issues. Since she was a well-known international jazz critic by the time they married, people knew and recognized her. Moreover, she was the major breadwinner and still used her maiden name professionally. People sometimes referred to her husband as "Mr. Gardner," provoking Carl Proctor's resentment in the already contentious relationship (Rich-McCoy, 1978, p. 214). They stayed married for two years because Barbara Proctor believed that was a "respectable amount of time" to do so and split on their second wedding anniversary in the summer of 1963 (Ingham and Feldman, 1994, p. 565). Believing herself not to be the marriageable type, Proctor once explained: "I require freedom. I'm not a marriageable person. You can be whole without being married" (Ingham and Feldman, 1994, p. 565). Since they were in the same profession, Barbara wanted to avoid seeing Carl Proctor on a regular basis after the split (Harrison, 1986; Rich-McCoy, 1978). Therefore, she resigned from Vee-Jay Records in the summer of 1963 – about the same time that the company was imploding – and divorced.

The twilight zone

Following the split with Carl Proctor, Barbara Proctor felt a need to reassess her life. She entered a period of her life which she referred to as "the twilight time" when she refocused and contemplated her employment options (Proctor, 1989). "This was a very bad time for me," she acknowledges, "I had left a glamorous lifestyle and exchanged it for the uncertainties of freelancing" (Harrison, 1986). She struggled financially for about the next 18 months while caring for her toddler son, relying on odd jobs, savings, and help from friends. Still doing free-lance writing for *Downbeat* magazine, she had received an advance from a publisher who wanted to turn one of her articles into a book and was helped by people such as secretaries, teachers, and other friends who would send her $20 to $30 dollars at a time (Rich-McCoy, 1978, p. 214). Although this period of her life was difficult, looking back, she recognized it as her "battle with destiny" (Ingham and Feldman, 1994, p. 565). She became intrigued with the advertising business. Although she was already a writer, she was fascinated with the persuasive aspect of advertising and writers' abilities to "write short" (Proctor, 1989). She realized:

> "In the space of 50–80 words you have to move millions of dollars worth of product. You have to persuade millions of people – not only to listen to you – but to go into their pockets and buy something which they may or may not need, based on your well-chosen 50–80 words."

With Proctor's sights now set on the advertising business, there are conflicting accounts as to how an opportunity to work in the industry came about. Proctor (1989) believed: "As late as 1963, there were no black professionals in the city of Chicago in advertising" – meaning that she had no connections. There *was* a black-owned agency in Chicago – Vince Cullers Advertising – which had been established in the late 1950s, however, it was not indicated whether Proctor was familiar with or had an interest in seeking employment with this company. Nonetheless, in 1964, Proctor applied for a position with the well-regarded Leo Burnett advertising agency, the largest and most prominent ad firm in Chicago, but was rejected because she was "overqualified" (Ingham and Feldman, 1994). However, several sources indicate that after the assassination of President Kennedy in November 1963, some advertising agencies, interested in cultivating a progressive image of equality, became interested in hiring African-Americans (Harrison, 1986; Ingham and Feldman, 1994; Rich-McCoy, 1978). After all, this era represented the height of the Civil Rights movement and Kennedy had been an ally to its leaders. Dr.

Martin Luther King Jr. led the famous March on Washington in August 1963 and over the next couple of years following Kennedy's death, some of the most significant and sweeping legislation of the times occurred, including the passage of the Civil Rights Act and the Voting Rights Act. As such, issues and images concerning opportunities for African-Americans were often featured in the media. Around this time, Proctor was approached by a white man who represented a large advertising agency, which "wanted to put a black in an important position" (Rich-McCoy, 1978, p. 215). At the interview for the job, Proctor's opinion was that the man "represented all the ignorance of the entire white establishment." The position, as he described it, may have been considered an "important" position for a black person, but in Proctor's view, it was merely a job for a "token black" (Rich-McCoy, 1978, p. 215). Proctor and the interviewer disagreed on the fundamental nature of the position and the extent to which it would involve teamwork, and the interviewer expressed discomfort as to how others at the agency would react to working with a black colleague (Rich-McCoy, 1978, p. 215). The interviewer's stance was upsetting to Proctor, as she considered her previous position as a well-regarded music industry writer and executive. Reflecting on the interview experience, Proctor despaired: "Oh, it was so humiliating ... the most humiliating experience of my life" (Rich-McCoy, 1978, p. 215).

Proctor's early advertising career

Despite Proctor's humbling experience at the advertising agency job interview, she was offered the position and decided to accept it because it was an opportunity to learn the advertising business (Krisman, 2005). In 1964, she began working at the Post-Keys-Gardner advertising agency. "I joined a firm and became the first black working for a general-market agency in Chicago," she claimed (Harrison, 1986, p. 158). She learned the business from the ground up, earning $8,500 per year – less than half of her former salary – and started out writing labels for consumer brands like the Pine-Sol cleaning product. The new job required another compromise: she was forced to alter her name. Although she had continued to use her maiden name "Gardner" after she married Carl Proctor, she had to use "Proctor" at the agency so as to distinguish herself from Mr. Gardner who was a principal with the Post-Keys-Gardner agency. At this point, she became known as Barbara Proctor or Barbara Gardner Proctor. In this setting, she was highly sensitive to the uniqueness of her situation and the challenges it presented. Recalling her grandmother's admonitions about accepting one's circumstances and moving forward, she mused (Sellingpower.com, n.d., p. 1)

> "In advertising, the only thing worse than being a woman, was being an old woman. I was over thirty, female and black. I had so many things wrong with me that it would have taken me all day to figure out which one to blame for my rejections. So I decided not to spend any time worrying about it."

Post-Keys-Gardner was a fairly new agency, created in 1963 through a merger of two smaller agencies, making it one of the five largest ad agencies in Chicago (Dattner and Dattner, 2003). Around the time that Proctor worked at the agency, Post-Keys-Gardner was billing about $30 million per year and, in addition to Pine-Sol, handled such accounts as: the Amana Refrigeration Company; Atchison, Topeka & Santa Fe Railway Company; Old Milwaukee beer, Primo beer, and Kona Coffee for the Schlitz Brewing Co.; the Florists' Transworld Delivery Association; candy maker E.J. Brach; the Sheaffer Pen Company; and several Brown and Williamson Tobacco Corporation brands – Kool, Viceroy, Raleigh, and Belair cigarettes – according to *Advertising Age*. Proctor did make a good friend at Post-Keys-Gardner – Creative Director Gene Taylor – who mentored her and gave her increasing responsibilities on a variety of assignments in the Creative Department. In her three years at the agency, her work won 21 awards and prompted recognition within the industry, especially in Chicago (Ingham and Feldman, 1994). Proctor's loyalty to Gene Taylor was such that – when he was fired from Post-Keys-Gardner around 1968 for political reasons – she quit too (Harrison, 1986; Rich-McCoy, 1978). Taylor subsequently ran his own small agency – Gene Taylor and Associates – and Proctor worked there for about a year as a Copy Supervisor. Interestingly, Proctor's reputation may have had an impact on the corporate culture at Post-Keys-Gardner because by 1975 – seven years after Proctor's departure – 3.3 percent of the agency's employees in professional/technical or managerial positions were ethnic minorities, placing it among the top agencies in terms of overall minority employee representation (*Chicago Reporter*, 1975). The agency's personnel director actively recruited for Post-Keys-Gardner by placing ads in minority-oriented newspapers like the *Chicago Defender* and *LaRaza*, which catered to the African-American and Latino communities, respectively.

In 1969, Proctor was hired at the North advertising agency (a.k.a. True North or Grey-North) as a Copy Supervisor in the creative department at a salary of $26,000 (Ingham and Feldman, 1994). But Proctor's tenure at North was brief and contentious. She was disgruntled when she was assigned work only on "women's accounts" – brands which catered to female consumers. Feeling that she had proven herself based on her track record – which included a 1968 American TV Commercial Award and a 1969 International Film Festival Award – she resented being cast in a stereotypical role (Ingham and Feldman, 1994). She also held a dim view of North's management practices, which seemed to be more focused on appeasing the clients rather than selling their products. The final straw came when she objected to a commercial concept for a hair product brand handled by the agency. The ad concept parodied the social justice marches which were common during the Civil Rights movement, and featured protesting women running down the street waving hair product cans demanding that hairdressers foam their hair (Krisman, 2005). Considering the idea to be "terribly offensive" to women, African-Americans, and the Civil Rights movement, Proctor refused to work on the campaign and was fired (Proctor, 1989).

As far as Proctor was concerned, the firing was just as well. Since leaving Post-Keys-Gardner, a seed had been planted in her mind about opening her own agency and she believed she had a good understanding of the advertising business. Reflecting on her prior experiences, she explained (Rich-McCoy, 1978, p. 216): "That's when I learned you really don't make decisions ... unless you are the boss." Seeking a situation where she would not have to "knuckle under," she considered the reality of her circumstances (Rich-McCoy, 1978, p. 216):

> "I'm well over thirty and advertising is the business of the golden girls ... under thirty, blonde and all that good stuff. Well, I wasn't any of that, so I thought I'd better find something very quickly I could control.... When have you ever seen an old ugly advertising woman who did not *own* something? Either the client or the company. You better be pretty or powerful. Preferably both."

Proctor also thought the time was right to capitalize on mainstream marketers' growing interest in the black consumer market coupled with the desire by black consumers to see themselves presented in positive, respectful manners in advertisements (Davis, 2013). The sensitivities among blacks revealed during the Civil Rights and Black Nationalist movements of the 1960s made the demeaning advertising portrayals of the past problematic, and many white-owned general-market agencies lacked the expertise as to how to effectively appeal to black consumers. Thus, during the late 1960s through mid-1970s, a number of African-American entrepreneurs, including Proctor, credibly positioned themselves to cater to the black consumer market as a means of getting a foothold into the advertising business, a period referred to as the "Golden Age" for black advertising firms (Chambers, 2008; Davis, 2002). Proctor was among the first black advertising entrepreneurs of this era to establish an agency, most of whom had prior experience with corporate clients. With great enthusiasm, she plunged into her venture with the attitude: "They loved my work when I worked for someone else. Let's see how much they love me now" (Ingham and Feldman, 1994, p. 566).

Barbara Gardner Proctor, advertising entrepreneur

The energetic Barbara Gardner Proctor – who was known for 15 hour workdays and only a few hours of sleep each night – launched Proctor & Gardner Advertising, Inc. in the spring of 1970 after securing financing from a variety of sources. She had received a $2,000 severance from her last agency job and one of Count Basie's band members sent her $1,000 when she telegrammed friends to "send what you can" (Blake, 1984). She approached and secured a collateral-free $80,000 loan from the Small Business Administration (SBA), after providing documentation indicating the value of her name and reputation in the advertising industry. By then, her track record and awards had made her a "hot property" in the advertising business and a magazine article called her the "black Mary Wells" (Rich-McCoy, 1978, p. 217), referencing the famous white advertising agency entrepreneur who became the wealthiest woman in the history of the advertising industry. These aspects elevated Proctor's professional stature such that her financing deal was the first unsecured service loan ever provided by the SBA (Rich-McCoy, 1978).

Initially, she established a small office at 619 N. Wabash Street in Chicago, in an old mansion upstairs over an Italian restaurant (Rich-McCoy, 1978, p. 217). Sensing that prospective clients would not be accepting of a black woman as the sole owner of an advertising agency, she combined her married and maiden names and named the company "Proctor & Gardner Advertising" to create an illusion that there was a male partner and that she was merely "a show pony," contending that this strategy "soothes the male chauvinists" who preferred a more "businesslike" male in the background (Dewitt, 1974, p. 18). Her initial staff consisted of an account person, a creative director, and a media director described as "malcontents" from other agencies (Ingham and Feldman, 1994, p. 566). Proctor hoped to inspire their loyalty by giving them lots of autonomy on the job, but, like many entrepreneurs, Proctor was a very hands-on CEO – writing copy, selling ideas, and chairing meetings while often working seven days a week (Ingham and Feldman, 1994). No campaign or piece of ad copy went out without her approval (*60 Minutes*, 1984). The first months were difficult, requiring an extensive selling effort and personal sacrifice – Proctor sold her car, clothes, and jewelry to raise cash for the fledgling enterprise (Proctor, 1989).

Eventually the hard work and sacrifices paid off, as Proctor explained in a magazine interview (Sellingpower.com, n.d., p. 5): "After six months of rejection, after rejection from potential clients – who had loved me when I was working for someone else but didn't believe a black woman 'had it' – I finally landed my first advertising contract with Jewel Foods in Chicago. That was in 1970." Jewel, a Chicago-based grocery store chain, had a problem with its generic food line which suffered from low sales (Encyclopedia.com, 2000). Proctor's approach helped to rescue the food line by targeting African-Americans, who preferred name brands and believed generics were poor quality "cheap junk" (Ingham and Feldman, 1994, p. 567). Using a variety of media, the advertising typified Proctor's style of clear and direct messages which underscored the idea of good value for money while tapping into consumers' desires in a realistic manner (Ingham and Feldman, 1994). For example, a 1979 ad shows a black working mother preparing for the day using a variety of Jewel brands to care for her busy family (see Figure 2.3). The advertising tagline: "People Helping People Make It" humanizes the Jewel brand, positions the store as a helpmate, and incorporates it credibly into a modern family's lifestyle. Other executions for the Jewel account were similarly family oriented, using black models while conveying traditional family values and loving familial relationships. For example, one ad shows three generations of a family – grandparent, parents, and children – enjoying fellowship at a sumptuous Thanksgiving dinner based on foods purchased at

Jewel – the tagline reads: "Together, we're good food people" (*Ebony*, 1978, p. 57). Another shows an African-American bride resplendent in her wedding dress with her groom and the phrase "Together Forever" (*CEBA*, 1978, p. 22). A print execution with the tagline: "Fathers and Families Make it Better" shows a black father celebrating by carrying his young son on his shoulders while the boy triumphantly holds up a trophy (*CEBA*, 1978, p. 6). Finally, an ad reminiscent of Proctor's relationship with Coralee Baxter shows a grandmother and granddaughter at the older woman's knee, reading with keen interest from a book featuring the tagline: "People Together Make it Better" (*CEBA*, 1978, p. 59).

Figure 2.3 Ads by Proctor & Gardner successfully positioned Jewel Food Stores as an important asset in the lives of black families.

Source: *Ebony*, September 1979, p. 123. Courtesy of New Albertson's, Inc. for Jewel Food Stores. Reprinted with permission.

High moral standards

The Jewel Foods account was the perfect type of account for Proctor & Gardner since its family-orientation and values were consistent with Proctor's ethical grounding and strong sense of social responsibility. Believing that advertising leads social change, she would not promote any products that she believed were stereotypical or adversarial to the image, dignity, or economic condition of black people or women. Therefore, she refused to accept assignments for cigarettes and hard liquor and she also avoided doing business with media companies which she believed had discriminatory employment practices. Defending her position, she told a magazine reporter (Sellingpower.com, n.d., p. 2):

> "Advertising is the highest form of persuasion ... We mold opinions, therefore we have a responsibility to those whose opinions we influence. My belief in the product is unimportant. What I resist is the business opportunity to sell questionable or stereotypical products to consumers, especially when there is evidence the product is detrimental or reinforces negative stereotypes.
>
> I do not presume to judge anyone's standards but my own. I do believe in the root and fruit chain of conduct. Whatever you plant or leave behind flowers into something you will see again. You profit or lose by those recurring encounters. So I try to live and utilize my resources in a positive manner.
>
> When I meet the fruits of my behavior, generally I am well-pleased. Occasionally I have lost revenue because there are some businesses I can't represent and some people I cannot be comfortable serving. Some business people can separate personal values from business accommodations. I am less complicated and more consistent. There are certain values which remain rock solid with me."

In contrast to Proctor's view, some others in the industry held that advertising followed social change or were unconcerned about the impact of the products they represented. Proctor acknowledges that she lost business because of her ethical stance. A question is – why was Proctor's moral position so important to her? She explains (Harrison, 1986, p. 159):

> "This is important to me because I remember back when I was poor and living in Black Mountain, how I looked up to Lena Horne. She stood for something – quality and dignity. Because of the positive influence she had on my life, I would like to think that I might serve as a positive role model for some child growing up today. My firm must reflect good images, strong values – not negative messages."

The toast of Chicago

From the beginning, Proctor and her agency were highly unusual in the advertising business. Proctor made it a point of explaining the differentiation (Blake, 1984):

> "We made it clear that we were kind of different. We said that we would not take liquor and cigarettes, which was kind of an interesting position for a small agency to come out with – starting out by saying who we weren't interested in. By the time we started approaching people, word had gotten out and people felt they were special if we wanted their business."

This positioning strategy worked for a while. Despite Proctor's refusal to engage in certain business practices, the Proctor & Gardner Advertising agency experienced a positive growth trajectory through the 1970s and early 1980s. A few years after launch, the agency's offices relocated to a large professional building at 111 E. Wacker Drive in the bustling downtown Chicago business district and employed an integrated staff of between 15 and 30 people over the years (*Black Enterprise*, 1973; Stantley, 2014). In 1972, the agency was billing $1.8 million (*Black Enterprise*, 1973, p. 67), $4.8 million in 1974, $5.4 million in 1976, and $6.8 million in 1978 (Ingham and Feldman, 1994, p. 567). By 1981, the agency was billing $12.2 million and increased to $13 million in 1983 (Ingham and Feldman, 1994, p. 567). In addition to Jewel Food Stores, the client roster grew to include other accounts such as Sears Roebuck of Chicago, the CBS station in Chicago, Kraft Foods, Alberto-Culver hair care products, Illinois Bell, E. & J. Gallo, and Wisconsin-based American Family Insurance.

During the 1970s, the Proctor & Gardner agency consistently listed among the top black-owned advertising firms (Proctor, 1989) trailing the well-regarded Burrell agency, also located in Chicago. These accomplishments earned Proctor a number of high-profile recognitions including the Advertising Women of Chicago's top award – Advertising Woman of the Year – in 1974 (*Jet*, 1974); followed by the Advertising Person of the Year award by the AAF in 1975 (*Jet*, 1975). In both cases, she is believed to be the first African-American woman to receive such acclaim. *Black Enterprise* magazine cited Proctor and two other black advertising women – Joan Murray of Zebra Associates and Sara Dancy of Burrell – as "black women who made their mark" in a 1974 special issue on black women in business and public life (DeWitt, 1974). Over her career, other awards were bestowed, including the 1974 Blackbook Businesswoman of the Year Award, the 1976 Mary McLeod Bethune Achievement Award, the 1978 Charles A. Stevens International Organization of Women Executives Achievement Award, the Black Media Outstanding Professional Award for 1980, the 1980 Headliner award by the Association for Women in Communications, and numerous Clio and CEBA awards for outstanding advertising (Krantz, 2004).

The self-assured Proctor regularly attended events hosted by Chicago business leaders and was invited to participate on boards of numerous business and civic organizations. She often attended business-related social affairs with George Miller, a white man and the de facto second-in-command at Proctor & Gardner, described as a private-school WASP and sometimes – for laughs – introduced as Proctor's "wife" (Rich-McCoy, 1978, p. 207). Noting that

Proctor often was the high point at such social gatherings, Miller noted (Rich-McCoy, 1978, p. 208): "White people are very anxious to know Barbara Proctor ... If you are trying to put together a hoitsy-toisty cocktail party, it's chic to have a well-known black." Perfectly coiffed and elegantly dressed in designer fashions, Proctor would circulate about the room with grace and charm, making small talk and business connections while selling the Proctor & Gardner brand. At an Illinois Chamber of Commerce reception, conscious of herself as a novelty among the crowd, Proctor acknowledged (Rich-McCoy, 1978, p. 209): "they think I'm so weird ... I have the greatest time among them because they just think I'm the strangest person they have ever met in their entire lives." But the influential men of this group insisted they invited Proctor to join their organization not due to her race or gender, but because she is intelligent, competent, and is a respected source of information about African-Americans. One of Proctor's staff members offered an interesting perspective on Proctor's effect on people in such settings (Rich-McCoy, 1978, p. 208):

> "I think white people are sincere ... The fact that she is black and she is the way she is – so outgoing, so positive – they get caught up in it, too. And I think the color stops right there. They want to help her. They see her as a human being, not a black, not a woman. And the bottom line the fact that she is black makes them want to do it more. Her color is a plus in her case. And on top of that she is woman, too."

Underscoring the opinion that being black and female could work in Proctor's favor, a feature article ran in *Ebony* magazine in August 1982 with the title: "Barbara Proctor: I made it BECAUSE I'm Black and a Woman." Responding to the question of which of the two – racism or sexism – hampered her career the most, Proctor answered confidently (*Ebony*, 1982, pp. 143–144):

> "Neither – racism and sexism were only challenges to me, not obstacles. I happen to be Black, but I am much more than that. To view every circumstance in one's life in terms of those two small biological characteristics is very self-limiting."

Despite the expressed opinions regarding race, the reality of Proctor & Gardner's opportunities is that advertising clients often *did* see color. Although she had not set out to limit the agency's work to African-American consumers, a majority of Proctor's clients were mainly interested in pursuing the black consumer market, believing that Proctor's agency had special insights into this segment. Their assignments also included some promotional and public relations work aimed at black consumers which tended to be less profitable than sales-oriented advertising projects (Ingham and Feldman, 1994). Originally, Proctor had planned to garner general-market accounts via relationships she had established with whites when she worked for agencies like Post-Keys-Gardner.

Ironically, prior to opening her own agency, she had never worked on brands specifically geared toward African-Americans and quietly felt somewhat frustrated at the thinking which confined her to that role. Nonetheless, she accepted the assignments and made the best of the circumstances. In doing so, she was successful in improving the corporate social responsibility images of her clients through effective advertising and public relations work. For example, she persuaded clients Jewel and Kraft to withdraw sponsorships of violent TV programming (Ingham and Feldman, 1994, p. 568). Kraft was a long-time major client for Proctor & Gardner, from the early 1970s through the 1990s, and the agency promoted a number of its brands including natural cheese, mayonnaise, salad dressings, barbecue sauce, and margarine. Kraft also sponsored some public relations advertising supporting themes such as recognition of Dr. Martin Luther King Jr.'s birthday. Often using the tagline: "Kraft means more than cooking," the work by Proctor & Gardner was particularly effective in bolstering Kraft's family-friendly image, often featuring black children in loving settings where they were served home-cooked meals and were obviously well-cared for (see Figure 2.4). Explaining the typical Proctor & Gardner advertising assignment, Proctor stated publicly (Ingham and Feldman, 1994, p. 568):

> "I have the opportunity to show the strength, beauty, humor and family respect that is a very proud tradition in the Black experience. And I have a magnificent client base which agrees with that projection and supports me in sharing it."

"Mompreneur"

Barbara Proctor's personal convictions as an entrepreneur and as a mother shaped many of her life decisions. Despite her failed marriage, she cherished her son Morgan and considered him the only positive result of her brief union with Carl Proctor (*Ebony*, 1982). "I have been blessed with the most gentle, supportive human being on earth for a son," she told a magazine interviewer (Sellingpower.com, n.d., p. 5). Barbara and Morgan enjoy a very close relationship, and George Miller once commented that Proctor had two priorities: "her son and her business" (Rich-McCoy, 1978, p. 222). Providing for Morgan was a major inspiration for her business success and – given her own impoverished upbringing – she explained on *60 Minutes* (1984): "I would not permit my son to be reared in poverty and I did whatever it took to get it done." Long before the term "mompreneur" emerged as a description for women business owners with children, Proctor's commitment to saying "good morning" or "good night" to her son daily when he was young also impacted her business choices. Therefore, she preferred to do business with client companies which had offices in or near the Chicago area, so she never had to travel too far from home and be away from her son for extended periods of time. As a child, young Morgan sometimes napped in his mother's conference room and also attended a school across the street from her office

Figure 2.4 Ads for Kraft brand products by Proctor & Gardner emphasized home-prepared foods in the context of loving family settings.

Source: *Ebony*, January 1980, p. 7. KRAFT Natural Cheese brand material used with permission from Kraft Foods.

(Rich-McCoy, 1978, p. 223). She had help with him when needed, sometimes relying on Miller to provide care (Rich-McCoy, 1978, p. 223). Barbara Proctor made sure to include quality time with Morgan – often having lunch together and cooking large meals on Sundays (Rich-McCoy, 1978, p. 223). When Morgan became older, he became involved in the business – employed at the agency in creative capacities concerning broadcast production and music, as well as participating with various fundraising and charitable efforts, such as the Youth Community of America, a non-profit subsidiary of Proctor & Gardner (*Jet*, 1983). Her experiences as a working mother made her very sensitive to the responsibilities and needs of working women. By now a millionaire, Barbara Proctor did not believe that women could "have it all" simultaneously and that women needed support to be successful as career women and mothers.

"1984"

The mid-1980s signaled a turning point for Proctor and her agency. Consistent with the opening line of Charles Dickens' classic novel *A Tale of Two Cities*, calendar year 1984 represented the best of times and the worst of times. On January 8, Proctor was featured on the *60 Minutes* television program and shortly afterwards on January 25, was highlighted by President Reagan during his State of the Union address, catapulting her name to prominence among millions of people and casting her firm into a national spotlight. However, later in 1984, the agency lost its largest client, Alberto-Culver, which accounted for about 20 percent of the agency's billings (Ingham and Feldman, 1994, p. 567). Although the agency was billing $13 million in 1983, it lost nearly one-third of its billings between 1983 and 1985 (Smikle, 1985). To address the situation, Proctor reduced staff and overhauled the agency's management team. Although Proctor's agency had survived and emerged as one of the few successful black-owned agencies from the 1970s Golden Age for such enterprises, she was wary about the future (Alexander, 1976). She complained about the way major advertisers forced ethnic agencies to prepare new presentations for every potential opportunity, which is a very expensive way to do business. Costing about $3,500 to prepare in exchange for a 15 percent media commission on a modest advertising assignment, she said: "we couldn't play the presentation game … we killed ourselves" (Dougherty, 1981). Although she had hoped to nurture Proctor & Gardner into the caliber of a Leo Burnett agency, changes in the national social and political climate after the 1970s undermined that goal in her opinion (Proctor, 1989; Ryan, 1992). She told *Black Enterprise* (Smikle, 1985):

> "We have concluded that the long term prognosis for black agencies is not good and I do not see us existing 20 years from now as we do today. This is not the 1970s where the Administration and the corporate leadership of America felt that affirmative action goals should have priority. When the decade closed, the

cap went on and we got less business. This means that there are going to be fewer black agencies and few of us will survive, but those of us who do will survive big."

Changing times and shifting fortunes

In the late 1980s and early 1990s, the Proctor & Gardner agency stabilized to some extent, but never regained its status and momentum of the 1970s and early 1980s (Smikle, 1985). By 1988, the agency had acquired E. & J. Gallo winery and the G. Heileman Brewing Company as clients. Heileman hired the agency to handle the Old Style beer brand for the black consumer market. Since the agency had gone many years without a liquor account, some observers began to speculate – had Proctor compromised her principles to shore up her firm's financial footing (Ingham and Feldman, 1994, p. 568)? According to Suzanne Stantley, a Vice President and Account Manager who worked at Proctor & Gardner during the time, these accounts were justified in Proctor's mind since she saw a distinction between hard liquor versus beer and wine products because they contained less alcohol. Stantley (2014) explained: "She would not take tobacco or alcohol accounts – hard alcohol. There were plenty of times when hard alcohol come after her, but she wouldn't do it. She would not take on 90–100 proof alcohol."

As noted, the corporate business climate had shifted away from public relations and corporate social responsibility campaigns directed at black consumers which had been popular during the 1970s. Moreover, compared with the 1970s, by the 1990s there were considerably more agencies – black- and white-owned – with interest and expertise in black consumers that had excellent track records, intensifying the competition for accounts. Corporations were also becoming extremely interested in courting Hispanic consumers, thereby allocating greater portions of their "ethnic" marketing budgets away from the black consumer market and agencies which catered to black consumers. Former Proctor & Gardner account executive Suzanne Stantley, who handled the Kraft account, recalled many client meetings related to the growing interest in the Hispanic market and explained:

> "In the 1990s, the Hispanic market was really beginning to take hold. We were – and other black agencies were victims in this way – always having to defend why there was value in having an agency to reach this [African-American] target segment. I recall having several meetings at Kraft – over time – defending our role and the segment and why it was important to have a black agency."
>
> (Stantley, 2014)

As her participation in the advertising business evolved, Proctor began to acknowledge difficulties circumventing issues faced by women and black people in the advertising field and recognized ongoing race-related problems in America and business. She criticized the dominance of the rich, white, and male establishment in marketing, a group she referred to as the "Green Giants" – named for the popular vegetable brand advertising character – claiming that women were little "sprouts" who must exercise their options in order to challenge "the old boy network" (Ingham and Feldman, 1994, p. 568). In her early years in the business, she had held out hope that blacks would eventually have the same advantages as whites, but in the wake of news coverage concerning the notorious police beating of Rodney King, an unarmed African-American man in Los Angeles in 1992, she commented: "I'm convinced it will not come in my lifetime. This one event, more than anything, has crystallized, for me the depth of racism" (Ryan, 1992). Relating the beating incident directly to her own experiences in business, she conceded that because she was a black woman, working with white men was an "uphill battle" (Ryan, 1992). Acknowledging that corporate America had made efforts to bring minorities and women into their organizations beginning in the 1970s, Proctor noted that such efforts typically ceased when the proportion of management rose to about 15 percent or so. She observed (Ryan, 1992):

> "I'm not nearly as successful as I would be if I were a white male. If I were a white male, I'd be among the Fortune 500 companies ... Fifteen percent is the critical mass. That's when they say 'that's enough'. I go to industry and community meetings and sit on corporate boards. The composition is the same. It's a network of good ol' boys."

A number of factors led to Proctor's diminution in the advertising business. By the late 1980s and early 1990s, several other agencies had black female CEOs – including Caroline Jones, Joel P. Martin, and Carol H. Williams – so Barbara Proctor was no longer the anomaly that she had been in the early 1970s. Moreover, from an account acquisition standpoint, Proctor's reputation for family oriented and "conscience advertising" and her refusal to accept certain kinds of products likely put her at a competitive disadvantage since other agencies would willingly accept those types of accounts. Most of the other successful black-owned agencies handled a cigarette or hard liquor account – or both. Keenly aware of the challenges facing her business, but refusing to change her stance, Proctor (1989) acknowledged:

> "Other agencies had by far surpassed us because of the caliber of clients they were taking and the kinds of advertising they were producing for those clients. That's the price you pay. That's why it's important for me that I own it. I can afford to lose it or not grow it as I will."

In 1995, Proctor & Gardner Advertising, listing more than \$1.8 million in debts and \$361,000 in assets, filed for Chapter 11 bankruptcy protection and underwent a reorganization (*Jet*, 1995). Barbara Proctor was the main decision maker since George Miller had retired and moved to another state a few years earlier (Stantley, 2014). According to *Crain's Chicago Business*, the agency was beset by several problems including inadequate financial controls, the lasting impact of an economic recession, and increased competition from black-owned and general-market agencies courting the black consumer market (Cahill, 1995). Under the terms of the restructuring, the firm of Shakir Coleman & Barbour, Ltd. was appointed to exercise control over the agency's finances (Cahill, 1995). By this time, the company had billings around $5 million and three loyal clients – Jewel Food Stores, Kraft Foods, and American Family Insurance – all of which committed to remain with the agency while the company reorganized. In addition, new business specialists were brought on board to shore up revenues. However, it is unclear as to whether they were unable to attract new clients or if Proctor was unwilling to take on the types of brands interested in working with the agency. Thus, Barbara Proctor decided to dissolve Proctor & Gardner and launch a new company. She and son Morgan, along with a business associate who was a computer systems expert, recognized the technological changes impacting the marketing industry and planned to capitalize on it (Cahill, 1995). Believing the future belonged to digital communications, they launched Proctor Communications Network (a.k.a. Proctor Information Network) in 1996 to embrace the internet as a marketing tool (Encyclopedia.com, 2000). However, this approach pitted the new venture against much larger, resource-rich advertising firms, who were also expanding their services into the digital realm. At this time, the internet was relatively new as a marketing vehicle and many firms had difficulty navigating this unfamiliar platform. Small tech start-ups entered the ad business to help marketers utilize this new medium and large agencies acquired concerns which could provide the digital expertise they needed. Against this backdrop, unfortunately, the new Proctor venture did not gain sufficient traction and Barbara Proctor, now in her mid-sixties, decided to close shop and retired from advertising.

Barbara Gardner Proctor, business and social activist

One would think that the dissolution of the Proctor enterprises would spell the end of the Barbara Gardner Proctor saga. However, she recognized the significance of advertising with respect to its impact on the broader society. Proctor acknowledged: "Once I got in, I began to see that advertising had the ability to lead social change" (*Essence*, 1990). In that sense, Proctor's activities had influence beyond the practice of advertising itself. *Ebony* magazine praised Proctor's ethical grounding and contributions to the industry, noting that the industry was often associated with "deceit and Machiavellian manipulations" (Burgen, 1977). Throughout her advertising career, Proctor's status served as a platform for work in advocacy and social activism. Moreover, her reputation as a high-profile leader with a conscience kept her in the spotlight with respect to social and economic issues concerning women and people of color. Her opinions were widely sought after and she was a favorite in civic and community service organizations and listed in the International Who's

Table 2.1 Partial listing of Barbara Proctor's memberships in trade, civic, and community service organizations

Black United Fund	Leadership Academy of the Chicago Young Women's Christian Association (YWCA)
Boy's Club	Louisville *Courier-Journal*
Chicago Media Women	Mid-City Bank of Chicago
Chicago Unban League	NAACP – life member
Cosmopolitan Chamber of Commerce (Chair, 1976)	National League of Black Women (president, 1978–1982)
Council of Chicago Better Business Bureaus	Northwestern Hospital
DuSable Museum of Black History	Operation PUSH (People United to Save Humanity)
Economic Club	United Way
Gannon-Proctor Commission	White House Task Force for the Small Business Council
Girl Scouts of Chicago	Window to the World Communications, Inc.
Illinois Bell Telephone	WTTW-TV, Chicago public television
Illinois Olympic Committee (1988)	
Illinois State Bar Association Institute for Public Affairs	

Who of Community Services. She was a member of many boards and lent her name, time, and expertise to numerous trade and service organizations (see Table 2.1).

Two of Proctor's service appointments were particularly significant. In 1976 she was elected the first African-American woman to chair the Cosmopolitan Chamber of Commerce in Chicago, an interracial trade group (Ingham and Feldman, 1994). Founded in 1933 as the Negro Chamber of Commerce because blacks were not permitted to join the local Chicago Chamber of Commerce, the group changed its name and mission in 1955 when white counterparts were invited to join. As a result, the Cosmopolitan Chamber of Commerce became the largest interracial trade group in the United States. Under Proctor's leadership, the organization's direction shifted to become more community-service oriented (Ingham and Feldman, 1994).

Another major appointment occurred in 1983–1984, when Proctor was invited by Illinois Governor James Thompson to serve as co-chair of the Gannon-Proctor Commission, a private, bipartisan body convened to study the types of legal, social, and economic discrimination faced by women in the state of Illinois. The Commission members represented a virtual "who's who" of civic, business, religious, and social action leaders in the state (Gannon-Proctor Commission, 1983). The final Commission report issued to the governor provided four main recommendations (Gannon-Proctor Commission, 1984, pp. 1–2):

1 Provide women and men with opportunities to choose their roles in society according to ability unhindered by traditional restrictive stereotypes;

2 Recognize the impact of the interrelationship of family and work responsibilities;
3 Provide women with assistance needed to enable them to have equal access to employment opportunities;
4 Eliminate barriers which prevent women from achieving economic equality in society.

The Gannon-Proctor Commission's final recommendations aligned with many of Proctor's personal views concerning women's roles in society, including equal pay status, the need for flexible working conditions to accommodate family responsibilities, and career paths which are free from gender-based stereotyping. Proctor admitted to having "a special kind of compassion" for the Women's Liberation Movement – even though she didn't fully understand it – suggesting that she saw it as mainly driven by white women's concerns about having careers outside of the home and achieving personal fulfillment (Leavitt, 1985, p. 218). Growing up without a male provider and seeing black women work as a matter of survival, Proctor attributed her personal drive and self-sufficiency to her own upbringing and the fact that she never had to rely on a man for support (*Ebony*, 1982; Leavitt, 1985). Nonetheless, she urged black women to join the white feminists' struggle, to "work for female equality across the board," noting a widening gap between men's and women's salaries since the 1950s (*Jet*, 1978, p. 16). Commenting on the Gannon-Proctor Commission's findings, she wrote (Gannon-Proctor Commission, 1984, p. 50):

> "If we are to be remembered as a sane and viable society, we must accept the serious responsibilities of closely examining the findings of this report, understanding its implications, and acting decisively to rid our society of all socio-sexual inequities."

Believing that many women would continue to occupy the "pink ghettos" of labor, Proctor encouraged women to take risks and not to be afraid of failure, noting that women hold less than 10 percent of corporate management jobs and make up less than 3 percent of corporate boards, where decisions are made (Krause, 1981; Leavitt, 1985; Sellingpower.com, n.d.). Proctor predicted that more women would start their own companies given barriers to advancement in corporate environments, explaining (Sellingpower.com, n.d., p. 4):

> "If men are objective enough to allow them access, fine, they will be rewarded. If they continue to reject women in top management, more and more women will simply walk away and begin their own businesses. Women-owned businesses are the fastest growing segment of all business. Never mind that our little businesses gross less than $100,000 annually. The women starting up and struggling today will soon be joined by their better trained, better funded, and more liberated sisters."

Although Proctor advocated for women's rights she did not believe that women should be subjected to the "superwoman squeeze" – the constant pressure of having two full-time jobs: one as a full-time paid worker and another as a homemaker (Krause, 1981). Proctor (1989) explained that it was unrealistic for women to be perfect mothers, lovers, bosses, and so on concurrently. In offering solutions as to how women's work and home life could be managed, Proctor advised (Sellingpower.com, n.d., p. 4):

> "The family will have to divide up responsibilities more equitably. An entire wave of 'liberated' women have determined that the superwoman is dead. They simply cannot be all things to all people. The guilt is diminishing daily, and they have determined that goals and responsibilities are joint commitments by all members of a family. This need not lead to conflict between career women and homemakers. It should lead to a quantification of the home career and stronger protections for the homemaker."

She said what?

Throughout her career, Proctor used her visibility and status to champion business and social causes which she deemed important. In her mind, her position as a business leader put her in place to help establish policies which she believed could address some of the problems and inequities that she observed in the marketplace and society. However, at times she took positions and made comments which were construed as unpopular or controversial, both in the black community and in the advertising industry. For example, she criticized the use of affirmative action policies in some organizations, arguing that blacks were sometimes too quickly placed in positions they were unsuited for, to their detriment in the long term (Klose, 1984). As a member of the White House Task Force on Small Business, she discouraged government support of low-quality enterprises, such as those lacking cleanliness or providing poor service. Some people took offense and interpreted her stance as denigrating to black businesses. Asked why black consumers did not support black-owned businesses, she replied (Ingham and Feldman, 1994, p. 569):

> "It's not that blacks do not support black businesses, they don't support shabby businesses. Blacks are some of the most sophisticated shoppers in the world. They have less money to spend so they have to be good shoppers. They are not going to buy a product just because it is black. If the service is not up to standards, they are not going to buy."

A firestorm erupted in summer 1974 when Proctor announced that her agency would make advertising media placements based on the race of the owner, prioritizing black-owned media over white-owned outlets (*Advertising Age*, 1974a; Chambers, 2008, p. 242). In addition, when a white-owned media company was the only alternative, she requested that a black representative be provided to service her account. Her purpose was to aggressively support black media and encourage equitable treatment of minority employees of white broadcast stations. However, industry insiders viewed Proctor's position as a form of reverse discrimination and the trade press labeled her a black racist (*Advertising Age*, 1974b). Her clients were also criticized for supporting her decision. Defending her position, Proctor explained (Harrison, 1986, p. 159):

> "I thought it was important for my agency to take a stand regarding discrimination on the part of radio stations that had predominantly black audiences, but did not pay their black salespeople the same amount of money as their white salespeople. I was determined that Proctor & Gardner would buy air time for commercials on black-owned and oriented radio stations whenever possible. We would also refuse to buy time for commercials on any white owned stations that had unfair hiring and paying practices."

Reflecting on the dispute, Proctor continued:

> "Many of my friends in the advertising community were surprised that I would take what they thought was a losing stand. I told them it may not be a winning position, but it is a moral one. My clients agreed with the position I had chosen and stayed with me. That year I was chosen Chicago Advertising Woman of the Year."

In light of the ongoing controversy, in order to quell the storm and silence her critics, in late summer 1974 Proctor announced that she would rescind the policy and select advertising media on a non-racial basis (*Advertising Age*, 1974b).

Interestingly, given her outspokenness and high visibility in the business community, Proctor's accomplishments were disparaged by some members of the African-American community. *Black Enterprise* published an article in 1974 on the progress that black women were making in business, attributing such gains to the Civil Rights Movement and the Women's Liberation Movement (DeWitt, 1974, p. 18). However, the article indicated that some people saw successes such as Proctor's – with women serving in middle- or upper-management roles – as impeding the progress of black men, or serving to compete with black men directly. Other critics derided black women in such positions as reinforcing the stereotype of black society as matriarchal. Finally, others believed it was acceptable for black women to work – so long as they did not pursue opportunities in fields that were just opening up to black men. Taking umbrage to these views, Proctor responded, acknowledging the long history of black women in the workforce, including their involvement in business enterprises (Morton, 1975):

> "Black people now are unfortunately assuming some of the attitudes that whites have had about women. The result is that black female heads of business are, just like their white counterparts, now viewed to some extent as an oddity and their historical track record is forgotten."

In other instances, there appeared to be outright enmity toward Proctor, her activities, and prominence. A columnist for *Jet* magazine, a popular black news weekly, complained that Proctor's infamous mention by President Reagan "skyrocketed ... the executive to instant celebrity status, but did little else for blacks in minority enterprise," suggesting that there was envy of Proctor's stature among the black business community (Booker, 1984). In another example, after her retirement, the prestigious AAF Advertising Hall of Fame, which inducted many of the high-achieving black male advertising pioneers after they retired from their careers, failed to recognize Barbara Proctor.

The un-conventions of Barbara Proctor

It is worthwhile to consider why Barbara Proctor did as well as she did for as long as she did, given her unlikeliness for a prominent career in advertising. Despite never receiving an Advertising Hall of Fame invitation, her accomplishments were significant and worthy of recognition. In addition to the Advertising Woman and AAF Advertising Person of the Year awards, the Smithsonian Institution acknowledged Proctor and featured her in its traveling exhibit: "Black Women Achievement Against the Odds." A national special report "Risk to Riches: Women and Entrepreneurship in America," concerning women entrepreneurs, focused on Proctor as a key subject (Fraser, 1986). Proctor was also featured in *Supersisters*, a set of 72 trading cards highlighting women who were important to the fight for women's rights, created by Lois Rich, a founding member of the Ohio Chapter of the National Organization for Women (Zanis, 2014).

Proctor's accomplishments belie that fact that she had – in her own estimation – many factors working against her given the traditions of the advertising industry: race, gender, age, and temperament. She had no role models in the industry to pattern herself after and had ideas and values which countered many practices in the business. She also took positions which – she acknowledges – likely cost her business and relationships. Thus, from every point of view, she was a highly unconventional advertising pioneer. Looking back on her career, she laughed (Proctor, 1989):

> "Had I had any idea what I was doing, I never would have done it, because there was no reason for me to succeed. I had a strong gut feeling that I had something to say in this business and nobody was going to tell me how to do it!"

Examination of Proctor's life and career illustrates matchless ambition, resolve, and determination to move forward on her pioneering path in advertising. Proctor was once asked if she ever grew weary of all of the hard work and aggressiveness which was instrumental to her success. She replied (Sellingpower.com, n.d., p. 2):

"Of course I do. I feel exploited at times. I feel overworked, misunderstood, misused … all the negatives. My solution is to push those feelings into absurdity. When I realize how absurd it is, and have a great laugh, the feelings are over for another year or so. I never go back and I seldom look back. I've made my share of mistakes and I've learned from them. Energy spent living in the past diminishes your time now and in the future."

Offering additional perspective on her life, Proctor reflected (Sellingpower.com, n.d., pp. 2–3):

"I have been poorer, uglier, lonelier, and more scared than most women … and I survived that childhood. Life has been a piece of cake since I got an education. I have enjoyed the freedom which comes only from knowing what's on the other side. I also know that when you buy inclusion and acceptance with conformity, the price bankrupts us spiritually. My greatest wealth is not financial. It is peace of mind."

A former Proctor & Gardner executive offered a final observation on Barbara Gardner Proctor and her unusual ascent in the advertising world (Stantley, 2014):

"She came from another school. She fought and scraped and clawed her way. When she came along, there were very few women business owners – there were few role models – so she had to figure it out by trial and error. The Caucasian women in advertising who hit the big time also came up in the '60s. You also cannot overlook the fact that those people had the support of men to help them create and develop. She didn't really have that.

I think when you come out of that environment and manage to get yourself to a point where you are mentioned by the President and on *60 Minutes* – she climbed a very, very tall mountain to get there."

References

60 Minutes (1984) 'Getting to Know Barbara' CBS News, January 8.

Advertising Age (1974a) 'Proctor & Gardner Won't Buy Media if Blacks Excluded,' June 17, p. 116.

Advertising Age (1974b) 'Black Agency Owner's Practice is Pure Racism,' August 19, p. 24.

Alexander, M. (1976) 'Black Agencies Ride a Roller Coaster through the Advertising Field,' *Black Enterprise*, June, pp. 150–160.

Billboard (1963) 'Ewart Abner Exits Vee Jay: Big Shake-Up,' August 3, pp. 1, 8.

Billboard (1966) 'Curtain Down on Vee-Jay as Liquidation is Ordered,' August 13, p. 7.

Black Enterprise (1973) 'Advertising Agencies,' June, p. 67.

Black Enterprise (1974) 'Black Women Make Their Mark,' August, pp. 37–40.

Blake, B. (1984) 'Barbara Gardner Proctor, President, Proctor & Gardner Advertising, Chicago, Ill.,' *Asheville Citizen Times*, January 28 [Online]. Available at: www.wresfm.com/files/barbara_proctort.pdf (Accessed: May 17, 2014).

Booker, S. (1984) 'Ticker Tape USA,' *Jet*, February 27, p. 12.
Burgen, M. (1977) 'Women in Business: They are Owners, Bosses, Workers,' *Ebony*, August, p. 122.
Cahill, J. (1995) 'Debt Swaps Star who Beat the Odds: Proctor Battles to Save Ad Firm; Files Chap. 11,' *Crain's Chicago Business*, September 18 [Online]. Available at: www.chicagobusiness.com/article/19950916/ISSUE01/10008828/debt-swaps-star-who-beat-the-odds-proctor-battles-to-save-ad-firm-files-chap-11 (Accessed: May 17, 2014).
Callahan, M. (2006) 'The Vee-Jay Story' [Online]. Available at: www.bsnpubs.com/veejay/veejaystory1.html (Accessed: June 16, 2015).
CEBA Exhibit Journal (1978) New York: World Institute for Black Communications.
Chambers, J. (2008) *Madison Avenue and the Color Line: African-Americans in the Advertising Industry*. Philadelphia, PA: University of Pennsylvania Press.
Chicago Reporter (1975) 'Blacks are Most Hidden Persuaders in Chicago's Billion Dollar Advertising Business,' March, p. 1.
Dattner, D. and Dattner, A. (2003) 'Post-Keys-Gardner, Inc.,' in J. McDonough and K. Egolf (eds.) *Advertising Age Encyclopedia of Advertising*. New York: Fitzroy Dearborn, vol. 3, pp. 1261–1263.
Davis, J. F. (2002) 'Enterprise Development under an Economic Detour? Black-Owned Advertising Agencies 1940–2000,' *Journal of Macromarketing*, 22(1), pp. 75–85.
Davis, J. F. (2013) 'Realizing Marketplace Opportunity: How Research on the Black Consumer Market Influenced Mainstream Marketers, 1920–1970,' *Journal of Historical Research in Marketing*, 5(4), pp. 471–473.
Dewitt, K. (1974) 'Black Women in Business,' *Black Enterprise*, August, pp. 14–19.
Dougherty, P. (1981) 'Advertising: Ethnic-Ad Budgets Holding Up,' *New York Times*, December 17 [Online]. Available at: www.nytimes.com/1981/12/17/business/advertising-ethnic-ad-budgets-holding-up.html (Accessed: May 17, 2014).
Ebony (1978) Jewel Food Stores advertisement, November, p. 57.
Ebony (1982) 'Barbara Proctor: I made it BECAUSE I'm Black and a Woman,' August, pp. 142–144.
Essence (1990) 'Women in Advertising,' January, pp. 35–40.
Encyclopedia.com (2000) 'Proctor, Barbara Gardner,' in *Gale Encyclopedia of U.S. Economic History* [Online]. Available at: www.Encyclopedia.com/doc/1G2-3406400755.html (Accessed: May 31, 2014).
Fraser, E. (1986) 'Risk to Riches: Women and Entrepreneurship in America. A Special Report,' *National Federation of Independent Businesses*.
Gannon-Proctor Commission (1983) 'Names.' Available at: www.lib.niu.edu/1982/ii821235.html (Accessed: May 29, 2014).
Gannon-Proctor Commission (1984) *Final Report*. Springfield, IL: The Commission.
Harrison, P. (1986) *America's New Women Entrepreneurs*. Washington, D.C.: Acropolis Books.
Ingham, J. and Feldman, L. (1994) *African-American Business Leaders: A Biographical Dictionary*. Westport, CT: Greenwood Press.
Jet (1967) 'Jazz takes a Blow, Chicago Radio Switches to Rock,' April 6, p. 55.
Jet (1974) 'Best in Ads,' March 7, p. 17.
Jet (1975) 'Barbara Proctor Selected for Top Advertising Award,' May 8, p. 16.
Jet (1978) 'Black Women Told to Join White Feminists' Struggle,' August 24, p. 16.
Jet (1983) 'California All-Stars Play Basketball to Aid School,' February 28, p. 51.

Jet (1995) 'Black Woman Advertising Entrepreneur Files Chapter 11 Bankruptcy,' October 9, p. 24.

Kimbro, D. and Hill, N. (1991) *Think and Grow Rich: A Black Choice*. New York: Random House.

Klose, K. (1984) 'In the Spirit of Enterprise,' *Washington Post*, January 27 [Online]. Available at: www.washingtonpost.com/pb/archive/lifestyle/1984/01/27/in-the-spirit-of-enterprise/4e83667f-5d64-4909-98f3-8db958193c8a/?resType=accessibility (Accessed: June 24, 2015).

Krantz, R. (2004) *African-American Business Leaders and Entrepreneurs*. New York: Infobase Publishing.

Krause, J. (1981) 'Caught in the Superwoman Squeeze?' *Milwaukee Journal*, April 8, p. 9.

Krisman, C. (2005) *Encyclopedia of American Women in Business: From Colonial Times to the Present*. Westport, CT: Greenwood Press.

Leavitt, J. (1985) *American Women Managers and Administrators: A Selected Biographical Dictionary of Twentieth Century Leaders in Business, Education and Government*. Westport, CT: Greenwood Press.

Morton, C. (1975) 'Black Women in Corporate America,' *Ebony*, November, pp. 106–107.

PBS.org (2012) 'American Experience: The Great Depression' [Online]. Available at: www.C-Span.org/wgbh/americanexperience/features/general-article/dustbowl-great-depression/ (Accessed: June 15, 2015).

Proctor, B. (1989) 'An American Profile: Life and Career of Barbara Proctor.' Interview by Susan Swain for C-Span.org, March 31 [Online]. Available at: www.c-span.org/video/?6903-1/life-career-barbara-proctor (Accessed: March 1, 2014).

Pruter, R. (1997) *Doowop: The Chicago Scene*. Urbana, IL: University of Illinois Press.

Reagan, R. (1984) *Address before a Joint Session of the Congress on the State of the Union*. January 25, 1984 [Online]. Gerhard Peters and John T. Wooley, the American Presidency Project. Available at: www.presidency.ucsb.edu/ws.?pid=40205 (Accessed: October 7, 2013).

Rich-McCoy, L. (1978) *Millionairess: Self-Made Women of America*. New York: Harper & Row.

Ryan, N. (1992) 'Barbara Proctor Founded Proctor & Gardner Advertising Inc.,' *Chicago Tribune*, May 10 [Online]. Available at: http://articles.chicagotribune.com/1992-05-10/news/9202110657_1_foote-cone-leo-burnett-white (Accessed: May 17, 2014).

Sellingpower.com (n.d.) 'Selling Power Magazine Article: Superachiever Barbara Proctor' [Online]. Available at: www.sellingpower.com/content/article/?i=1254&ia=8213/superachiever-barbara-proctor (Accessed: May 31, 2014).

Smikle, K. (1985) 'The Image Makers,' *Black Enterprise*, December, pp. 44–52.

Stantley, S. (2014) Interview with the Author, June 25, 2014.

Wickman, F. (2013) 'How a Black Label Brought the Beatles to America,' *The Slate.com*, January 10 [Online]. Available at: www.slate.com/blogs/browbeat/2013/01/10/the_beatles_and_vee_jay_records_ how _it_took_a_black_owned_label_to_bring.html (Accessed: June 16, 2015).

Zanis, L. (2014) 'Collecting Inspiration with Supersisters,' *Metropolitan Museum of Art* [Online]. Available at: www.metmuseum.org/about-the-museum/now-at-the-met/2014/supersisters (Accessed: April 3, 2015).

3 Caroline Robinson Jones

Tenacious advertising trailblazer

Figure 3.1 Caroline R. Jones.

Source: courtesy of Tony R. Jones.

References to Caroline Jones' advertising career often emphasize how she started in the industry as a secretary. That fact, by itself, is unremarkable since many adwomen of her era started in clerical positions. What is significant is that she was a trailblazer in many other respects and rose to become one of the most respected and influential women in the advertising profession. Named as the Advertising Woman of the Year by the Women's Advertising Club of New York in 1990, sources called Jones a "role model" and the "preeminent black woman in advertising" (Tharpe, 1988; Vagoni, 2001). Given her accomplishments, Jones' career is typically described as a "success story" (Fleming, 1996). Yet, despite the accolades, Jones believed her professional career was limited by what she termed "caste-typing" – opportunity constraints based on race and gender. In 1990, reflecting on her career after many years in advertising, Jones explained her opinions, using the "caste-typing" terminology:

> "As a member of a double minority – female *and* Black – I've learned the biggest problem in America is the existence of castes within society, business and advertising ... Some might think there's been progress. But look around advertising today and you'll find there are *fewer* Black men or women than in the 1970s. Even more disturbing, there's not much talk about equal opportunity ... Caste-typing by color or sex or nationality injures everybody; especially the businesses that are deprived of the enormous talent and energy minorities can provide."
>
> (*Wall Street Journal*, 1990)

Jones' career path was characterized by a zig-zag pattern of trailblazing positions with large general-market advertising firms interspersed with significant entrepreneurial ventures in the field. As such, this chapter organizes her biographical narrative around two major career trajectories rather than a chronological scheme: (1) her experiences in important pioneering roles in major general-market advertising agencies; and (2) her experiences with entrepreneurial advertising ventures where she was a key executive or owner of the establishment. Her experiences not only tell a compelling personal story, but also underscore the significant challenges faced by women of color in the advertising business. Jones apparently sensed her significance in history and donated her personal and business papers and artifacts to the archives of the National Museum of American History at the Smithsonian Institution in 1996, providing a rich source of information about her life and career. This chapter relies on these resources and supplemental materials to reconstruct Jones' career and gain insight into her views and experiences. Secondary sources concerning conditions in the broader society and advertising industry culture during Jones' lifetime are included to provide appropriate context.

Caroline Jones, advertising pioneer

By the time Jones had established her own agency and won the prestigious Advertising Woman of the Year award, she reported that she was often asked, "What's it like at the top?" Her thoughtful reply:

> "It's like climbing a mountain ... I've often said, with your bare hands. And when you reach the summit, scraped, bleeding and bruised from the jagged rocks you look around – it's lonely sometimes ... and cold sometimes ... but you can also feel the sunshine."
>
> ("Ad Woman of the Year," 1990)

Born in 1942 in Benton Harbor, Michigan, Jones, the eldest girl among ten siblings, was recognized early on as a leader: tall, attractive, dependable, resourceful, energetic, dynamic, charismatic, a risk-taker, and a perfectionist ("Product of Benton Harbor," n.d.). Growing up, she was industrious and regularly involved in activities where she could earn money – picking and selling berries, magazine subscriptions, cosmetics, greeting cards, and so on. "I was always out selling something," she told a reporter (Fleming, 1996, p. 6). The first of her family to attend college, she won a full scholarship to the prestigious University of Michigan where she graduated in 1963 with dual degrees in Science and English. Wanting to help children with physical disabilities, she originally planned to study medicine and become an orthopedic surgeon. She applied to Michigan after learning that Harvard – her first choice – did not accept women into its pre-med program. However, she abandoned the idea of becoming a doctor when she became ill at the sight of a dead cat during an anatomy class and changed majors (Fleming, 1996, p. 7).

She also earned a teaching certificate in case she needed to pursue teaching as a career option. Given this backdrop, Jones' entry into the advertising profession occurred by happenstance.

"Any Monday morning": Jones at the JWT agency

As a college senior, Jones attended a campus recruiting seminar hosted by a woman from the JWT company and completed an application for "some kind of advertising agency" (Jones, 1968). Traveling to New York City that summer to investigate employment opportunities, Jones visited the agency and within two days was offered a secretarial position. Friday turnover among the secretarial ranks was so high that the personnel director assured her that a position would be available "any Monday morning." Jones remembers encountering a series of pre-existing "female-oriented stereotypes" immediately at Thompson, one of the largest agencies, noting that racial stereotyping would come later (Jones, n.d.). Although Thompson was considered among the most progressive agencies of the era, all women – regardless of educational background or experience – started as secretaries. Men, however, could be hired directly into junior copywriter positions with "little more than a part of a portfolio and a little bit of promise" (Jones, 1987, p. 34). Jones was strongly encouraged to accept the offer by two black women journalists, Tomasina Norford and Ellen Tarry, who hosted her during her New York visit arguing that they "couldn't have paid for a job in advertising" when they finished college (Jones, 1968). Despite her father's objections and lacking secretarial skills – she twice failed Thompson's mandatory typing test – Jones accepted the job offer, and its "woman's salary" of $75 per week. She recalled:

> "I wasn't qualified to be a secretary, but Thompson only let women enter the firm as secretaries at that time. The turnover in workers was incredible. A new group would be coming in as an old one would be leaving."
>
> (Fleming, 1996, p. 8)

Jones started at Thompson in August 1963 and quickly began to understand the agency culture, referring to it as a "very much cutthroat business, fueled by a glamorous, good-ole-boy network and a prep school and Ivy League image" (Jones, 1987, p. 34). New to the company, she asked a high-level manager why women had to start as secretaries, not realizing that the question was *verboten*. The manager responded to her query, explaining:

> "That's an interesting question, Caroline. But I don't know the answer. I guess because that's the way we've always done it – it's historical."
>
> (Jones, n.d.)

Within three weeks after being hired, Jones was assigned as the secretary to Arnold Grisman, the Creative Director for the agency's largest account – Ford Motor Company. Shortly thereafter, she was encouraged to pursue the competitive try-outs for Thompson's famed Copywriter's Workshop, a training program offered annually to female employees. Unaware that this opportunity offered practically the only escape from a secretary's existence, she competed successfully among 200 other women and was among 18 accepted as copy trainees (Jones, n.d.). Unbeknownst to her, Jones' hiring and acceptance into the Copywriter's Workshop coincided with an initiative spearheaded by Dan Seymour, then chairman of JWT, who encouraged his management team to recruit blacks for clerical jobs with the objective of training them in professional advertising skills such as copywriting, media research, and account services (Chambers, 2008, p. 171). Sensitive to the efforts of civil rights groups concerning minority hiring practices in advertising agencies, and wanting to develop its own cadre of skilled minority staffers, JWT made such hiring a priority during that period. As such, the percentage of black employees increased from 0.6 percent in 1963 – the year Jones was hired – to nearly 5 percent in 1968 (Chambers, 2008, p. 172). In 1964 Jones assisted in writing a special publication commemorating the 100 Year Anniversary of Thompson and was stunned to learn that she was the first black person ever trained as a copywriter at the agency. She also learned that while copywriting was considered an acceptable career path for women, they were shunned from non-creative account management positions, which were gateways to agency management roles. To her knowledge, there were no female account supervisors at the agency. Bored with clerical work and eager to take advantage of whatever advancement opportunities might be available, Jones spent her free time digesting advertising trade publications and analyzing successful advertising campaigns in order to learn the elements of effective advertisements. Less than eight months into the job, Jones received an excellent performance review from Ilene Clark, a woman executive at the agency:

> "I'm told by Messrs. Grisman, Wells, and Fillippo that her performance to date has been excellent. They report that Caroline is most dependable and resourceful, and that she appears able to assume greater responsibilities. Arnold has remarked on several occasions how well she is doing. He says she is the best secretary he has had with this Company. From my own experience with Caroline, I can support these observations. I would like, in addition, to say that she deports herself well and presents a most agreeable appearance."
>
> ("Miss Georgia Demarest," 1964)

Observing that Thompson was one of the few agencies which had female vice presidents – six – Jones wanted to be one of them because they were in managerial roles (Fleming, 1996, p. 10). She noticed that many of the top women in the advertising industry worked for Thompson, such as Rena Bartos and Georgia Demarest, who had hired Jones in 1963 (Jones, 1987, p. 35). The culture at Thompson was influenced by Helen Lansdowne Resor, wife of Thompson's longtime President, Stanley Resor, one of the most influential leaders in the history of the agency. Mrs. Resor had been a member of Thompson's board of directors and a well-known women's rights advocate. Women executives at Thompson typically worked in areas outside of account management, such as creative and research (Jones, n.d.). Jones noticed that individuals had to be aggressive and assertive to move ahead in advertising and needed to present a polished personal style. Therefore, Jones mimicked the style of dress and presentation of Thompson's women executives, noting: "They wore hats and white gloves to work, so I did the same" (Fleming, 1996, p. 10). These female executives served as role models and sources of inspiration for other women. Although Fleming (1996, p. 12) suggests that Jones received limited support from her white colleagues at Thompson, Jones praised her experiences with the women supervisors: "At that time it was unusual for a woman to be an Executive Vice President and many of these women were. They all looked after me and helped me in every way" (*Entrepreneurial Woman*, 1989, p. 66).

Despite her ambition, initiative, and completion of the Copywriter's Workshop, Thompson was slow in providing Jones with copywriting opportunities. Instead, the company managers decided to have her trained as a researcher in the Consumer Research Department, responsible for conducting door-to-door interviews to learn consumers' likes and dislikes. Thompson had a long history of using research as a basis for advertising strategies (Kreshel, 1990) and Jones' training proved valuable to her overall development as a copywriter. After a year in Research, incensed at seeing other secretaries obtain copywriting assignments, she threatened to leave. She was finally offered a junior copywriter's position on the Prince Matchabelli fragrance account which, she says, "was headed by one of the nicest women in the agency" (Jones, 1968). This assignment underscored another norm at Thompson – female copywriters were assigned to "women's products" accounts while men were assigned to "men's products." During her five-and-a-half years at Thompson, Jones honed her copywriting skills on such national brands as Chesborough-Ponds, Lux, Lady Scott, Listerine, and Murine International. Her first ad featured a line of women in towels with the phrase: "Don't go Near the Water without your Albano Bath Oil" which appeared in the *New Yorker* in 1965 (Dicker, 1985). She moved between writing and research assignments, at one point supervising the Consumer Research Group, overseeing transcribing typists and managing daily operations (Fleming, 1996, p. 12). Although she preferred copywriting, the research skills she learned provided a foundation which improved the quality of her work in future areas of advertising practice.

Eventually, Thompson promoted Jones to a full-fledged copywriter and she was able to improve her standard of living, moving out of her small walk-up apartment in New York City. In 1965 she married Edward H. Jones, a manager with the Small Business Administration (*Jet*, 1965, p. 40). Jones juggled family and work responsibilities as the couple raised one son, Anthony (Tony). When Tony was old enough, he sometimes accompanied his mother on trips in the United States and abroad where she directed recording sessions for commercials. Through his mother's work, he enjoyed meeting celebrities and seeing her ads in the media, although he felt resentment at times when her career obligations interrupted family time (Jones, 2016). Tony described his mother as a smart, no-nonsense, and very resourceful person. Once she knew what she wanted "she'd figure out a way to get it," Jones (2016) explained.

Most of Caroline Jones' work at Thompson concerned advertising for mainstream consumer products, but she was sensitive to the potential of multicultural marketing opportunities and the viability of the black consumer market. Believing fruitful opportunities for multi-ethnic marketing to exist in the cosmetics segment, she submitted a research report in 1965 indicating the variety of skin tones among "non-European women" (Jones, 1965). She believed the inclusion of ethnic models in ads would appeal to various consumers. Jones was dissatisfied with the agency's practice of excluding blacks and Hispanics from advertisements geared toward the general market, even in group settings. At the time, Thompson handled the Breck account, which featured the famous Breck Girls in its hair coloring ads. Attractive models like Cheryl Tiegs and Cybill Shepherd appeared in 1960s Breck ads. "I wondered if we could use a black woman as the Breck Girl," Jones pondered, since it was the height of the Black Power movement in the United States and "everything was black, black, black" (Fleming, 1996, p. 14). Noting that the ad shoot had only blonde women, Jones suggested to her superiors that Breck would sell more products if black women were included in the ads. However, she was told there were no black blondes, an explanation which upset Jones. Later, she was further angered when client Alberto-Culver refused to include ethnic models in ads for a new hair coloring product called "For Brunettes Only," since most black and Latino women have dark hair. Noting the resistance to her efforts to increase and improve the image of multi-ethnic women in advertising portrayals, Jones commented: "The few of us who were in the ad business were fed up with the racial politics of the industry" (Fleming, 1996, p. 14).

Beyond Jones' work at Thompson, she joined several trade groups including the NAMD, a networking and support group of black advertising and marketing professionals established in the 1950s; and the Group for Advertising Progress (GAP), an organization of professional men and women working for advertising agencies, their suppliers, or clients, committed to the advancement of blacks within the advertising industry. Established in 1968 in New York City, GAP was affiliated with the mainstream trade group – the 4 A's. GAP's mission was to bolster the ranks of black professionals working in advertising and enhance the professionalism of those already employed in the industry by providing resources and support (Chambers, 2008, p. 197). GAP also served as an advocacy group for people of color in the advertising profession and assisted civil rights and government organizations in investigating discriminatory practices in the industry (Chambers, 2008, p. 199).

Jones was an early participant with GAP while working as a copywriter. She appeared as the only female speaker at GAP's 1968 Annual Conference on a panel titled "Closing the Gap: Minority Groups in Advertising Agencies," chaired by GAP President Doug Alligood, a black Account Executive with BBD&O, a large mainstream advertising agency in New York. Reflecting on the poor perception of blacks in the industry and the typical shortage of opportunities for blacks in agencies, Jones remarked in her presentation:

> "Non-whites are underpaid in terms of their relative merit and experience ... because of the small percentage of non-whites in advertising. Management is often at a loss as to how to determine the true value of a non-white employee. A few agencies are still 'show-casing' their non-white employees."
>
> (Group for Advertising Progress, 1968)

Frustrated regarding her observations of the advertising business and compensation, Jones left Thompson in 1968, critical of some of the practices she observed. She wrote an essay summarizing her tenure at the agency, reflecting in part:

> "As I look back on my career at J. Walter Thompson, I feel that I have been associated with a greater variety of advertising activities than most young writers. Yet as I look around me and into the future, I feel I am at the crossroads of my career. Ironically, for having been faithful to my company, I have fallen behind in salary. Daily, I see younger people being given greater compensation for less experience and talent. I like my work and my surroundings, and I feel that it is unfortunate that traditionally in advertising, companies are remiss in rewarding their own, and it is indeed those people who choose to move around and 'get all they can' who get ahead in this game."
>
> (Jones, 1968)

Caroline Jones, Vice President, BBD&O

Seven years later, in 1975, Jones' appointment as a Vice President at BBD&O made her the first black woman named to an executive position at a major Madison Avenue advertising agency (Jakobson, 1985). Recruited by Jim Jordan, then President of BBD&O, Jones was told, "we need someone good who can help on accounts committed to black advertising" ("Caroline Jones is an advertising pioneer," n.d.). Jones was hired to help BBD&O shore up its marketing to black consumers and her main responsibilities concerned copywriting (Jones, 1987, p. 37; Jones, 2016). Yet, evidence indicates that her experience at BBD&O was bittersweet. BBD&O was not new to placing black professionals in high-profile roles, having hired Clarence Holte in 1952 as the first African-American to hold an executive position in a major New York agency – to head its newly established Ethnic Markets division. Holte had retired from BBD&O three years prior to Jones' arrival and – similar to Holte's selection – Jones' appointment generated intense media publicity and accolades. Inside BBD&O, however, Jones claims that she felt alone, self-conscious, and ostracized, which she attributed to envious co-workers including an immediate supervisor (Berger, 1989). In a magazine interview Jones stated, "Some whites wondered how I could possibly come in as a Vice President" ("Caroline Jones, a heroine...," n.d.). In another, she acknowledged that some viewed her $40,000 salary as "excessive" (Jakobson, 1985). She explained how widespread publicity worsened her situation:

> "To be black and female is always to be noticed, and standing out in a crowd is not always good in corporate life. There were people who had been there for years and who were not profiled, as I was, in magazine and newspapers stories."
>
> (Jakobson, 1985)

> "A great many people resented my coming to BBD&O. I was shocked at the degree of hostility that my appointment aroused. But, despite the obstacles, I did some things there that I am very proud of."
>
> (Nivens, 1982)

Jones did notable creative work during her tenure at BBD&O. For example, she helped Campbell's soup revitalize its advertising approach, using emotional appeals aimed at black consumers, based on the rationale: "food is love." Where Campbell's traditional approach had been to depict the product and its features, Jones convinced the client that average people – black models in this case – had to be shown enjoying the soup in loving familial settings. This approach was so successful in courting black consumers, that Campbell's adapted the concept into its general-market advertising. With the support of Jordan, Jones also successfully did work for the Armstrong Company and promoted national membership drives for the NAACP in 1976–1977 and the National Urban League. Despite Jones' notoriety at BBD&O, her time there was brief. She left BBD&O in 1977 after less than two years, the last time she would be employed by a large general-market agency. Jordan, while disappointed, was supportive and complimentary: "I'll always be a Caroline Jones fan," he said. "She has maintained a first-rate reputation in the industry" ("Caroline Jones: a heroine...," n.d.).

Caroline Jones, entrepreneur

Beginning around the late 1960s and continuing through the late 1970s, a variety of socioeconomic phenomena contributed to the establishment of a significant number of new advertising agencies with black ownership (Davis, 2002). Heightened interest in black consumers by mainstream marketers, the impact of the Civil Rights movement, and a rising standard of living among African-American consumers prompted black entrepreneurs to capitalize on the business climate and position themselves as experts in targeting the black consumer market. Scholars called this period the "Golden Age" for black agencies (Chambers, 2008; Davis, 2002) and Jones was an important figure of that era.

Jones at Zebra Associates

Having received superb training at JWT, Jones left in 1968 and participated in the establishment of a new agency named Zebra Associates which launched in 1969, serving as a Vice President and Co-creative Director between June 1969 and October 1971. Zebra introduced itself as a black-owned agency with a racially integrated staff, hence, the name "Zebra" and developed a snazzy company logo utilizing a black-and-white zebra-print motif to underscore the integration theme. Its two principals were Raymond League, formerly an account executive at JWT, and Joan Murray, another pioneering woman who had been the first black woman hired as a newscaster by CBS. *Newsweek* magazine noted that Zebra opened just three weeks before the premiere of the quirky 1969 movie *Putney Swope*, a satire about a black man running an advertising agency. Yet, Zebra's leadership insisted their endeavor was legitimate and there was significant fanfare surrounding the launch of the agency including national media coverage by *Time* magazine, *Advertising Age*, and the TV news program *60 Minutes* (Chambers, 2008, p. 219). Zebra's clients included Clairol, Polaroid, the Bronx Zoo, Fabricators, Inc., and a number of small black companies. Focused on targeting black consumers, expectations for the agency were high and, by 1972, it was the second largest among all black-owned advertising firms, billing $4.7 million (Davis, 2002).

The New York press noted that Jones' position at Zebra made her the first black female Vice President in the advertising industry (Vagoni, 1988). While at the agency, Jones was named one of the "Foremost Women in Communications" in 1970 and won several creative advertising awards, including a Clio for a Polaroid radio commercial in 1971 ("Black Creative Group...," 1973). She increased the size of Zebra's creative staff from two to ten, engaged in training and development of the creative staff, and was a highly visible and popular speaker in the general advertising community (Chambers, 2008, p. 222). Despite these accomplishments, Jones left Zebra late in 1971, unhappy. There were rumors of internal issues among Zebra personnel and top management which threatened the reputation of the agency (Chambers, 2008, pp. 222–223; Davis, 2002). Always mindful of her professional image, Jones decided to leave, providing an explanation in her letter of resignation to Zebra's Chairman and President, Raymond League, in October 1971:

> I am very sorry that I can no longer continue with Zebra after these 2½ years. I sincerely feel that the quality of the creative department was no longer up to the standards that I, as a professional, felt they should be. Consequently I felt overworked and underpaid, but more importantly, frustrated in my attempts to give Zebra the finest advertising possible.
>
> ("Termination of Employment," 1971)

Indeed, there appeared to be a number of significant problems facing Zebra Associates. Jones complained to League about witnessing discriminatory personnel practices within the agency and believed that management was doing too little to curb such behaviors, leading to diminished staff morale ("Memo to Raymond League," 1971). At the same time, she believed that the agency suffered from prejudice exercised by people outside of the agency. Although she typically avoided speaking out on race-themed topics, she told a newspaper reporter about her experiences at Zebra and her perceptions of racism. Referring to the establishment of Zebra, she said:

> "We got a lot of attention, but there was resistance on the part of the mainstream agencies whose billings would have to be cut in order for clients to redirect some of their budget to minority consumers. We didn't know there was such racism in the agency business until a black agency got started. The same people who wished us well were stabbing us in the back."
>
> (Vagoni, 1988)

Zebra's tenure in the advertising industry was brief, lasting only about six years – by 1976, the agency was closed. League had departed Zebra in 1973, citing health reasons, and his successor, Bill Castleberry, clashed mightily with co-owner Joan Murray over managerial and financial issues (Chambers, 2008, pp. 223–224). Blaming Castleberry for the firm's demise, their relationship deteriorated to the point where Murray was alleged to have conspired to have him murdered. The bizarre situation was resolved in court with Murray pleading guilty to a lesser charge and serving no jail time. Castleberry then moved on to briefly run another advertising agency and Murray exited the advertising business permanently. For a detailed discussion of the history of the Zebra Associates agency, please see Chambers (2008, pp. 218–224).

The Black Creative Group

After a short stint as a senior copywriter for mainstream agency Kenyon and Eckhardt during 1972–1973 where she worked on such accounts as Ford Corporate, Lincoln-Mercury, and Brown and Williamson, Jones co-founded the Black Creative Group (BCG), a creative boutique, in 1973 with Kelvin Wall. Wall was another African-American who had worked at Zebra and was a former Vice President of marketing for Coca-Cola USA, a Harvard Business School lecturer, and marketing consultant. BCG's mission was to work with advertising agencies on a project basis to conduct research, determine positioning, and develop creative material for the black consumer market, with Jones as the firm's Creative Director. Recognizing increased competition among black agencies for assignments, Jones and Wall believed that the targeting of black consumers required a more sophisticated approach. A BCG press release stated:

> "Superficial, non-strategy approaches relying primarily on Black models and cool Black talk no longer work … Segments of the [black consumer] market differ among each other as well as from segments of the white market."
>
> ("Black Creative Group…," 1973)

High quality research was a hallmark of BCG's work and Jones used it to develop a creative approach referred to as "soul with sophistication" (African American Registry, 2012). Research was the foundation of creative efforts oriented toward black lifestyles in a manner which was stylish, cultured, and devoid of common stereotypes. Jones and Wall lectured regularly at trade meetings and universities on effectively reaching black consumers. One was a presentation at *Advertising Age*'s seventeenth annual creative conference in New York in July 1974 titled "Critical Factors for Development of Marketing and Creative Strategy" which focused on black perceptions of banking, photographic, and alcoholic beverage products (Wall and Jones, 1974). By this time, Jones had become a recognized expert whose advice and ideas were widely sought after. Around this time, she was recruited to the vice-presidency position at BBD&O.

Mingo-Jones Advertising, Inc.

In 1977, Jones left BBD&O – recruited by Frank Mingo – to establish one of the most significant entrepreneurial ventures the advertising industry had ever seen. Mingo, another industry pioneer who had been the first black account executive at JWT and a Senior Vice President and management supervisor at McCann Erickson, was one of a handful of blacks with significant management experience in large, general-market agencies. An early partner was Richard A. Guilemenot III, who held an MBA from Northwestern University and also had been a Vice President at BBD&O. The trio brought an unprecedented level of mainstream experience to a black-owned agency: Mingo's expertise was in management, marketing, and finance; Jones was known as an excellent copywriter; and Guilemenot was experienced in sales and business acquisition (Jones, 2016; Mingo, 1985). *Advertising Age* (1977a) praised Mingo's "solid general-marketing reputation" while press releases touted his master's degree in Advertising from Northwestern. Mingo was credited with supervising the introduction of Lite Beer from Miller Brewing at McCann Erickson – the most successful new product introduction in the history of beer marketing and the second largest account at McCann (Mingo, 1985; "New Black-Owned Affiliate...," 1977). With great promise, Mingo-Jones-Guilemenot set out to redefine "minority" advertising at a time when many black-owned agencies were failing (Mitchell, 1979). Suggesting that the black agency "golden era" – sometimes based on social responsibility efforts rather than bona fide selling opportunities – had ended, Mingo commented, "The white guilt market is at a very low ebb now. You've got to earn all your accounts" (Pope, 1981). Mingo explained that the agency's goal was to seek mainstream assignments and not engage in tokenism. Mingo stated, "We position ourselves as a first-class agency – as professionals, not as blacks. We happen to be black" (Longshore, 1982). However, Mingo (1985) conceded that the firm had to start out focused on the black consumer market niche in order to have a reasonable chance for viability in the competitive ad agency landscape.

The establishment of Mingo-Jones Advertising (Mr. Guilemenot left the partnership by 1981 for undisclosed reasons) was unique in another regard: it was affiliated with the IPG, a mainstream holding company, from where Mingo-Jones would purchase media, research, accounting, and billing services, while retaining independent ownership and decision authority (Funding Universe, n.d.). Mingo (1985) acknowledged the chairmen of IPG, Paul Foley and Carl Spielvogel, were instrumental to the establishment of Mingo-Jones because they helped him establish relationships with banks so that financing could be secured. *Advertising Age* claimed that the affiliation provided Mingo-Jones with "the strongest start any black-owned shop has ever had," but some critics viewed the reliance on IPG as a form of "white paternalism" and prompted rumors of Mingo-Jones "being a sharecropper on the Interpublic plantation" (*Advertising Age*, 1977a; *Advertising Age*, 1977b). Despite the controversy, the relationship with Interpublic provided access to the Miller Brewing client. Starting out with a staff of four, Mingo-Jones' first account was a $1,000,000 assignment for Miller High Life oriented toward black consumers. Jones' creative work for Miller, sometimes featuring black or white athletes, resonated with black consumers resulting in increased market share. Mingo-Jones became regarded as one of the hottest shops on Madison Avenue, quickly securing accounts with Kentucky Fried Chicken and L'Oréal, and developing an impressive roster of clients over the next few years including other Miller brands, Disney, Goodyear Tire and Rubber, Liggett and Myers Tobacco (Omni brand), the National Urban League, Pepsi-Cola (Pepsi and Mountain Dew brands), Seagram's, Uncle Ben's Rice, and Westinghouse Electric. Several of its clients and brand themes were featured in a trade ad published in an industry awards journal in the early 1980s (see Figure 3.2).

Among black-owned agencies, Mingo-Jones not only enjoyed great financial success, but made significant contributions in terms of how the black consumer market was perceived and ways in which black people were portrayed in advertisements. For example, advertisements for L'Oréal's "Look of Radiance" beauty brand showcased a variety of attractive black women photographed by the famous Italian photographer Franceso Scuvullo (*CEBA*, 1980, p. 196), who was well known for his sophisticated celebrity and fashion photography that appeared in high-end fashion magazines such as *Vogue*. While some Mingo-Jones advertisements featured black professionals, entertainers, and celebrities, others featured average black people. Jones told *Advertising Age* (Trager, 1985),

> "We try to balance what blacks see ... not to show blacks [only] as doctors and lawyers. It's all right to show blacks living in [fine] houses and buying cars – and yet we know some don't live like that. But aspirations are what advertising can be about."

Commenting on her sophisticated approach to creative advertising, Jones explained: "We try to protect clients from themselves, because if an ad gets

Advertising you can feel.
"We do chicken right!"
KENTUCKY FRIED CHICKEN CORPORATION
After all the research and all the strategy development and before one word of advertising is put to paper—we stop! And we put ourselves into the shoes of the person we're trying to reach. The consumer.
The result is advertising that works a little harder. Sells a little deeper. Lasts a little longer. Advertising that's a little less subject to pre-emption by competitive claims or changing life-styles.
It's advertising based on the universal need for self-satisfaction. It's advertising you can feel. Mingo-Jones advertising.
To put the feeling to work for you, call Frank Mingo, President (212) 697-4515.
"If it's not Goodyear, it's not good enough for me."
GOODYEAR TIRE & RUBBER COMPANY
They'll never believe you did it yourself.
LOOK OF RADIANCE BY L'OREAL
Introducing the world's most elegant menthol.
OMNI Luxury Lights.
LIGGETT & MYERS TOBACCO CO., INC.
Mingo-Jones Advertising, Inc.
485 LEXINGTON AVENUE, NEW YORK, NEW YORK 10017
Gino's Inc.
Goodyear Tire & Rubber Co., Inc.
Heublein, Inc.
Hunter College
Kentucky Fried Chicken Corp.
Liggett & Myers Tobacco Co.
Look of Radiance by L'Oreal
Miller High Life
Lite Beer from Miller
Philip Morris Corp.
Scott Paper Co.
Westinghouse Electric Corp.

Figure 3.2 Mingo-Jones Agency Trade ad.

Source: *CEBA Exhibit Journal*, 1982, p. 66.

ghetto-ized, the consumer will be offended" (Trager, 1985). In addition to brand advertising, Mingo-Jones also did some public affairs work, such as the first birth control campaign for the National Urban League aimed at teenage boys with the theme: "Don't Make a Baby if You Can't Be a Father" (*CEBA*, 1985, p. 85).

While the majority of Mingo-Jones' assignments were oriented toward black consumers, a few were general-market accounts like Cuticura soap and

Porcelana skin cream (Grant, 2001, p. 89). Several assignments held "cross-over" appeal – meaning they were attractive to multiple consumer groups – and were subsequently adapted for general-market campaigns, such as Disney's – "Discover Disney: More Magic than Ever" – and Westinghouse Electric's – "Engineering your Future – And Ours" (Jones, 1979). A slogan for Kentucky Fried Chicken (KFC) – "We Do Chicken Right!" – developed in 1979 by an unnamed Mingo-Jones intern, was promoted by Jones to the client for a local New York black-oriented promotion. Appearing on bill-boards and in radio commercials, the advertising featured the catchy slogan with popular R&B artists such as Gladys Knight (see Figure 3.3). The award-winning theme prompted a brand turnaround in local markets like New York, Detroit, and Chicago and was so engaging that it was incorporated into all of KFC's national advertising of the early 1980s, replacing its old theme

Singers: WE DO ONE THING LIKE NO ONE ELSE CAN DO WE CONCENTRATE ON MAKING IT GREAT . . .
Announcer: Ladies and Gentlemen, Miss Gladys Knight.
Gladys Knight: When it comes to singing, I didn't just arrive on the midnight train. I've been at it since I was four years old. Practice makes perfect! . . . Just like it's made Kentucky Fried Chicken number one. . . . Mmmm, Mmmm. Take it from a little girl from Georgia . . .
Singers: KENTUCKY FRIED CHICKEN . . .
WE DO CHICKEN RIGHT

AWARD OF EXCELLENCE

Title: Gladys Knight
Advertiser: Kentucky Fried Chicken Corporation
Agency: Mingo-Jones Advertising, Inc.
Copy: Allan Corwin
Recording studio: Sigma Sound/CSS Las Vegas
Agency producer: Caroline Jones Inc.
Music production company: Jana Productions, Inc.
Director: Debbie McDuffie
Composer: Lucas/McFaul

Figure 3.3 CEBA Award for Kentucky Fried Chicken radio commercial.

Source: *CEBA Exhibit Journal*, 1982, p. 93.

"It so nice to feel good about a meal." In a subsequent testament to its general-marketing capabilities, in 1981, Mingo-Jones was selected to introduce the Omni cigarette brand to a general test market, rather than the black consumer market (*Adweek*, 1981). As Creative Director, Jones was recognized in the trade press as a well-rounded problem-solver, responsible for the innovative creative aptitude of Mingo-Jones. She told *Adweek*: "The biggest asset in advertising is to know how to analyze problems and spot a good idea. I consider myself a pretty good judge of good ideas" (Dicker, 1985).

In spite of its crossover successes and the backgrounds of its principals, in 1982, at its five-year anniversary, Mingo-Jones found that the majority – 60 percent – of its assignments were still oriented toward the black consumer market, with another 10 percent directed at the Hispanic market. Both Mingo and Jones were disappointed with this outcome, believing that barriers within the industry limited their business opportunities. For example, despite the success of the KFC "We Do Chicken Right!" campaign, the client assigned only the black consumer portion of the account to Mingo-Jones, directing a much larger general-market assignment, which included lucrative TV commercials, to Y&R, its general-market agency (Grant, 2001). Similarly, Mingo-Jones was allowed to handle black-targeted advertising for Pepsi's Mountain Dew brand, but BBD&O kept the general-market assignment. However, trade reports indicated that Mingo-Jones was the second largest black-owned agency in the country by 1981 (Funding Universe, n.d.; Mingo, 1985). While *Advertising Age* applauded the agency's performance and reputation (Longshore, 1982), a *New York Times* article concluded that the firm had fallen short of its goal to build a business based primarily on significant general-market advertising assignments (Dougherty, 1982). Other black-owned agencies also claimed they were not allowed to handle significant mainstream business. Mingo explained: "It's tough to break through the perception of us as a black-only agency" ("Black-Owned Agency aims…," 1985). "It was hard to swallow the fact that, although I had handled $100 million accounts for big agencies, some people were inclined to question my ability to handle a $3 million account because I have a black face" (Pope, 1981). Jones added: "They choose to see us as black only. If we win a creative shoot-out, they'll [prospective clients] have another excuse to award the account to another agency. It frustrates you, but you can't let it embitter you" ("Black-Owned Agency aims…," 1985). Mingo continued: "It's a real struggle and seems to be mainly a cultural thing and not something people overtly want to do. They believe that if they are advertising to white, WASPy consumers, they need white, WASPy people to talk to them" (Trager, 1985). "The ad business is not so different from society at large. There isn't any overt racism, but stumbling blocks are still placed," Mingo concluded ("Black-Owned Agency aims…," 1985). In light of the difficulties in securing sizeable mainstream accounts, in the mid-1980s, Mingo-Jones decided to pursue opportunities in the growing multicultural marketing segment, beyond the black consumer market, as a growth strategy. In 1983, the agency acquired a Miami, Florida-based agency with Hispanic marketing expertise and called the subsidiary Mingo-Jones-Garrido, which did Spanish-language ads for Anacin, Goodyear and KFC (Mingo-Jones-Garrido, 1983).

Jones departs Mingo-Jones

Jones shocked the advertising community late in 1986 when she abruptly left Mingo-Jones to form her own company, Creative Resources Management, later renamed Caroline Jones Advertising, Inc. (Seaman, 1986). By then, Mingo-Jones had been built into nearly a $50 million enterprise, ranking it among the top two or three among all black-owned agencies. What led to the demise of the Mingo-Jones partnership? Close-lipped at the time of her departure, Jones later told *Crain's New York Business*, "I felt that I was doing a lot of work and not getting the rewards" (Rigg, 1987). Sources indicate that Jones and Mingo regularly clashed on ideological topics concerning direction of the firm, financial versus creative issues – and compensation (Jones, 2016; Rigg, 1987). A memo from Jones to Mingo underscores her dissatisfaction with her financial status in the agency:

> "My contributions to Mingo-Jones, in my opinion, far exceed the present $65,000. I am, without question, the most hard-working and producer of the most consistently-quality work in the agency ... My department is also recognized as 'the reason to go to Mingo-Jones' and never has the creative work been the reason for our termination. Creative Directors at my level and less make a great deal more than the $150,000 I am requesting."
>
> ("Salaries and other Compensations," 1986)

Beyond compensation, other factors contributed to Jones' exit. In the early years of the company, Jones and Mingo were in agreement with respect to business issues, but as time went on, they disagreed on major decisions (Jones, 2016). There was also a sense that Jones felt marginalized and believed her best opportunities were to be had through independent entrepreneurship. Moreover, an *Advertising Age* (1987) article suggested that some women employed at Mingo-Jones thought Mingo was too controlling and perhaps even chauvinistic. A former college football player and Army lieutenant well over six feet tall, Frank Mingo was an imposing figure with strong leadership skills (American Advertising Federation, 2012). Both Mingo and Jones were smart, strong-willed individuals and Jones maintained that Mingo controlled the business, that her stake in the agency was too small, and that she was not making enough money (Berger, 1989). Quoted in *Newsday*, Jones complained: "Men just don't listen. I wasn't sharing in the [agency's] success" (Kahn, 1987). After leaving Mingo-Jones, Jones told a reporter, "I just find that women work harder than men. People at my old company would agree to that" (Rigg, 1987). Mingo countered that his choice of Jones as a business partner indicated that he held no biases against women, but acknowledged, "some people who get involved in feminist issues might see things differently" (Rigg, 1987).

A closer examination of Jones' business arrangement with Mingo reveals startling revelations. When the Mingo-Jones-Garrido subsidiary was dissolved for undisclosed reasons, Mingo-Jones sought to acquire several smaller minority-owned agencies in California in order to expand its presence to the West Coast among multicultural consumer markets (Grant, 2001). A merger between several firms, all with African-American, Hispanic, and Asian principals, created a new venture called Muse-Codero-Chen & Beca Advertising (later Muse-Codero-Chen) and Mingo formed a partnership with them (Funding Universe, n.d.). This made sense because, for several years, the idea of consolidating several minority-owned agencies to form a "superagency" had been touted as a means to gain tactical and financial advantages which would enhance their viability and competitiveness (Davis, 2002). Such an arrangement would provide important strategic advantages allowing minority-owned agencies to compete more equitably with the resources of white-owned agencies, who were now also courting black and multicultural consumers. However, negotiation of terms with the California companies exposed a rift between Frank Mingo and Caroline Jones which became irreparable. Although her name was on the company logo, sources indicate that Caroline Jones held little to no ownership stake in the Mingo-Jones agency, a circumstance implied in Jones' memo regarding her compensation status ("Salaries and other Compensations," 1986). As discussions concerning the partnership progressed, Jones reportedly demanded 50 percent of the Mingo-Jones company or she was leaving. Frank Mingo refused and late that year – 1986 – Jones left to launch her own agency. Explaining her actions, Jones told the *New York Times*, "I want to be independent and make a lot of money," saying that she had been dissatisfied with her stake in the agency (Dougherty, 1987). Although Mingo attempted to convince her to stay, Jones' mind was made up and she was determined to leave. She left him a resolute handwritten note confirming her decision (see Figure 3.4).

After Jones' departure, Frank Mingo renamed the agency The Mingo Group and the agency continued to thrive. Interestingly, three years later in the fall of 1989, Frank Mingo suffered a stroke and heart failure and died at the relatively young age of 49 (*New York Times*, 1989). Mingo's widow inherited a majority stake in the agency and business associate Samuel Chisholm assumed the lead, operating the firm as Chisholm-Mingo. Later, in 1996, Frank Mingo was elected, posthumously, to the AAF's Advertising Hall of Fame – the first African-American so recognized. However, losing Mingo – considered the "ringmaster" of the agency – hurt the company tremendously (Grant, 2001). Although the agency experienced revenue growth for several years, by mid-2004 the agency, hampered by account losses and managerial challenges, filed for bankruptcy and was closed permanently (Brown, 2004).

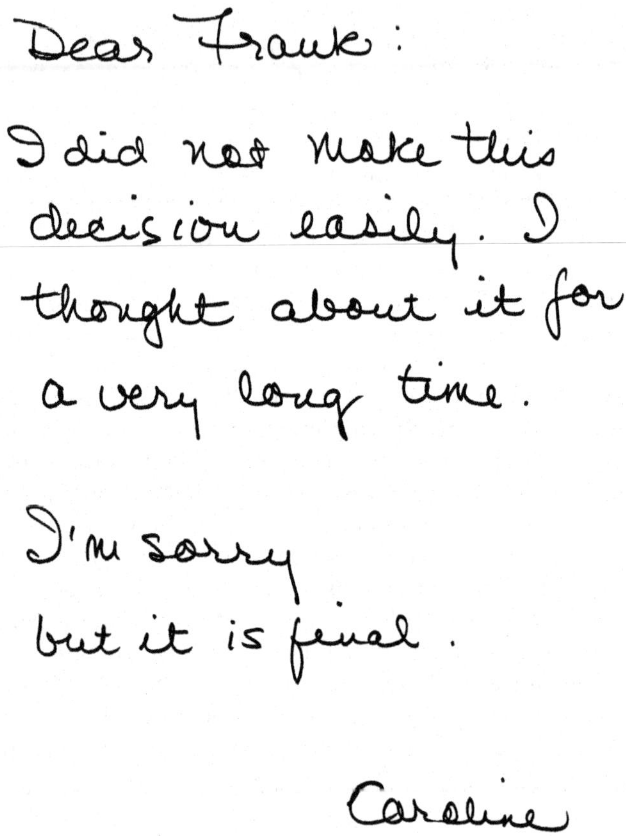
Dear Frank:

I did not make this decision easily. I thought about it for a very long time.

I'm sorry but it is final.

Caroline

Figure 3.4 Caroline Jones' handwritten resignation letter to Frank Mingo, 1986.

Source: Caroline R. Jones Collection, Archives Center, Series 3G, Box 18, National Museum of American History, Smithsonian Institution.

Caroline Jones Advertising/Caroline Jones, Inc.

Noting the significance of Caroline Jones' exodus from Mingo-Jones and the decision to launch her own shop, *Newsday* columnist Daniel Kahn (1987) wrote: "FEW WOMEN RUN [*sic*] their own advertising agencies, and even fewer are black." Kahn continued: "In Chicago, there's Barbara Proctor of Proctor & Gardner. And in New York, there are Joel Martin of J.P. Martin and, most recently, Caroline Jones."

Mindful of the careers of trailblazing adwomen such as Mary Wells Lawrence, Jo Foxworth, Barbara Proctor, Joel Martin, and others, Jones believed the best opportunities for women in advertising came about as a result of leaving the "big brother hen" to start their own agencies (Jones, 1987, p. 35). After breaking away from Mingo-Jones, Jones was on her own, taking none of Mingo-Jones' clients, confident that "my reputation will bring me new accounts" (Jones, 1987). A major believer in the power of reputation, especially in an industry where "we promote our clients, not ourselves" (Jones, 1987), Jones advised in a magazine interview:

> "No matter how many times you change jobs or agencies, your reputation will go with you. So take care of it, build it and never forget it's your most valuable asset – more valuable than a big salary, more durable than an impressive title, more meaningful than any creative awards."
>
> (Jones, 1991)

Taking advantage of her reputation and contacts, Jones established her agency with financing arranged through Leo-Arthur Kelmenson, a former colleague at Kenyon and Eckhardt, held by Lorimar Telepictures (Kahn, 1987). Initially, Caroline Jones Advertising was 40 percent held by Lorimar until Jones bought out that interest a short time later. The new full-service agency desired to break out of the ethnic-only mode, although Jones acknowledged that she must first build her firm by pursuing black and Hispanic-oriented assignments where her reputation was established (Kahn, 1987). The agency's credentials stressed professional management, commitment to research-based communication strategies, and successful case studies which indicated quantitative results of past campaigns, with Jones at the top as President and Creative Director. Her ultimate goal was to build a general agency with "clout and respect," according to *Newsday* (Kahn, 1987).

As head of the agency, Jones now spent most of her time on account management efforts, recruiting and advising clients, writing for trade publications, engaging in public speaking, and networking at industry-related events. By her own admission "happily divorced" since 1974, she maintained a high profile in the business community, usually attending functions alone, often the only black person present ("Caroline Jones is an Advertising Pioneer," n.d.). She was a member of or served on the Board of Directors of numerous organizations including the Advertising Council, Advertising Women of New York, the National Urban League, Long Island University, the Women's Forum, New York City Partnership, New York State Banking Board, the Academy of Television Arts and Sciences, 100 Black Women, the Committee of 200, the International Women's Forum, the NAACP, the National Urban League, and others. For many years, she moderated and hosted radio and television programs in New York under the titles "Focus on the Black Woman" and "In the Black: Keys to Success" which focused on business topics (Elliott, 2001). Believing in giving back to the community, she also spent significant time hiring and mentoring young women, speaking at colleges, and encouraging people of color to consider careers in the advertising business. Within the first five years of her firm's existence, Jones built up an impressive client roster, increased staff to 22 and was named the 1990 Advertising Woman of the Year (see Figure 3.5).

Caroline Jones Advertising, Inc.
More Than Ads.
Our Mission:
To sell products, through advertising and promotion, by accurately reflecting the colors and cultures of the consumers who buy those products.
Our Management: Second to None
Headed by the "Advertising Woman of the Year, 1990," our uniqueness stems from our team of well-rounded creative and marketing professionals whose skills have been honed solving advertising, public relations and special events problems for domestic and international clients.
We've Done It All
From packaged goods to tourism; financial services to recruitment; public relations to special events; our work is powerful, relevant and effective.
Find out how we can do ads, and more, for you.
Contact:
Caroline R. Jones
CAROLINE JONES ADVERTISING, INC.
1290 Avenue of the Americas
New York, NY 10104
Phone (212) 262-8181 • Fax (212) 333-4208
CAROLINE JONES
ADVERTISING, INC.

Figure 3.5 Promotional material for Caroline Jones Advertising, Inc.

Source: Caroline R. Jones Collection, Archives Center, Series 3H, Box 23, National Museum of American History, Smithsonian Institution.

Clients of Jones' agency included American Express, Anheuser-Busch Companies, Bahamas Ministry of Tourism, DeKuyper's Peachtree Schnapps, E. & J. Gallo, Greyhound, Kenmark Optical (Billy Dee Williams Eyewear), Lorimar, Partnership for a Drug Free America, Prudential, Ryder, Tone Soap, the Trump Organization (real estate development and community relations), and Western Union. The firm billed about $8 million dollars in 1987 and $12–13 million by the end of 1991 (Agency Fact Sheet, 1994). Several accounts were oriented toward corporate affairs advertising, such as a late 1980s campaign for Anheuser-Busch Companies titled: "People who Make Things Happen," which featured prominent black civil rights figures and role models such as NAACP President Benjamin Hooks and activists Dorothy Height and Coretta Scott King. Caroline Jones Advertising ran with a high degree of professionalism and provided opportunities for women and people of color to advance in the field. For example, Troy Ellen Dixon served as management supervisor over account services, Angela Spears and Flo McAfee were public relations directors, and Oscar Gonzalez was production manager. At various times, her sisters Dinah, Patricia, and Kimberly Robinson also worked at the agency (Jones, 2016). The agency's approach provided strategic focus on clients' objectives, research-based and results-oriented campaigns. For example, when the Bahamas Ministry of Tourism faced declining market share for travel to its islands given increased competition for travelers from destinations such as Hawaii, Mexico, and other Caribbean locations, a campaign developed by Jones' agency: "It's better in the Bahamas" was able to successfully persuade black travelers, increasing their visitation to the Bahamas by 25 percent ("CJA Case History," n.d.). When the human resources department of the Prudential insurance company realized that African-Americans and Hispanics had low awareness of the company as an employment option, the agency developed a campaign called: "The Biggest is Looking for the Best" (see Figure 3.6) which was successful in increasing the number of diverse job applicants by 32 percent between 1991 and 1992 ("CJA Case History," n.d.).

As agency chief, Jones focused on management of the agency's finances and its ability to be profitable, prompting a restructuring of financial arrangements with some clients. For example, in early November 1991, Jones wrote letters to executives with the Anheuser-Busch Corporate Affairs division, which had been a client of the agency since 1987, seeking a restructuring of the account's business arrangement with Caroline Jones Advertising, complaining: "THE AGENCY DOES NOT NOW, NOR HAVE WE EVER, MADE ANY PROFIT ON THE ANHEUSER-BUSCH COMPANIES ACCOUNT" ("Ms. Thelma Cook," 1991; "Mr. Wayman Smith," 1991a). In the correspondence, she noted a *Mediaweek* news item which indicated that Anheuser-Busch was planning to boost its advertising spending by $100 million in the following year (Brunelli, 1991). The financial arrangement with Anheuser-Busch had put her agency at a distinct disadvantage, since the client's general-market agency of record – Darcy, Massius, Benton & Bowles – was placing all of the media and collecting the media commissions. Given this information, Jones requested that Caroline Jones Advertising be designated as the agency of record for Anheuser-Busch Corporate Affairs Department, be compensated with a standard 15 percent commission rate for media purchases, a 17.65 percent agency markup for production work, and other items. She also approached John Jacob, President of the National Urban League and a member of the Anheuser-Busch Board of Directors for help in re-negotiating terms. By mid-November, Jones received a response from Anheuser-Busch, agreeing to a revised compensation arrangement between the agency and the client, with Caroline Jones Advertising named as agency

"Some jobs pay well.
Some make you happy.
I held out for both."
If you've been holding out for a job that pays well, but doesn't short-change you in other ways, you're the kind of person we want to talk to. If you have a lot to offer, The Prudential has a great deal to offer you in the way of challenge, responsibility, personal growth, opportunity and financial rewards.
In other words, we have the kind of jobs that'll make you eager to get up in the morning and get to work. In financial services, information systems, actuarial and insurance services and general administration.
At The Prudential, we feel that when *you* feel that way about your work, personal growth and financial success are inevitable.
If you're interested in career opportunities, direct inquiries to: Manager, College Relations, The Prudential Employment Center – Dept. SCT, 56 North Livingston Avenue, Roseland, NJ 07068. An equal opportunity employer.
The Prudential
The biggest is looking for the best.

Figure 3.6 Prudential advertisement "The Biggest is Looking for the Best" by Caroline Jones Advertising, Inc.

Source: *Ebony*, February 1990, p. 125. Reprinted with permission of the Prudential Insurance Company of America.

of record for Anheuser-Busch Corporate Affairs, receiving a monthly fee, and collecting media commissions ("Mr. Wayman Smith," 1991b).

Over her career, Jones experienced significant rewards as well as challenges. Her creative work and campaigns that she supervised earned awards in nearly all of the industry's major competitions such as the Clio Awards, the One Show, CEBA Awards, Telly Awards, EFFIEs, International Film and TV Festival of New York, Obie Award for Outdoor, Cannes Film Festival, Andy Awards, Galaxy Awards for Public Relations, and the Direct Marketing Association ECHO Awards ("Our Creativity Shows", n.d.). Jones also served as co-chairman of the 1988 CEBA Awards program, the only other woman besides Joel P. Martin to serve in this capacity, as discussed in Chapter 4. Jones' white male co-chair of the CEBA Awards was G. Robert Holmen, Chairman and CEO of the Backer Spielvogel Bates advertising agency. In Jones' opinion, these awards were a clear indication that her creative work was on par with the best – regardless of audience – which included general-market agencies with major corporate accounts ("Our Creativity Shows", n.d.).

Jones was presented with two major honors in 1990. The Advertising Women of New York named her its Advertising Woman of the Year and the *Wall Street Journal* featured her in its prestigious "Creative Leaders" trade advertising series, which saluted significant individuals in the advertising business and presented their views on the industry. While a few other African-American women were similarly recognized in their respective cities, in these cases, Jones was the only black woman ever so recognized by the New York advertising establishment. While these recognitions prompted abundant favorable publicity, she lamented the difficulty in breaking out of the black consumer market niche: "When I walk in the door to pitch an account, people automatically think 'black advertising,'" Jones told a reporter, indicating that the problem was ingrained in the industry (Berger, 1989). She explained that the problem was exacerbated by client interest in courting Hispanic and Asian consumers, which siphoned dollars away from the black consumer portion of multicultural advertising budgets. Jones was candidly dissatisfied about the minority niche market snare when she made her statements about the "caste-typing" which existed in the industry and quoted in the *Wall Street Journal* (1990) "Creative Leaders" article. Privately, Jones fumed about her disappointments in the industry and wrote lengthy, rambling musings expressing these frustrations (Jones, n.d.):

> "First of all – let's look at the category: Black, female, small advertising business owner. Each part represents an obstacle or challenge. Or opportunity – depending on what definition you want to apply to it.
>
> The only part in all of this that I want to or can change is the small part. I want to be big.
>
> And, perhaps if I should be later described as a Black, female big advertising business owner, many of the obstacles I face would go away. But until that day comes, I have to deal with obstacles every day.
>
> Number One
>
> Being Black carries with it a lot of weight-baggage. I was the first Black person ever trained as a copywriter at J. Walter Thompson in its 100 year history. That was 23 years ago.

> Fortunately – I have survived in this industry – but unfortunately I am one of the few survivors.
>
> Just as Adam Clayton Powell said many years ago, I find myself answerable to anyone and everyone who [*sic*] to do any business in the industry – who wants to work in the industry. That's a challenge. That's a real challenge.
>
> I get hundreds of letters and people must understand, I <u>cannot</u> answer them all – particularly the ones that start 'I'm writing my exam about _____, please send me the answers to these questions by Friday.'
>
> <u>Number Two</u>
>
> Being female is perhaps the biggest obstacle – you have to maintain your reputation, get people to do things for you, learn to accept criticism, how to be a leader and get people to work <u>with</u> you <u>and</u> for you.
>
> I use a <u>lot</u> of humor. I say what I want – usually tongue in cheek.
>
> One thing is for sure – when you are Black and female, you get noticed. Use it to your advantage. You can't do <u>everything</u> you want in this world, you have to accommodate others, but many people <u>do</u> want to be able to contribute to your success – later take credit. That's OK.
>
> <u>Number Three</u>
>
> Small. Is self-explanatory. But if you are small, don't <u>think</u> small – but you'd be wise to act small. In other words, don't get caught up in the glamour of being <u>in</u> business until you have a good solid business.
>
> Often Black people get more credit than they deserve – like me. Pictures in all the press. Stories. Awards. That's great, but until you have money to pay the bills, <u>Be</u> <u>Honest</u>.
>
> There's nothing wrong in saying, 'we cannot afford this. We are small. If you give me tickets I will be there. Otherwise, we cannot afford it.'
>
> <u>Number Four</u>
>
> The advertising business is one of the toughest to be in. It's an underground business – you don't hear much about the agencies – we project our clients' products or services."

On top of Jones' frustrations with the advertising business, she would encounter her most formidable foe around 1993: a diagnosis of breast cancer. Although the Smithsonian documents make no direct reference to the disease or its treatment, other sources revealed that she had the disease (Jones, 2016; Smikle, 2001). While Jones kept meticulous files of Caroline Jones Advertising records, only a few items appear in the records for 1993 and most correspondence is provided by Angela Spears, Director of Public Relations for the agency. In June and August of that year, Jones is pictured with close-cropped natural hair, in contrast to the longer, straightened hair styles shown in photographs from previous years, suggesting hair loss from cancer treatments.

Jones' illness had a disastrous effect on the agency's business. Internal company documents show that the agency lost nearly half its billings in one year, falling from $12.6 million in 1992 to $6.4 million in 1993 (Agency Fact Sheet, 1994). During this time, the agency lost several key clients, including Ryder, Prudential, Western Union, and the Bahamas Ministry of Tourism, which had been the agency's largest account (Agency Fact Sheet, 1994). By late 1993 and into 1994, the firm would have difficulty paying its bills, according to correspondence from various creditors. In a letter printed in a local trade paper dated December 12, 1994, Angela Spears confirmed that Caroline Jones Advertising had filed for bankruptcy protection, adding, "we're confident the current status is temporary" ("Jones Agency retains…," 1994). A business brief in the February 1995 issue of *Black Enterprise* provided details of the agency's financial troubles, reporting that Caroline Jones Advertising had incurred significant media and other costs for three client accounts which had not paid the agency (Lowery, 1995). The Bahamas Ministry of Tourism account was the most significantly delinquent and the agency spent $300,000 in legal fees in efforts to collect $750,000 from the Bahamian government. Two other unnamed accounts owed the agency about $240,000 combined. At the time of the bankruptcy filings, the firm had $1.48 million in liabilities and only $316,500 in assets, according to court records (Lowery, 1995).

Aunt Jemima is alive and cookin'

Battling health and business problems, Jones was still sought after for her creative expertise and wisdom. She accepted a consulting assignment in 1993 for Quaker Oats' Aunt Jemima brand and its advertising agency Jordan, McGrath, Case and Taylor (JMCT). Jones helped the companies avoid a potential public relations fiasco in connection with a proposed controversial advertising slogan for its Aunt Jemima breakfast foods (Davis, 2007). Planning a major relaunch of the brand for the fall of 1994, JMCT provided concept ads for TV commercials and print ads with the following proposed advertising slogan (Davis, 2007, p. 30):

> "If you want a better breakfast, you can just stop lookin',
> 'cause Aunt Jemima is alive and cookin'."

Mindful of the history of the iconic Aunt Jemima image and its association with the happy plantation slave Mammy stereotype – often perceived as derogatory or demeaning – Jones was aware that the Aunt Jemima brand had historically been promoted via live public appearances and television commercials featuring black women dressed as Aunt Jemima, in addition to print ads featuring the character. Given ongoing racial tensions between African-Americans and other ethnic groups in the United States, Jones feared backlash from those who might be offended by the connotation of a "live" Aunt Jemima as suggested by the ad slogan; or by a black actress who might be perceived as a slave/cook who is subservient to whites. Jones was eventually successful in convincing JMCT and Quaker Oats to alter their plans and produce a less provocative advertising theme – a TV commercial with singer Gladys Knight enjoying a pancake breakfast with her real-life grandchildren accompanied by the phrase "Now you're cookin'!" In addition to the consulting assignment, Jones' advice led to her agency being hired to handle the 1994 Aunt Jemima relaunch aimed at the black consumer market.

Rebounding

After recovering from cancer treatments, Jones was back at work full time by early 1995 feverishly pursuing new business, under the new name Caroline Jones, Inc., since Caroline Jones Advertising was "subject to Chapter 7 proceeding and is in the hands of a trustee" Jones told a creditor ("Ms. Farnese Haynes," 1995). Jones sent out numerous letters of solicitation to prospective clients, hired a white New Business Associate to pursue general-market assignments, registered with firms seeking diversity among their suppliers, and exhorted her staff to be very aggressive in courting new business. Claiming to represent "some of the best brains in the business, Black or White," she emphasized in a staff memo the gravity of the firm's situation:

> PLEASE KEEP TRACK OF YOUR CONTACTS, KEEP CALLING OR WRITE UNTIL YOU GET SOME RESPONSE … TRY TO LAND AN ACCOUNT WITH BILLINGS 3 TIMES YOUR OWN SALARY … THANK YOU. THIS IS VERY IMPORTANT TO OUR SURVIVAL.
>
> ("New Business Letters…," 1995)

In time, Jones was able to navigate the firm out of its financial crisis, however the struggle proved difficult. In correspondence to prospects, Jones would often tout the "Advertising Woman of the Year Award" and the *Wall Street Journal* "Creative Leaders" feature. Yet, in the summer of 1995, when asked to supply information to U.S. Congresswoman Cardiss Collins regarding opportunities for minorities in advertising, she attached copies of publicity related to both awards and cryptically noted by hand on each ("Congresswoman Cardiss Collins," 1995):

> "One would think this would help get business. It doesn't."

In a draft of comments prepared for a speech, Jones' irritation with the advertising business had clearly grown. She wrote (Jones, 1995):

> "The so-called 'rules' keep changing. Or perhaps I should say, the whims of Whites keep changing. Fluctuating. Finding reasons for keeping budgets for ethnic programs down. Looking for band-aid solutions to keep competition out. Not always keeping the interests of the clients in view as much as keeping the

money in their pockets. Let's look briefly at the issue of minority personnel. Agencies have yet to acknowledge the Catch-22 that we as an industry have created. Not having employed minorities at the entry level has resulted in fewer minorities to full [*sic*] meaningful-level jobs today. There [*sic*] simply not enough seasoned Blacks, and soon, Hispanics and Asians in the business. That isn't the way it's 'supposed' to be. It's the way it is."

"Clients seem extremely uncomfortable with the notion that we have a country of different ethnic groups. Groups large enough to be addressed effectively and efficiently in their own media. Or in their own language. One example – if the Black Consumer Market's gross income were measured as a Gross National Product, it would rank as the ninth largest country in the world. But you knew that, didn't you?"

Despite her health and business challenges, Jones believed she had something to offer to others who might benefit from knowing about her life experiences. She donated her personal and business papers and artifacts to the Smithsonian Institution in 1996, where they are archived as a permanent collection in the Archives Center of the National Museum of American History. Around this same time, she participated in the development of a book aimed at educating youths about advertising careers, published in 1996 (Fleming, 1996). Titled *The Success of Caroline Jones Advertising Inc.*, the 80-page book provides highlights of Jones' career, an overview of her agency, and addresses fundamentals of the advertising business including a glossary of advertising terms and a list of schools offering advertising education. The book is an important example of Jones' commitment to youth, which included the establishment of a four-year Dean's Merit scholarship in her name at the University of Michigan for minority students interested in advertising careers. The book was also an effort to help preserve Jones' legacy after the breast cancer scare, and includes a variety of photographs of her and her staff working in the Caroline Jones agency offices, examples of advertisements, and awards the agency won. One photo shows Jones at a black-tie affair with former U.S. President Bill Clinton, with the caption: "small-town girl goes bigtime" (Fleming, 1996, p. 6).

By 1997, Caroline Jones Inc. had been rebuilt into a viable enterprise, although a greater proportion of the firms' work had shifted to public relations, event marketing, and various types of marketing communications other than advertising. Clients of this era included Anheuser-Busch (corporate affairs), Toys R Us, the U.S. Postal Service, Quaker Oats' Aunt Jemima brand, Heineken, U.S.A., the United Negro College Fund, and McDonald's Tri-state (Connecticut, New Jersey, New York) Co-op. The McDonald's assignment launched the Gospelfest, an annual live event featuring top gospel artists which debuted in New York's Madison Square Garden in the late 1990s (Jones, 2016). According to annual advertising agency rankings published by *Black Enterprise* each June, from 1998 to 2001, the firm's billings were between $12 million and $15.2 million, earning Caroline Jones, Inc. a consistent spot among the largest 15 black-owned advertising firms in the United States (Davis, 2002).

Although Caroline Jones, Inc. was revived, unfortunately for Jones, her advertising career ended tragically. Around 2000, a virulent form of the breast cancer recurred and spread rapidly (Jones, 2016). In the spring of 2001, Jones entered hospice care in New York City and died June 28 at the age of 59. Tony Jones served as agency President in the final months of his mother's illness and for some time after her death, but, unfortunately, the company could not be sustained. In light of the aftermath of the September 11, 2001 terrorist attacks on New York City and a major global advertising recession, Caroline Jones, Inc. quietly folded (Hayes, 2002).

Over her 40-year career, Jones achieved several impressive "firsts" in the advertising business and garnered top industry awards and recognitions. At the time of her death, *Advertising Age* reported, "Her importance to the industry was not fully understood" (Vagoni, 2001). Sam Chisholm, CEO of Chisholm-Mingo (formerly Mingo-Jones) said,

> "people don't know how much of a pioneer she was in this industry. Most people think of her as a hard-driving entrepreneur. But [she was a] good writer and a superior editor of the creative product. She was able to zero in on what was right for a client. It's just too bad that most people probably won't remember her for that."
>
> (Smikle, 2001)

Industry leader Tom Burrell reflected: "She understood the concept of establishing relationships. She had terrific social skills, and that's one thing I always envied about her" (Smikle, 2001). Tony Jones described his mother as "kind and generous," who advocated for the "betterment of women in business" (Jones, 2016). He acknowledged that she wanted to give more to the advertising business, but ran out of time. "She did a lot for advertising, a lot for black people, and a lot for women," Jones (2016) reminisced. On September 24, 2012, Jones finally received recognition befitting her status and contributions to the industry. *Advertising Age* (2012), the industry's leading trade publication, featured Jones on its front cover and inside story which named the "100 Most Influential Women" in the history of advertising.

References

(Excerpts in this chapter were originally published in: Davis, J. F. (2013) 'Beyond Caste-Typing? Caroline Robinson Jones, Advertising Pioneer and Trailblazer,' *Journal of Historical Research in Marketing*, 5(3), pp. 308–333.)

'Ad Woman of the Year' (1990) [article] Caroline R. Jones Collection, Archives Center, Series 2A, Box 2, Folder 12, National Museum of American History, Smithsonian Institution.

Advertising Age (1977a) 'Interpublic Move Creates New Entry in Black-Owned Area,' May 9, p. 1.

Advertising Age (1977b) 'Interpublic's Opener,' May 23, p. 12.

Advertising Age (1987) 'Mingo Aims to Build First-Class Agency,' February 23, p. 89.

Advertising Age (2012) 'The 100 Most Influential Women in Advertising,' September 24, Front Cover and p. 28.

Adweek (1981) 'L&M picks Mingo-Jones for Menthol Introduction,' June 29, p. 3.

African American Registry (2012) 'Caroline R. Jones is a Marketing Genius' [Online]. Available at: www.aaregistry.org/historic_events/view/caroline-r-jones-marketing-genius (Accessed: November 10, 2012).

Agency Fact Sheet (1994) [document] Caroline R. Jones Collection, Archives Center, Series 3H, Box 23, National Museum of American History, Smithsonian Institution.

American Advertising Federation (2012) 'Frank L. Mingo, Advertising Hall of Fame' [Online]. Available at: www.advertisinghalloffame.org/members/member_bio.php?memid=720A (Accessed: February 7, 2012).

Berger, W. (1989) 'Caroline Jones Advertising,' *Inside Print*, March, pp. 30–34.

'Black Creative Group Formed by Kelvin Wall and Caroline Jones' (1973) [article] Caroline R. Jones Collection, Archives Center, Series 3E, Box 15, Folder 2, National Museum of American History, Smithsonian Institution.

'Black-Owned Agency aims to Win White Market Over' (1985) [article] Caroline R. Jones Collection, Archives Center, Series 3G, Box 17, National Museum of American History, Smithsonian Institution.

Brown, C. (2004) 'Pioneering Black Ad Agency Closes Doors Forever,' *Black Enterprise* [Online]. Available at: www.blackenterprise.com/2004/08/01/pioneering-black-ad-agency-closes-doors-forever/ (Accessed: February 12, 2012).

Brunelli, R. (1991) 'Anheuser-Busch will Boost Spending by $100 million in 1992' [article] Caroline R. Jones Collection, Archives Center, Series 3H, Box 23, National Museum of American History, Smithsonian Institution.

'Caroline Jones: A Heroine in a Lot of Ways' (n.d.) [article] Caroline R. Jones Collection, Archives Center, Series 3H, Box 23, National Museum of American History, Smithsonian Institution.

'Caroline R. Jones is an Advertising Pioneer' (n.d.) [article] Caroline R. Jones Collection, Archives Center, Series 3G, Box 17, National Museum of American History, Smithsonian Institution.

CEBA Exhibit Journal (1980) New York: World Institute for Black Communications.

CEBA Exhibit Journal (1982) New York: World Institute for Black Communications.

CEBA Exhibit Journal (1985) New York: World Institute for Black Communications.

Chambers, J. (2008) *Madison Avenue and the Color Line: African-Americans in the Advertising Industry*. Philadelphia, PA: University of Pennsylvania Press.

'CJA Case History' (n.d.) [document] Caroline R. Jones Collection, Archives Center, Series 3H, Box 23, National Museum of American History, Smithsonian Institution.

'Congresswoman Cardiss Collins' (1995) [memorandum] Caroline R. Jones Collection, Archives Center, Series 3H, Box 25, National Museum of American History, Smithsonian Institution.

Davis, J. F. (2002) 'Enterprise Development Under an Economic Detour? Black-Owned Advertising Agencies 1940–2000,' *Journal of Macromarketing*, 22(1), pp. 75–85.

Davis, J. F. (2007) 'Aunt Jemima is Alive and Cookin'? An Advertiser's Dilemma of Competing Collective Memories,' *Journal of Macromarketing*, 27(1), pp. 25–37.

Dicker, S. (1985) 'Caroline Jones: Well-Rounded CD,' *Adweek*, July, p. W-17.

Dougherty, P. (1982) 'Advertising: Minority Marketing,' *New York Times*, June 28, p. D6.

Dougherty, P. (1987) 'Caroline Jones Back in Business,' *New York Times*, February 5 [Online]. Available at: www.nytimes.com/1987/02/05/business/advertising-caroline-jones-back-in-business.html (Accessed: February 12, 2012).

Elliott, S. (2001) 'Caroline Jones, 59, Founder of Black-Run Ad Companies,' *New York Times*, Obituaries, July 8 [Online]. Available at: www.nytimes.com/2001/07/08/nyregion/caroline-jones-59-founder-of-black-run-ad-companies.html (Accessed: February 11, 2012).

Entrepreneurial Woman (1989) 'Who's Your Role Model?' Summer, p. 66.

Fleming, R. (1996) *The Success of Caroline Jones Advertising, Inc.: An Advertising Success Story*, New York: Walker & Co.

Funding Universe (n.d.) 'Chisholm-Mingo Group, Inc. History' [Online]. Available at: www.fundinguniverse.com/company-histories/chisholm-mingo-group-inc-history/ (Accessed: June 10, 2016).

Grant, T. (2001) *International Directory of Company Histories*. Chicago, IL: St. James Press, vol. 41.

Group for Advertising Progress (1968) *Closing the Gap: Minority Groups in Advertising Agencies*, Panel Discussion, October 22, American Association of Advertising Agencies. [document] Caroline R. Jones Collection, Archives Center, Series 2A, Box 2, Folder 25, National Museum of American History, Smithsonian Institution.

Hayes, C. (2002) 'Crossing the Color Line,' *Black Enterprise*, June, pp. 99–204.

Jakobson, C. (1985) 'The Entrepreneurial Spirit,' *Savvy*, March, pp. 54–55.

Jet (1965) 'Something to Smile About,' May 13, p. 40.

'Jones Agency retains Clients' (1994) [article] Caroline R. Jones Collection, Archives Center, Series 3H, Box 23, National Museum of American History, Smithsonian Institution.

Jones, C. (1968) 'A Glance at My Life up Till Now at J. Walter Thompson' [manuscript] Caroline R. Jones Collection, Archives Center, Series 3A, Box 10, Folder 1, National Museum of American History, Smithsonian Institution.

Jones, C. (1979) 'Advertising in Black and White,' *Madison Avenue*, September, pp. 52–58.

Jones, C. (1965) 'Cosmetics and the Negro Market' [report] Caroline R. Jones Collection, Archives Center, Series 3A, Box 10, Folder 5, National Museum of American History, Smithsonian Institution.

Jones, C. (1987) 'Opportunities for Women and Blacks: Not Enough … But More Than Ever' [Career Directory] Caroline R. Jones Collection, Archives Center, Series 2B, Box 2, Folder 34, National Museum of American History, Smithsonian Institution.

Jones, C. (1995) [personal notes] Caroline R. Jones Collection, Archives Center, Series 3H, Box 23, National Museum of American History, Smithsonian Institution.

Jones, C. (n.d.) 'Images and Stereotypes of Women' [manuscript] Caroline R. Jones Collection, Archives Center, Series 2A, Box 2, Folder 25, National Museum of American History, Smithsonian Institution.

Jones, M. (1991) 'Caroline Jones Advertising, Inc.: the Right Moves,' *About Time*, September, pp. 8–10.

Jones, T. (2016) Interview with the Author, May 22, 2016.

Kahn, D. (1987) 'Black and Female and On Her Own' [article] Caroline R. Jones Collection, Archives Center, Series 3H, Box 23, National Museum of American History, Smithsonian Institution.

Kreshel, P. (1990) 'John B. Watson at J. Walter Thompson: The Legitimization of "Science" in Advertising,' *Journal of Advertising*, 19(2), pp. 49–59.

Longshore, S. (1982) 'Their Marketing Homework Rates an A+,' *Advertising Age*, November 29, pp. 14–15, 17.

Lowery, M. (1995) 'Caroline Jones Advertising Seeks Protection from Creditors,' *Black Enterprise*, February, p. 18.

'Memo to Raymond League' (1971) Caroline R. Jones Collection, Archives Center, Series 3B, Box 2, Folder 3, National Museum of American History, Smithsonian Institution.

Mingo, F. (1985) 'Blacks in Advertising' [audio recording]. Interview with John Hansen for *In Black America*, University of Texas-Austin, November 8.

'Mingo-Jones-Garrido' (1983) [document] Caroline R. Jones Collection, Archives Center, Series 3G, Box 17, Folder 7, National Museum of American History, Smithsonian Institution.

'Miss Georgia Demarest' (1964) [memorandum] Caroline R. Jones Collection, Archives Center, Series 2A, Box 2, Folder 25, National Museum of American History, Smithsonian Institution.

Mitchell, G. (1979) 'And Then There were 13,' *Black Enterprise*, September, pp. 43–49.

'Mr. Wayman Smith' (1991a) [correspondence] November 7, Caroline R. Jones Collection, Archives Center, Series 3H, Box 23, National Museum of American History, Smithsonian Institution.

'Mr. Wayman Smith' (1991b) [correspondence] November 18, Caroline R. Jones Collection, Archives Center, Series 3H, Box 23, National Museum of American History, Smithsonian Institution.

'Ms. Farnese Haynes' (1995) [correspondence] Caroline R. Jones Collection, Archives Center, Series 3H, Box 25, National Museum of American History, Smithsonian Institution.

'Ms. Thelma Cook' (1991) [correspondence] November 5, Caroline R. Jones Collection, Archives Center, Series 3H, Box 23, National Museum of American History, Smithsonian Institution.

'New Black-Owned Affiliate of the Interpublic Group Announced' (1977) [Press release] Caroline R. Jones Collection, Archives Center, Series 2, Box 6, Folder 3, National Museum of American History, Smithsonian Institution.

'New Business Letters Follow-up' (1995) [memorandum] Caroline R. Jones Collection, Archives Center, Series 3H, Box 25, National Museum of American History, Smithsonian Institution.

New York Times (1989) 'Obituary, Frank Mingo,' November 1, p. D-26.

Nivens, B. (1982) 'Caroline Jones: Advertising Trailblazer,' *Elan*, February, pp. 28–30.

'Our Creativity Shows' (n.d.) [document] Caroline R. Jones Collection, Archives Center, Series 3H, Box 23, National Museum of American History, Smithsonian Institution.

Pope, L. (1981) 'Ethnic Expertise Helps but Black Agency Viability Depends on Non-Ethnic Success,' *Business Today*, April 8, p. 4.

'Product of Benton Harbor' (n.d.) [Video recording] Caroline R. Jones Collection, Archives Center, CRJ 552.100, National Museum of American History, Smithsonian Institution.

Rigg, C. (1987) 'Black Ad Agency Redefines Minority,' *Crain's New York Business*, February 9, p. 1.

'Salaries and other Compensations' (1986) [memorandum] Caroline R. Jones Collection, Archives Center, Series 3G, Box 18, Folder 5, National Museum of American History, Smithsonian Institution.

Seaman, D. (1986) 'Mingo-Jones Founder Quits for Own Shop,' *Adweek*, November 8, p. 4.

Smikle, K. (2001) 'Caroline Jones, Advertising Pioneer, Dies,' *Target Market News*, July 2 [Online]. Available at: www.targetmarketnews.com/latestnews/ (Accessed: September 13, 2012).

'Termination of Employment' (1971) [memorandum] Caroline R. Jones Collection, Archives Center, Series 3B, Box 11, Folder 5, National Museum of American History, Smithsonian Institution.

Tharpe, P. (1988) 'Caroline Jones: More than Ads,' *New York Post*, May 3, p. 12.

Trager, C. (1985) 'Mingo-Jones Builds Long-Term Relationships,' *Advertising Age*, December 18, pp. 18–20.

Vagoni, A. (1988) 'Rising from the Secretarial Ranks,' *New York Observer*, June 20, p. 7.

Vagoni, A. (2001) '"Role Model" Jones, 59, Dies,' *Advertising Age*, July 16, p. 4.

Wall, K. and Jones, C. (1974) 'Ad Age Workshop: Critical Factors for Development of Marketing and Creative Strategy' [manuscript] Caroline R. Jones Collection, Archives Center, Series E, Box 15, Folder 7, National Museum of American History, Smithsonian Institution.

Wall Street Journal (1990) 'Charisma is Caroline,' Creative Leaders series [article] Caroline R. Jones Collection, Archives Center, Series 2D, Box 6, National Museum of American History, Smithsonian Institution.

4 Joel P. Martin

Transformative artist

Figure 4.1 Joel P. Martin.

Source: courtesy of Joel P. Martin.

As an eight-year-old schoolgirl, Joel Prendergast suffered a traumatic experience at her Ohio elementary school. One day her teacher gave the class an assignment to write a poem. The young student, inspired by the opportunity, excitedly delved into the assignment with enthusiasm and recalls:

> "That night, the words flew. I assumed this ability to create pictures out of words came from my mother who wrote poems and was a voracious reader. I figured she passed this love on to me. So after I finished my poem, I remember feeling PROUD."
>
> (Martin, 2014)

The next day, Joel stood in front of her classmates and read the poem, beaming the entire time.

> "I was excited about it because I had been raised to honor education; to do your best; to respect your elders. When I delivered my poem to the class, I was expecting praise. Instead – harsh, angry words came from the teacher's mouth demanding – 'who wrote that? I know *YOU* didn't!'"
>
> (Martin, 2015)

Confused, embarrassed, and shocked into numbness by the teacher's verbal assault, the young girl thought: "the teacher must be speaking the truth, as she's an adult" (Martin, 2014). The damaging emotional impact created feelings of humiliation and shame which remained long after the incident such that young Joel stopped writing altogether. Recalling that painful ordeal, she reflects: "What I remembered was being ordained by this teacher to be an eight-year-old who was not only dumb, but a liar who was incapable of writing poetry" (Martin, 2014). Observing how negative childhood experiences – particularly among young black children – can have long-term, damaging psychological effects, Martin (2015) explained: "If we don't have some transformational opportunity, like I did, it stays with us forever and it dictates the path of our lives."

Years later, Joel (pronounced "jo-EL") Prendergast Martin would become one of the first black female Art Directors in the advertising industry and the first African-American woman to establish a full-service advertising agency in New York City. By the mid-1980s, her company – J.P. Martin Associates – would be recognized as one of the leading black-owned advertising agencies in the United States. How did the humiliated eight-year-old girl evolve into to a high-achieving advertising pioneer and entrepreneur?

The early years: in pursuit of happiness

An only child born in New York City in 1944, Joel Prendergast moved to Ohio at a young age when her parents divorced. Living with her mother, who had friends in Ohio, the two moved around frequently to different towns in the state including Toledo and Lorain while her mother worked odd jobs including waitress and nanny positions. Although she had a large extended family, she believed that her father had abandoned his family and felt a sense of loss growing up without a father (Martin, 2007, p. 22). After high school, she attended Ohio State University in Columbus during the mid-1960s. Initially planning to major in Math and Education, she found the curricula uninspiring. She was also struggling with self-esteem issues stemming from her past. She found herself attracted to the fine arts program, where she studied art history, graphics, and aspects of visual art. Martin (2015) recalls choosing the Visual Art major because, in her opinion, "in art, no one would judge you, there was free expression and there was a lot of personal fulfillment in it." She also enjoyed painting and doing graphic design work.

During this period, following the passage of major new U.S. civil rights laws, large corporations were keen on bringing college-educated black people into their organizations and recruited heavily at top colleges. At Ohio State, corporate recruiters often came to the campus, including companies like IBM. Known as "Big Blue," IBM was a "very wonderful corporation" in her view and she was recruited by "a wonderful African-American man who gave me the choice of two jobs or career paths" (Martin, 2015). One option was to be a computer programmer and the other was to be a graphic designer in IBM's Audio-Visual Department. She chose the audio-visual path since it fit in with her major and – in her mind – "an unconscious desire to do great" (Martin, 2015). After graduation, she moved to White Plains, New York to work in IBM's Audio-Visual department where she honed her production and graphic design skills for the next two years. However, she had a desire to return to her birthplace, having "a romantic idea of what it was like to live in New York City" (Martin, 2015).

Joel Martin, Art Director

"I was really very fortunate at each path in my career," Martin (2015) reminisces. Relocating to New York City, she was hired as an industrial designer for Fulton and Partners, doing fiberglass and other design projects which drew on her fine arts training. About two years later, her industrial design experience led to work in advertising, where she was hired at the McCaffrey & McCall advertising agency – also known as LaRoche, McCaffrey & McCall – around 1969. Martin (2015) noted that several African-Americans and women were already employed in professional, non-clerical jobs at the agency when she started – including in creative and art direction positions – indicating that McCaffrey & McCall was one of the more progressive and liberal agencies of the time. As an example of its liberal leanings, the agency coordinated with volunteers from the advertising industry to produce an anti-Vietnam War campaign called "Unsell the War" (Saxon, 2001). Martin (2015) recalls that there seemed to be an emphasis during this period to bring black professionals into advertising agencies. Given her previous experience, Martin was hired as an Assistant Art Director and was later promoted to full Art Director, making her possibly the first black female Art Director in New York City. Her roles at McCaffrey & McCall gave her the opportunity to do innovative design work and was a fulfillment of the creative subjects she studied in college. She did creative work for such clients as JP Stevens, a fabrics and carpeting company; Westvaco, a paper and chemical company which eventually merged with Mead; and British West Indies Airlines (BWIA) for whom she did graphic design work and television commercials (Martin, 2015).

The McCaffrey & McCall agency enjoyed a good reputation in the advertising industry. Co-founded by James J. McCaffrey and David B. McCall in 1962 when they purchased the LaRoche & Company advertising firm, the agency did work for such brands as Tiffany, Mercedes, Norelco razors, and Canadian Club whiskey, and was known for campaigns which conveyed understated elegance (Saxon, 2001). Jim McCaffrey, who served as President of leading trade group the 4 A's between 1972 and 1973, retired from the industry shortly after his term ended and pursued such interests as community affairs and local politics (Saxon, 2001). In addition to advertising work, Dick McCall served as President of the Urban League of New York in the late 1960s, creating outstanding projects like the Emmy-winning Schoolhouse Rock educational program for children's television and was heavily involved in philanthropy. Tragically, McCall, his wife, and two others were killed in a car accident in 1999 while helping refugees in Kosovar during an aid mission in Albania (O'Leary, 1999). By then, he had also retired from advertising and the McCaffrey & McCall agency had been acquired by the Saatchi and Saatchi advertising company in 1983 (Dougherty, 1983).

Martin was thrilled to be working for a top advertising agency which was involved with high-profile fashion accounts in Manhattan. She enjoyed the atmosphere at McCaffrey & McCall, calling it "a very friendly environment" (Martin, 2015). Agency colleagues would collaborate on work projects, socialize, and have fun. She appreciated the nurturing she received and the relationships she developed, describing agency chief Dick McCall as "a wonderful mentor and friend" (Martin, 2015). While at McCaffrey & McCall, Martin was also able to exercise her interests in social activism, consistent with the personalities of the agency's leadership. To that end, she did pro bono creative design work for the Poor People's Campaign which had been spearheaded by the late Dr. Martin Luther King, Jr. in his commitment to achieving equality and justice. Describing her volunteer work as "meaningful and motivating," Martin (2015) explained: "This was a culmination of my family background; living in upstate New York not far from the home of Harriett Tubman; belief in education; my mother's humbleness; a large extended family and me being an only child."

While working at McCaffrey & McCall, Martin joined the trade association GAP, like many other black advertising professionals in and around New York. Established in 1968 in New York City and affiliated with the 4 A's, GAP aimed to increase the number of black professionals working in advertising agencies and served as a resource for those already employed in the industry (Chambers, 2008, p. 197). Although membership was not bound by race, its members had to be in some way involved in the advertising industry so that services and outreach program could be designed for current professionals. As such, its membership consisted mainly of black professionals who worked in agencies, in the advertising or marketing departments of corporations, and as freelancers. Joel Prendergast met her future husband Robert (Bob) Martin, an import/export entrepreneur, at a GAP meeting through friends who were advertising film producers. "He was celebrating his birthday with friends and I tagged along," Martin (2015) recalled, adding: "We had great conversations and have been talking ever since!" She and Bob fell in love and decided to marry. She resigned from McCaffrey & McCall, which gave her a "great sendoff" and she and Bob married and moved to Wingdale, New York, a rural town about a two-hour drive north of New York City where Bob's parents lived. Soon thereafter, Joel was expecting a child and daughter Cybel was born in 1971. Joel enjoyed life as a stay-at-home mom, wanting to be a "good mom," give Cybel her first steps, and have a degree of success. She started doing freelance work while her daughter was a preschooler and "was very blessed to have [Bob's] parents live next door to us in Wingdale" (Martin, 2015). "I wanted to raise my daughter so I started freelancing out in the country and going into the city." According to Martin (2015), "From freelancing, one thing led to another and the work I was getting grew to the point where my husband and I decided to move back to New York City." Joel and Bob Martin both loved New York's access to culture which included jazz, music, art, and the Metropolitan Museum. Moreover, both were artists at heart – Bob was a fine artist and oil painter who understood what Joel was doing artistically and creatively. He also understood the advertising business. Through his friends in GAP, he was familiar with the rigors and expectations which went along with agency work, especially in a field where blacks lacked significant representation. Together, they believed that their best opportunity to succeed in advertising was to launch an advertising agency. It helped that Cybel was now old enough to attend school full time and required less attention at home. With respect to the decision to open an advertising agency, Martin (2015) explained: "I wanted to create my own lifestyle. Could I have gone and worked for another agency? Probably, but that would not have given me the kind of freedom and flexibility I felt I wanted to have." On her husband's role in the decision, she continued: "We decided bit by bit to move into the city and launch a company. There's just really a great affinity between he and I. He has always been very supportive of me and whatever makes me happy."

J.P. Martin Associates Advertising agency

Reflecting on her interest in becoming an advertising agency entrepreneur, Joel Martin (2015) commented: "The reason why I went into advertising was because it fit my passion and lifestyle." However, a *New York Times* writer, noting her relatively limited advertising experience, said: "Going out on her own took a considerable amount of courage, since at the time she really did not know that much about advertising" (Dougherty, 1985). However, Joel Martin replied: "But ambition, desire and drive don't show up in a resume" (Dougherty, 1985) justifying her decision to open shop in the big city. Under this scenario, J.P. Martin Associates was established and incorporated in 1974 in New York City, with Joel P. Martin as President and Creative Director and husband Bob Martin as partner. Explaining the set-up of the agency, Joel Martin (2015) said: "Bob was in the back office while I ran the creative team – handling all creative elements and product development, client meetings, and that kind of thing." At the time, there was no other full-service advertising agency in New York City headed by a black woman and few owned by any women. Taking notice of workforce advancements among black women in government, law, and business, the *Crisis*, a civil rights magazine and official publication of the NAACP, featured adwomen Joel Martin and Caroline Jones (who was then at the Mingo-Jones agency) on the same page in a 1983 issue pointing out: "in recent years, there has been a marked increase in the number of black women … entering the work place at higher and higher levels – assuming positions never before held, in some cases, by black women" (*Crisis*, 1983, p. 46). Identified by *Fortune* magazine in a "People to Watch" article, Martin noted that the most difficult part of her transition to ad agency chief was the sales aspect: "I came from an Episcopalian background," she explained, "and nice women didn't sell" (Kupfer, 1985).

Joel Martin obtained her first agency client – Ashanti Bazaar, an African boutique in New York focused on black women – by going door to door in 1974 (Dougherty, 1985). In those days, the professional environment for African-American advertising entrepreneurs – men and women – was centered on black consumers. Martin (2015) recalls: "Those were the days of 'targeted' marketing and black consciousness and the black consumer market was really a focus for our agency." Martin recalls that other black agency professionals in New York in the 1970s – such as Byron Lewis, Sam Chisholm, Frank Mingo, and Caroline Jones – were all involved in marketing to black consumers, in addition to her agency. Although Martin was a member of GAP, she was heavily involved with another trade group, the NAMD. Established in the 1950s by African-American men who worked in sales and marketing positions for major corporations, the NAMD was a primary resource for education, support, and networking among black marketing professionals who were often shut out of such opportunities within their employers' organizations (Chambers, 2008, pp. 63–64). From the 1950s through the 1970s, NAMD members actively promoted the black consumer market on behalf of large corporations such as Coca-Cola, Pepsi-Cola, Carnation, Anheuser-Busch, Standard Oil, and others; they were instrumental in conducting research and developing techniques to cultivate the black consumer market (Davis, 2013a). Martin (2015) acknowledges that the men of the NAMD supported her fledgling agency claiming: "Without the NAMD, I don't think I would have had my clients." She also suggests that it may have helped that the NAMD members who helped were men:

> "There was a pre-conceived notion [in agencies] that men would be the ones to get the contracts. I don't know if I got the same kind of billings that the men did – as far as I am concerned – I did, but I don't know that to be a fact."
>
> (Martin, 2015)

Elaborating on the role of the organization with respect to her agency, Martin (2015) said:

> "NAMD was about the marketers within the corporations who sought to deliver a Civil Rights commitment through the corporations. We were all looking to see how we could serve our communities and be marketing professionals at a time when we could say we had the inside information on what it took to market to African-American consumers."

About ten years later, Martin was in a position to give back to the NAMD and was elected as board chair and served as President of its New York Chapter (*Black Enterprise*, 1984). Martin (2015) also expressed a philosophical orientation with respect to her agency's mission and culture, explaining:

> "There was a commitment that I had and was expressed to my agency to support a social commitment to our community. We worked on the United Negro

> College Fund and the Jesse Jackson [presidential] campaign. We had a lot of initiative in serving our community. I remember we participated in a walk-a-thon as a company and we had our sweatshirts and our banners because we were out there representing. We did a lot of things like that – because we could. And because it mattered to us. I could because it mattered to me. So we invested in ways that could serve the community."

Over the next ten years, J.P. Martin Associates grew substantially in terms of billings, size, and reputation, securing a number of clients including several national brands (see Table 4.1). Beginning around 1979, Bob Martin often traveled on the road working with the Budweiser Superfest, a popular soul music and R&B concert series sponsored by agency client Anheuser-Busch in cities across the United States, featuring headliners such as Michael Jackson, Stevie Wonder, Aretha Franklin, Parliament, Luther Vandross, and other top black entertainers. For its tenth anniversary in 1984, the agency moved its offices to 100 Fifth Avenue, in a district of New York dubbed "the new Madison Avenue" by industry insiders (J.P. Martin Associates, 1984). By the end of 1985, Martin's agency was recognized by *Black Enterprise* magazine as one of the six largest black-owned agencies in the United States: Burrell Advertising, Mingo-Jones Advertising, the Uniworld Group, Lockhart & Pettus, J.P. Martin Associates, and Proctor & Gardner, respectively, which collectively billed about $155 million (Smikle, 1985). That year, J.P. Martin Associates billed $12.5 million and employed a multicultural staff of 28, including those with experience from large general-market and other black-owned agencies (Dougherty, 1985).

Table 4.1 Client Roster, J.P. Martin Associates, 1984

Amalgamated Publishers, Inc.	Black Theater Alliance	National Banker's Association
American Savings & Loan League	BOCA (Black Owned Communications Alliance)	National Black Network
Amerada Hess	Budweiser Superfest	New York Health and Hospital Corporation
Anheuser-Busch, Inc.	Carnation	Pawling Savings Bank
Anheuser-Busch Companies, Inc.	Council of Concerned Black Executives	Pfizer, Inc.
Ashanti Bazaar	Essence Communications	Revlon
Associated Black Charities	Hoffman La Roche	Simmons Market Research Bureau
Benta's Funeral Home	John Atchison	State of South Carolina
Black Consumer Inserts (BCI)	Michelob Region One	Tennessee Valley Authority
Black Enterprise Magazine	National Association of Market Developers	U.S. Army ROTC

Source: J.P. Martin Associates (1984) 'Come Grow with Us' trade ad, *Black Enterprise*, June, p. 104.

The little agency that could

By 1986, J.P. Martin Associates was promoting itself as "the Little Agency that Could ... And Did" – touting awards it had won, its ability to offer big agency service and personal attention – while maintaining small agency enthusiasm (J.P. Martin Associates, 1986). The shop, known for compelling creative work, promised: "You get a full-service agency with pizzazz" (J.P. Martin Associates, 1986). Among its award-winning work, the agency did a breakthrough corporate advertising campaign for Anheuser-Busch, intended to enhance the reputation of the company among black consumers, titled: "Being black in America: a Real Picture." The campaign series, which appeared in the black press during 1984, featured African-Americans in uplifting portrayals which underscored positive family relationships and various bonding rituals relevant within the black community. For example, one ad featured an older father enjoying time with his adult son with the theme "My buddy ... my dad"; another pictured a young black father rocking his infant child to sleep with the headline "He took the time to care"; and another showed a young girl lovingly combing her great-grandmother's hair as the older woman tells stories of the family's history and culture (see Figure 4.2). Research showed that the campaign increased the positive brand perception of Anheuser-Busch from number eight to number two among black consumers in less than one year (Martin, n.d.).

Successful work for corporations including the "Being Black in America" series for Anheuser-Busch, the "Super Rich" campaign for Clairol hair products aimed at black women, and corporate recruitment advertisements for Pfizer, led to increased assignments and responsibilities from various accounts, including work on TV commercials. The agency's track record with Anheuser-Busch led to a breakthrough assignment in 1985 to introduce the King Cobra malt liquor brand to the marketplace, with J.P. Martin Associates as the agency of record, thereby putting it in charge of all of the brand's advertising and media, a significant accomplishment for a black-owned agency (Dougherty, 1985). Anheuser-Busch was so impressed with Joel Martin, that they featured her in a corporate ad highlighting her accomplishments as a successful advertising entrepreneur (see Figure 4.3). Joel Martin explained to *Black Enterprise* in late 1985:

> "A lot of the business that we get is not because we've pitched for it. It's because we have been working for the clients for a long period of time and have acquired a certain degree of trust and respect from them for our work and they have rewarded us by increasing responsibility and billings."
>
> (Smikle, 1985)

By the mid-1980s, a *New York Times* article suggested that the agency's successful relationships with corporate clients could be leveraged to gain access to more general-market business, expanding its scope beyond the black consumer market (Dougherty, 1985). Like some other black-owned agencies,

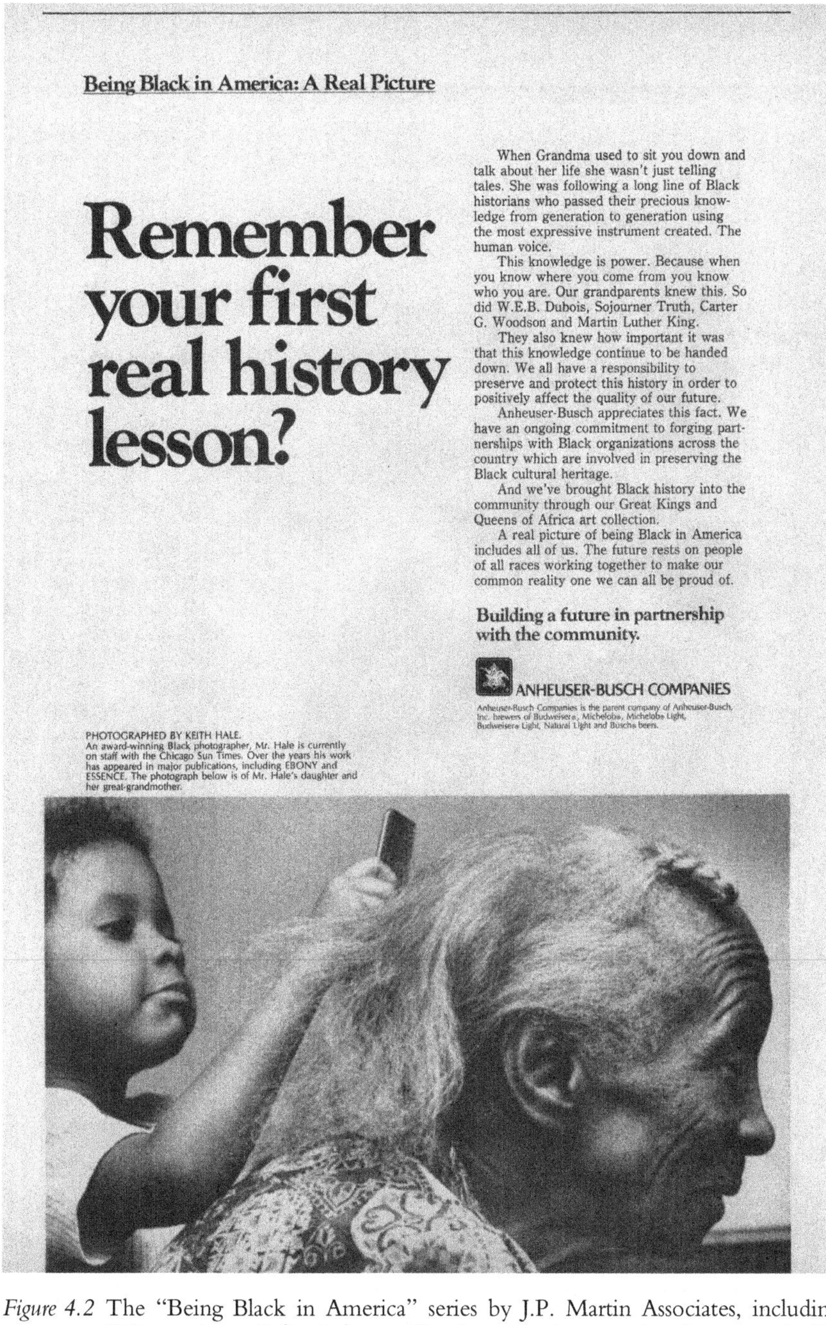

Being Black in America: A Real Picture
Remember your first real history lesson?
When Grandma used to sit you down and talk about her life she wasn't just telling tales. She was following a long line of Black historians who passed their precious knowledge from generation to generation using the most expressive instrument created. The human voice.
This knowledge is power. Because when you know where you come from you know who you are. Our grandparents knew this. So did W.E.B. Dubois, Sojourner Truth, Carter G. Woodson and Martin Luther King.
They also knew how important it was that this knowledge continue to be handed down. We all have a responsibility to preserve and protect this history in order to positively affect the quality of our future.
Anheuser-Busch appreciates this fact. We have an ongoing commitment to forging partnerships with Black organizations across the country which are involved in preserving the Black cultural heritage.
And we've brought Black history into the community through our Great Kings and Queens of Africa art collection.
A real picture of being Black in America includes all of us. The future rests on people of all races working together to make our common reality one we can all be proud of.
Building a future in partnership with the community.
ANHEUSER-BUSCH COMPANIES
Anheuser-Busch Companies is the parent company of Anheuser-Busch, Inc. brewers of Budweiser®, Michelob®, Michelob® Light, Budweiser® Light, Natural Light and Busch® beers.
PHOTOGRAPHED BY KEITH HALE.
An award-winning Black photographer, Mr. Hale is currently on staff with the Chicago Sun Times. Over the years his work has appeared in major publications, including EBONY and ESSENCE. The photograph below is of Mr. Hale's daughter and her great-grandmother.

Figure 4.2 The "Being Black in America" series by J.P. Martin Associates, including "History Lesson" for Anheuser-Busch, used relevant cultural cues to significantly increase positive perceptions of the brand among black consumers.

Source: 1985 *CEBA Exhibit Journal*, p. 109. Anheuser-Busch ads used with permission of Anheuser-Busch, LLC. All rights reserved.

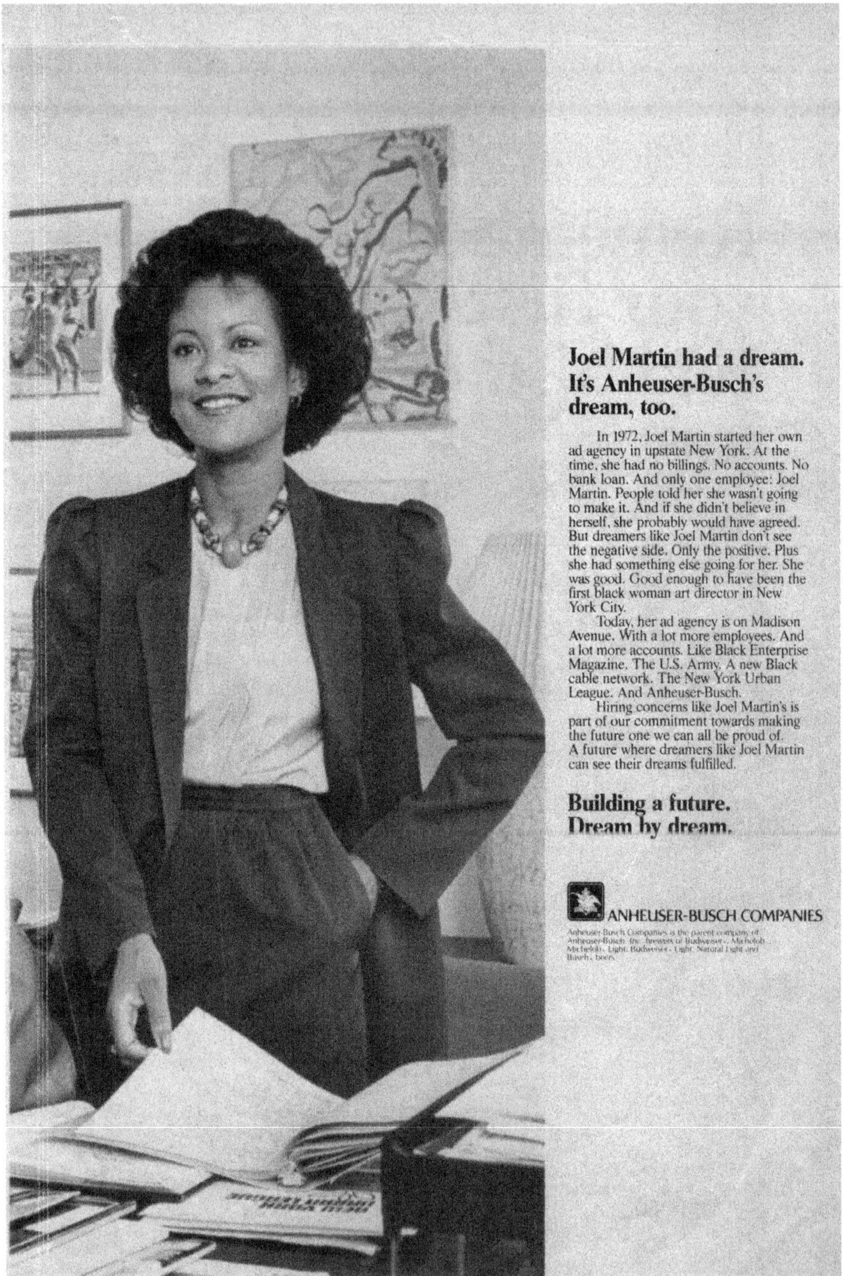

Joel Martin had a dream. It's Anheuser-Busch's dream, too.
In 1972, Joel Martin started her own ad agency in upstate New York. At the time, she had no billings. No accounts. No bank loan. And only one employee: Joel Martin. People told her she wasn't going to make it. And if she didn't believe in herself, she probably would have agreed. But dreamers like Joel Martin don't see the negative side. Only the positive. Plus she had something else going for her. She was good. Good enough to have been the first black woman art director in New York City.
Today, her ad agency is on Madison Avenue. With a lot more employees. And a lot more accounts. Like Black Enterprise Magazine. The U.S. Army. A new Black cable network. The New York Urban League. And Anheuser-Busch.
Hiring concerns like Joel Martin's is part of our commitment towards making the future one we can all be proud of. A future where dreamers like Joel Martin can see their dreams fulfilled.
Building a future. Dream by dream.
ANHEUSER-BUSCH COMPANIES

Figure 4.3 Anheuser-Busch featured agency President Joel P. Martin in a corporate ad praising her business accomplishments.

Source: *CEBA Exhibit Journal*, 1982, p. 20. Anheuser-Busch ads used with permission of Anheuser-Busch, LLC.

J.P. Martin Associates attempted to secure a greater share of general-market accounts. However, the agency mentioned in a trade advertisement the difficulty in getting corporations to see past the color of the agency's principals (J.P. Martin Associates, 1985). Martin (2015) commented:

> "We had the skills and ability to do general-market work. We were entrepreneurs – and you go after what you can go after. While the bulk of our work was in 'targeted marketing,' we did have [some] general-market accounts and we did go after them."

At the most, however, J.P. Martin Associates had 15–20 percent from general-market billings in a given year, as estimated by Martin (2015). Examples of these accounts included Jodee Bras for post-mastectomy women and a vendor purchasing program for Pfizer. However, Martin (2015) noted: "The readiness of general market companies to do business with black-owned companies in those days was limited." Therefore, the vast majority of the agency's work remained oriented toward black consumers. But Martin (2015) had no regrets about serving in that capacity, explaining: "The work that we were doing was so much about honoring and respecting the black community – that was our culture."

By 1986, the agency's reputation climaxed with Joel Martin being named as a co-chair of the CEBA Awards – the first woman to do so since the program's inception (*CEBA*, 1986, p. 5). As discussed in Chapter 1, CEBA was an annual awards program event which ran from 1978–1991 and recognized outstanding marketing communications directed at black consumers. Sponsored by the World Institute for Black Communications, each year an elaborate awards program was held in New York City and a 200-plus page exhibit journal was published which featured exemplary advertising work and other forms of marketing communications aimed at black consumers. Entries for the CEBA Awards were judged by leaders in the advertising and marketing industries. Each year, two top executives from advertising, media, or brand companies – one black and one white – were named as co-chairs of the awards program and served as ambassadors for the event. Both black and white advertising agencies received CEBA Awards for their work in about 30 various categories, but since the work of black agencies was usually black oriented, black agencies were well represented among the winners. During Martin's year as co-chair, she served with Ed Wax, President and CEO of Saatchi & Compton, Inc., a large general-market advertising agency. The only other black woman to co-chair the CEBA Awards was Caroline Jones, who served in 1988 along with G. Robert Holmen, Chairman of the Backer, Spielvogel Bates agency (*CEBA*, 1988, p. 5). In addition to being named as 1986 co-chair, Martin's agency won 13 CEBA Awards that year for its work on campaigns for the Anheuser-Busch corporate account, Budweiser, and Carnation brands. In fact, the J.P. Martin Associates agency was featured on 21 pages of the

1986 *CEBA Exhibit Journal* (p. 404). Reminiscing about her opportunity to serve as CEBA co-chair and the agency's winning record, Martin (2015) remarked:

> "It was fun! I was honored to represent my company. We walked off the stage with 13 CEBA awards. It was significant recognition of the creative ability of my agency. It validated how we were serving our clients and how we were presenting their goods and services in the corporate ads. I was quite proud. It was really based on performance – not just because I was a woman – but because my agency, my company was doing great work."

Creative activism

A significant body of work by J.P. Martin Associates was a series of ads produced for BOCA, a consortium of black communications executives who owned media outlets such as *Black Enterprise* magazine and black-owned broadcast stations. In the early 1980s, BOCA was founded by radio station owners Eugene Jackson and Percy Sutton; publishers Earl Graves, Ed Lewis, and Clarence Smith; and other black media owners, along with Joel Martin and public relations executive Terrie Williams, who served as BOCA's Executive Directors. The goal of BOCA was twofold: (1) to bring attention to advertisers of the spending power of black consumers in an effort to help black media get their share of advertising dollars which was representative of black spending power; and (2) to educate black consumers of their value and worth in the marketplace and as citizens. BOCA not only sought advertising dollars, but respect for black media. For example, at the time, *Essence* – a magazine aimed at contemporary black women – was told it could not carry perfume advertising because such targeting was considered to be a stigma on the perfume companies' brand images (Martin, 2015). Martin (2015) explained:

> "We were about busting stereotypes and at the same time educating the men and women in our communities about what their purchasing power was about; and to create pride and self-esteem and community esteem through our advertising. Basically, we wanted to wake people up."

The agency's work for BOCA served as a form of activism and provided some of the most provocative creative themes of the 1980s. For example, a BOCA ad encouraging black voter participation evoked memories of black slaves and sharecroppers, showing a prominent image of black adults picking cotton in a field, with the headline: "The hands that picked cotton now pick Presidents. Nov. 4th. Vote like your life depended on it" (*CEBA*, 1981, p. 29). Another BOCA ad presented stark text with no images, challenging black people to consider their worth as consumers and to behave accordingly. The ad, opening with a headline in large bold typeface, stated the following (*CEBA*, 1980, p. 32):

> "**Who cares what Black people think anyway?**
> If you think nobody gives a damn what Black people think, think again. Some people care a lot. Especially when they need something from you. Take corporations. They want you to buy their products. And banks care about whether you're going to give them your money. Politicians. They care about what you think and they're looking for your vote. And TV and radio stations hope you'll pay attention to their shows. The point is, all these people want something *from you*. We should learn to use that power wisely to make the changes we need to make. Give your money, your votes and your loyalty to people who deserve it. People who are going to *give you* something in return. People who are doing the most for Black people. Who cares what Black people think? Right now there are 25 million Black people in this country and last year alone we earned 110 billion dollars. That's clout. Write us. Because we care what Black people think."

Perhaps the most compelling BOCA ads featured black children, which suggested the psychological harm created by continuous exposure to negative black images and media stereotypes. In one version, an African-American girl rejects the black baby doll she is holding and complains: "Mama, something's wrong with this baby" (*CEBA*, 1982, p. 21). The baby doll ad, which garnered a CEBA Award of Excellence, was reminiscent of the famous 1940s studies conducted by black psychologist Dr. Kenneth Clark, which illustrated that black children tended to show preferences for white dolls and assigned positive attributes to white figures while assigning negative attributes to black figures. This evidence of psychological injury such as internalized perceptions of inferiority and low self-esteem by black children was provided as part of the legal rationale for outlawing "separate but equal" school segregation policies in the landmark *Brown* vs. *Board of Education* case before the U.S. Supreme Court in 1954. In another version, an African-American boy peers into a bathroom mirror and sees a white superhero in his reflection (see Figure 4.4) with a caption which asks: "What's wrong with this picture?" (*CEBA*, 1980, p. 67). Thus, these ads for BOCA challenged readers to consider how societal norms and symbols inflicted psychological harm on black children, who were often exposed to negative black stereotypes along with positive white stereotypes – but were limited in the range of positive black images they were exposed to.

Over and out

Considering all of the accomplishments of the J.P. Martin Associates agency through the mid-1980s, it would appear that Joel P. Martin was at the top of the advertising game. The recognition and visibility associated with the 1986 CEBA Awards attracted new business to the agency (Martin, 2015). However, as the decade continued, Joel Martin's passion for the agency business started to wane and her interests shifted to other areas. While running the agency was exciting, the best aspects, in her opinion, involved the creative process. Providing perspective, Martin (2015) said:

Figure 4.4 Boy and Superhero ad for the Black Owned Communications Alliance.
Source: courtesy of Joel P. Martin, BOCA.

"I loved the creative process and working with Byron Jones, our music director; and Denise Young, our producer; and my husband – who is a very creative person with a brilliant mind. I am a writer. My favorite memories of running the agency is when we would get together to brainstorm the breakthrough ideas for different kinds of campaigns. Remember – my soul is of an artist. What is [the work] going to look like? How will people feel when they see it? What's

> the emotional content? My context is tied up into empowerment and fortunately in those days it led to some of the campaigns I'm really proud of – like BOCA and the Anheuser-Busch corporate account."

But in running the agency, there were myriad responsibilities such as media buying, account management, and working with clients, which did not involve the sort of creativity that Martin enjoyed. Martin (2015) observed: "The more we grew, the less I could be hands on all of the areas." She continued:

> "There were challenges typically that business owners have, that entrepreneurs have, that agencies have – getting clients, doing presentations, burning the midnight oil, servicing clients – so that you have something you are proud of which is strategic and on point and on target. Those things have not much changed; and that was part of running the business."

Around 1987, Joel and Bob Martin were introduced by a friend to Lifespring, Inc. a private, for-profit training company focused on helping individuals and institutions reach their full potential. Founded in 1974 by John Hanley and partners, the company helped to introduce and popularize experiential education techniques by which participants could transform their lives and organizations (Lifespringnow.com, 2015). "I loved my training," Martin (2007, p. 32) said, calling it her catalyst for change. "Through it I found my passion and a calling to be in service to others," she explained (Martin, 2007, p. 23). Martin's training experiences prompted her to reexamine her life, career, and purpose as the head of J.P. Martin Associates. She asked herself, "What do I want to do with the rest of my life? Make a difference with a human being, or sell another bottle of beer?" (Martin, 2007, p. 27). This was a personal turning point for Martin as her attention shifted toward new areas of passion and fulfillment and she became less focused on running the agency. She confessed: "My heart was no longer in the agency business. I hired staff to do what I was no longer interested in doing" (Martin, 2007, p. 28). Thinking back on that period, Martin (2015) reflected: "When a [client] hires you, they want 100% of your attention, particularly from the President and CEO, which I was. So when my focus shifted, my customer service and service delivery shifted because my heart was elsewhere."

Martin's new priorities had a detrimental effect on the agency's operations and, in 1989, its major client – which represented a significant share of the agency's business – fired J.P. Martin Associates. Considering the whole situation, Joel and Bob Martin decided to resign the remaining accounts and close the agency. Martin (2007, p. 28) admits: "Even though I knew advertising wasn't my passion any longer, closing my company was traumatic and humbling." Declining to identify the client which terminated the agency, she said,

> "I don't regret the firing – from a standpoint of accountability and responsibility – I can explain all of the things that that led up to the firing. But that was one of

> my rites of passage between my role as an agency owner and the transformational trainer I was to become and what I do internationally that matters so much to me now."
>
> (Martin, 2015)

"The one regret that I have – and I now speak about it – is that I wish that I knew how to sell a property. I would have sold J.P. Martin Associates, but I didn't know about that exit strategy then." The Martins auctioned off the furniture and closed the agency permanently, ending the tenure of the little agency known for its gutsy creative work.

The transformation of Joel P. Martin

After closing J.P. Martin Associates, Joel Martin concentrated on a total transformation of her life and professional career. Twenty-five year later, she was quoted in the book *Think and Grow Rich for Women* (Lechter, 2014, p. 45), saying:

> "You've probably heard the expression, 'Get out of the box.' Well transformation is inventing your box and making it large enough to handle and generate more of what you want personally, professionally and in your relationships."

In the 20 years following the closure of the advertising agency, Joel Martin drew on this way of thinking to transform herself into a well-regarded international trainer, executive coach, motivational speaker, event planner, and author. Her professional endeavors expanded on the values and perspectives she developed while running the advertising agency including the importance of education and leadership development; along with diversity, inclusion, and cultural competency in organizations. The Martins' departure from the advertising business offered the opportunity for a fresh start. Daughter Cybel had finished high school in New York and started college in Pennsylvania. Joel and Bob Martin moved across the country to Northern California because Joel was interested in becoming a trainer with Lifespring and wanted to live near the headquarters where her education would take place. Learning the business from the ground up and starting out as a rookie trainer for Lifespring, she eventually became a manager. In the meantime, she went back to school because she felt there were gaps in her knowledge and she didn't completely understand the foundation and terminologies that were used by the company she was working for. Martin (2015) explained:

> "I wanted to be able to engage in conversations about existentialism, oncology and other important ideas. The program I trained in was life-defining and I wanted to know the philosophical side of it. I wanted to know – when did the industry start? Who started it? How does experiential education work? What is transformation? I was curious. I went back to school so that I could be better at what it is I chose to do."

To that end, she entered graduate school and over the next several years earned a Master's Degree in Psychology, a Ph.D. in Communications, and became a Fellow of the Wharton Business School at the University of Pennsylvania. This advanced education and training played a key role in her new career focus. Her doctoral research and dissertation, *The Training Industry Guide and Reference Book* and *A Study of an Integrated Experiential Training, Development and Communications Program Designed for the Organizational Setting*, served as the foundation for the executive coaching firm she established a few years later.

The phoenix rises

With new credentials and experience, Dr. Joel Martin formed an alliance with several business partners to form a national integrated communications firm providing public relations, marketing, research, and training services to business executives in metro Los Angeles, Chicago, and New York under the Triad nameplate, which operated in the Western, Eastern, and Midwest regions of the United States, respectively (Martin, n.d.). Martin focused on the Western region and by 1997 had purchased rights to the Triad West name and established Triad West, Inc. in Scottsdale, Arizona, where she and Bob relocated. The company provides consulting and business development services, motivational events and public speaking, curriculum design, workforce training, executive coaching, and other services. As President and owner of Triad West, Martin's personal mission, and the mission of her company is "to transform lives and businesses for the better" (Woods, 2014). Through her company, Dr. Martin has worked with thousands of clients globally in countries including the United States, China, Russia, Malaysia, South Africa, France, the United Kingdom, and Norway, specializing in delivering vision-driven experiential education, developing leadership, fostering workplace culture change, creating breakthrough communications strategies, and growing diverse and inclusive work teams. Her clients have consisted of Fortune 500 companies, for-profit and non-profit organizations, and entrepreneurial ventures. Her professional memberships include the American Society of Training and Development, the National Association of Women Business Owners, and the Society of Human Resource Managers. Sought after as a respected behavioral scientist, her work has earned a variety of recognitions including the Distinguished Alumni of Ohio State University, Outstanding Young Women of America, Who's Who in the East, International Who's Who of Entrepreneurs, the Recipient of the Key to the City of Los Angeles, and a delegate to the White House Conference on Small Business. Her accomplishments with J.P. Martin Associates and Triad West, Inc. have earned her media coverage via outlets including the *Today* show, *U.S. News and World Report*, *Fortune*, *Black Enterprise*, *Essence*, and *Working Woman* magazines.

In addition to her work with Triad West, Inc., Martin has provided other work which promotes empowerment and inclusion for diverse professionals, two of her main causes. For example, she created the Positively Powerful

Woman Awards, an outgrowth of her commitment to women's leadership. The awards program recognizes women who excel as leaders in service or business through achievements in several areas including education, the arts, STEM (science, technology, engineering, and math), non-profit and philanthropic work, the faith community, and global business (Woods, 2014). Launched in 2007, the annual awards event became a popular full-day program which attracts hundreds of participants and provides transformational leadership, personal and professional development, inspiration, and networking opportunities. Beyond these accomplishments, Martin authored three books on personal growth and career development, using strategies drawn from her career as a trainer including *How to Be a Positively Powerful Person!* – first published in 2003; a revised fourth edition published in 2007 titled *How to Be a Positively Powerful Person! The Spirit-Filled Large Print Revised Edition*; and a guide to personal branding titled *Get The "Me" Brand Awareness: The Positively Powerful Way*, published in 2011. She also writes articles for an internet blog called "Positively Powerful Insights" which offers guidance and inspiration, publishes motivational speeches on YouTube, and provides branding and leadership presentations online via Slideshare.net.

Reflections on the advertising business

Joel Martin's work in executive training and coaching led her to the conclusion that "a company is merely the shadow of the man or woman that leads it" (Martin, 2015). Her transformative training work impacts organizational culture since it influences senior executives who in turn institute change from the top down. Considering the existence of "unconscious factors" within organizations' cultures, she recalls that at Anheuser-Busch Companies, most leaders during the J.P. Martin Associates era were tall, white men. Reflecting on insights drawn from working in advertising and with major corporations, she continues to be a champion of diversity, mindful of the historical problems with ethnic and gender roles in the advertising business. Martin (2015) says:

> "Diversity and inclusion is about creating a workforce which gets the best abilities to the foreground. Many advertising agencies are not inclusive – and they wonder why their talented people of color are walking out the door. They're walking out because they are not being included. For many, the [work] is about engagement – and for high-context people, it's about community."

Acknowledging that pressure has been exerted on ad agencies with respect to their hiring practices, Martin (2015) responds that "they should come under fire" for lack of diversity and inclusion. Martin discusses that diversity and inclusion training is important work on an international basis, since modern companies are more global in outlook.

Although she no longer follows the advertising business, there are aspects of her advertising experience which benefit her training career. She explained:

> "For the kind of executive training I do for high-achieving professionals in major corporations and education, my unique combination of skills and abilities plays well for them. The way marketing, advertising and promotion comes in – even though a lot has changed in advertising and marketing because of technology – I am still able to hear the promotional heartbeat of a client. The kinds of consulting work, presentations and graphics that I do draw on my advertising background."
>
> (Martin, 2015)

> "My mindset continues to be: to honor all people. The advertising background is still a part of the contributions I am able to make as a highly paid coach. Another of the ways that I use my advertising and marketing background is through the Positively Powerful Woman Awards."
>
> (Martin, 2015)

Whether put to use in an advertising agency or an executive training firm, Martin's best work typically centered on creativity in some manner. Although she decided to exit the advertising business, her memories of her experiences in the business are that advertising is "highly competitive, fulfilling, challenging, barrier-breaking and fun" (Davis, 2013b).

Joel P. Martin: survivor and poet

Added to Joel Martin's long list of life events is one she would have rather not had – a bout with breast cancer in 2009. "It's a traumatic experience being diagnosed with cancer," she reflected, "we caught mine early – thank goodness" (Martin, 2015). Given the circumstances, much of that year focused on medical treatments and recuperation which she addressed in another book she wrote: *There And Back ... A Book of Poems* (Martin, 2009). Focused on family and friends, writing the poetry book was therapeutic for Martin and aided in her recovery. "Fortunately, I had a very good team and my husband was incredible and supportive," she recalled (Martin, 2015.) One of the poems, "I Appreciate You," acknowledges Bob Martin's role in her healing and survival and serves as a testimony to their 40-plus year marriage and relationship commitment (Martin, 2009, p. 7):

> "You have been more gentle than I ever could have imagined
> Speaking in a tone that caresses me all over.
> I appreciate you.
> You pat me with a touch that speaks volumes
> About how you are afraid to hurt me.
> Timidly, hesitantly, you cause me to moan, though not with ecstasy.
> You notice it. 'I'm sorry,' you say. 'It's okay,' I reply.
> I appreciate you.
> The four months of daily meals, bills paying, doctor chauffeuring
> Bringing the pup to say 'hello'
> Your worried brow as you hold him
> As much for your own comfort as for mine.
> 'It will be okay,' you promise. And I believe you."

It took Martin months to recover from cancer treatments and unsuccessful breast reconstruction surgery. There came a point in the third year after the inception of the Positively Powerful Woman Awards event that she decided that there was not going to be an awards presentation that year because she was not well enough to do the work. But supportive women who knew Martin and her efforts stepped forward and volunteered to organize and execute the event, telling her: "you just sit!" and the program went on successfully (Martin, 2015). Today, as a breast cancer survivor, sought-after speaker, and thriving businesswoman, she has "put to rest the dumb little eight-year old liar conversation" she held in her mind for many years (Martin, 2007, p. 32). "I'm alive and happy to be here!" she exclaims (Martin, 2015). In sum, Joel P. Martin moved forward from that painful day as a humiliated schoolgirl to live her life in a positive and powerful way as a wife, mother, businesswoman, and advocate for diversity, inclusion, and change.

References

Black Enterprise (1984) 'On the Move,' October, p. 144.

CEBA Exhibit Journal (1980) New York: World Institute for Black Communications.

CEBA Exhibit Journal (1981) New York: World Institute for Black Communications.

CEBA Exhibit Journal (1982) New York: World Institute for Black Communications.

CEBA Exhibit Journal (1986) New York: World Institute for Black Communications.

CEBA Exhibit Journal (1988) New York: World Institute for Black Communications.

Chambers, J. (2008) *Madison Avenue and the Color Line: African-Americans in the Advertising Industry*. Philadelphia, PA: University of Pennsylvania Press.

Crisis (1983) 'Reaching for the Top,' June, 90(6), p. 46.

Davis, J. F. (2013a) 'Realizing Marketplace Opportunity: How Research on the Black Consumer Market Influenced Mainstream Marketers, 1920–1970,' *Journal of Historical Research in Marketing*, 5(4), pp. 471–493.

Davis, M. (2013b) 'Dr. Joel Martin: A Transformational Icon Impacts Lives Around the World,' *Exceptional People Magazine*, September/October [Online]. Available at: http://exceptionalmag.com/GuestArticles/ExceptionalPeopleMagazineSeptemberOctober2013Issue-Dr-Joel-Martin.pdf (Accessed: February 27, 2015).

Dougherty, P. (1983) 'Saatchi Agrees to Buy McCaffrey and McCall,' *New York Times*, June 25 [Online]. Available at: www.nytimes.com/1983/06/25/business/saatchi-agrees-to-buy-mccaffrey-mccall.html (Accessed: March 27, 2015).

Dougherty, P. (1985) 'Advertising: A Black Agency's Strategy'. *New York Times*, July 24 [Online]. Available at: www.nytimes.com/1985/07/24/business/advertising-a-black-agency-s-strategy.html (Accessed: January 21, 2015).

J.P. Martin Associates (1984) 'Come Grow with Us,' Agency trade ad, *Black Enterprise*, June, p. 104.

J.P. Martin Associates (1986) 'The Little Agency that Could ... And Did,' Agency trade ad, *Black Enterprise*, June, p. 97.

Kupfer, A. (1985) 'People to Watch,' *Fortune*, December 23 [Online]. Available at: http://archive.fortune.com/magazines/fortune/fortune_archive/1985/12/23/66797/index.htm (Accessed: August 31, 2015).

Lechter, S. (2014) *Think and Grow Rich for Women*. New York: Penguin.

Lifespringnow.com (2015) *About Us*. Available at: www.lifespringnow.com/2015/index.html (Accessed: February 24, 2015).

Martin, J. P. (n.d.) *Dr. Joel P. Martin: Herstory*. Unpublished biography.

Martin, J. P. (2007) *How to Be a Positively Powerful Person!* Scottsdale, AZ: Sugar Pup Productions.

Martin, J. P. (2009) *There and Back ... A Book of Poetry*. Self-published: Blurb Online.

Martin, J. P. (2014) 'Gift that Keeps on Giving: Hope, Encouragement and Praise,' Blog post, December 2 [Online]. Available at: www.positivelypowerful.com/Insights/2014/12/gift-keeps-giving-hope-encouragement-praise/ (Accessed: January 21, 2015).

Martin, J. P. (2015) Interviews with the Author, February.

O'Leary, N. (1999) 'David McCall Dies Aiding Refugees,' *Adweek*, April 26 [Online]. Available at: www.adweek.com/news/advertising/david-mccall-dies-aiding-refugees-24511 (Accessed: January 21, 2015).

Saxon, W. (2001) 'James J. McCaffrey, 79, Co-Founder of Top New York Ad Agency,' *New York Times*, July 27 [Online]. Available at: www.nytimes.com/2001/07/27/business/james-j-mccaffrey-79-co-founder-of-top-new-york-ad-agency.html (Accessed: March 27, 2015).

Smikle, K. (1985) 'The Image Makers,' *Black Enterprise*, December, pp. 44–52.

Woods, L. (2014) '2014 Positively Powerful Woman Award Honorees Announced' [Online]. Available at: http://the3000club.org/index.php/component/k2/item/57-2014-positively-powerful-woman-award-honorees-announced-may-19-2014 (Accessed: January 21, 2015).

5 Carol H. Williams

Marathon woman

Figure 5.1 Carol H. Williams.

Source: courtesy of the Carol H. Williams Advertising agency.

"WHOSE EYES ARE YOU LOOKING THROUGH WHEN YOU VIEW THE WORLD?" is the trademarked, thought-provoking inquiry which greets visitors who explore the credentials of the Carol H. Williams Advertising agency, a highly regarded multicultural-focused, independent advertising firm where Williams herself sits at the helm. Underpinning a strategic and razor-sharp focus on the minds of the target consumers, the question underscores Williams' approach to creative advertising, which produced the famous campaign theme for Procter & Gamble's Secret antiperspirant brand: "Strong Enough for a Man, But Made for a Woman." Williams' insightful thinking catapulted the brand, which was lowly ranked in its product category – and sinking – to the number one position within six months in the mid-1970s. Her work for Secret and other major brands resonated with consumers while producing measurable results for advertisers, establishing a reputation which earned Williams an Advertising Woman of the Year award by 1977. During her long career in advertising – spanning more than 45 years – she served in a number of highly visible, pioneering roles and started her own agency – the most successful advertising firm founded by an African-American woman in the history of the advertising business. Why was Carol Williams able to prosper in an industry where many others faltered? An examination of her life and career, based on personal interviews with Carol Williams and other sources, provides insight as to how she navigated the thorny world of advertising.

"Least likely to succeed": Carol Williams and the Basic Advertising Course

Born on Chicago's south side into a working class family with Southern roots, young Carol Henny Williams – who was energetic and very smart – never considered a career in advertising (Hayes, 1999). Her parents had high standards and insisted that their five children become "self-sufficient, productive citizens" (Hayes, 1999, p. 184). Williams worked at Sears as a catalog editor while a student at Northwestern University, a highly selective private institution located in Evanston, Illinois, where she majored in Biology intending to become a doctor. However, in 1969, a fortuitous meeting led to her participation in the Basic Advertising Course (BAC), a career training program which grew out of national concerns regarding the lack of opportunities for blacks in the advertising business. The BAC was a 13-week educational program sponsored by the 4 A's established by two men with extensive advertising experience: Bob Ross, a white man and chairman of the Chicago 4 A's chapter, and Bill Sharp, a black man and mentee of Ross. Over the years, Sharp led a stellar advertising career – working as a copy supervisor at JWT in Chicago, serving as Vice President of Advertising for Coca-Cola, and founding his own advertising agency in Atlanta. Sharp would eventually be inducted into the prestigious Advertising Hall of Fame. With a rigorous curriculum designed by Sharp, Ross, and Vernon Fryburger, chairman of Northwestern's Advertising Department, the program's mission was to counter agencies' claims that there were no "qualified" blacks with the capabilities demanded of the advertising profession; and to establish a pipeline of black talent trained in copywriting, art direction, media planning, and account management (Chambers, 2008, pp. 183–186). Unbeknownst to Ross, Sharp had already been in discussions with a small group of African-Americans who were already working in advertising, including future agency owners Tom Burrell and Frank Mingo, who were trying to figure out ways to get more blacks involved in the profession. Sharp – charged with implementing the BAC program – recruited white and black advertising practitioners from the Chicago area to serve as the program's instructors.

Seeking individuals who were highly motivated with excellent communication skills, BAC's first class of ten students met in September 1967 on Northwestern's campus. Later, classes would meet at different advertising agencies in the Chicago area. The coursework was difficult, providing mock assignments which featured general-market brands, so that the skill set learned would be applicable to a wide variety of marketing and job situations. Sharp wanted to be sure that the students would not be pigeon-holed into only being able to work on advertising directed at black consumers (Chambers, 2008, p. 188). During the program, students' work was thoroughly critiqued and subjected to the same level of scrutiny that occurred in professional environments. By the end of the course, the participants had built a portfolio of mock advertisements and other work. BAC's founders wanted to ensure that the quality of the students' work was top-notch and that the graduates would be taken seriously.

As word spread about the BAC, it attracted a lot of interest. At one point there were 165 applications for eight spots in the program and Sharp had to whittle down the numbers (Chambers, 2008, p. 187). Many of the BAC courses were taught by black instructors, including Sharp, Burrell, and Frank Daughton, along with Ross and others. Carol Williams met Bill Sharp in late 1968 at Northwestern when he happened to attend a play she had written for the campus theater (Hayes, 1999). Impressed with her writing skills, Sharp told Williams about the BAC. Although interested after learning about the class – which would be starting in a few weeks – Williams had missed the application deadline. Recounting her BAC experiences, Williams (2014) recalls: "I wasn't really in the Basic Ad Class – I audited it. By the time they began that whole thing I had missed the admission [process]. I met Bill Sharp and asked him to let me audit it." Impressed by Williams' talent, Sharp and Ross agreed to let her participate in the class. This decision apparently upset Frank Daughton, who was one of Williams' instructors. "He thought that was totally terrible that other students were privileged and had worked diligently to get themselves to get in position to be in this class and how dare Bill Sharp and Bob Ross allow me to audit that class!" Williams (2014) laughed. "I was considered the most unlikely one to succeed. I was very, very quiet, had this Southern family background, and was still in school. They didn't pay any attention to me," Williams (2014) chuckled. The following summer – 1969 – Williams sought out internship opportunities and landed at Leo Burnett in Chicago, one of the most prominent agencies in the advertising industry. Upon completion, she was offered two full-time jobs: one at JWT's Chicago office, where Bill Sharp worked, and a permanent offer from Leo Burnett. Considering her options, Williams reflected: "I loved the problem-solving aspect of strategic marketing and here I was invited into a field which was very rewarding, challenging and intellectually-driven. I went with my heart" (Hayes, 1999, p. 184). Deciding to remain at Burnett, she recounted her experiences, reflecting on her relationship with Bill Sharp. "Bill was one of my mentors and he taught me. I got a job. Next thing those boys [from the BAC] knew, I was a copy supervisor and moving around the bases" (Williams, 2014). Ironically, Williams acknowledged that most of her classmates who went through the BAC only lasted in the industry for a few years. Sharp, lamenting on the high attrition rate among BAC participants who went on to work for agencies, believed he had made a "major mistake" by not helping the graduates get acclimated to the organizational culture present in most advertising firms (Chambers, 2008, p. 190). In light of these problems, Sharp took what he had learned from the BAC experience and self-published a book titled *How to Be Black and Get a Job in the Advertising Agency Business Anyway* (Sharp, 1969), which was a primer on black survival in white general-market advertising firms. As a testimony to his mentorship of African-Americans in the advertising profession, the book was re-published in 2015, a few years after Sharp's death.

Happy days: Williams at the Leo Burnett agency

Carol Williams' career trajectory at Leo Burnett was unprecedented. Within seven years of being hired full time at the agency in August 1969, by the end of 1976 she had been named a Creative Director and Vice President of the agency. Initially hired as a copywriter, for a while she had two jobs simultaneously: one as a full-time student at Northwestern at night, and another as a creative professional at Leo Burnett during the day. Williams (2014) recalls, "I was a total workaholic, but it was fun to me." She won a number of Clio and Addy awards while at Burnett and, in 1977, the Women's Advertising Club of Chicago named Williams as Advertising Woman of the Year. Prior to that time, the only black woman ever so recognized was pioneering adwoman Barbara Gardner Proctor. "I thought I was big time – making money," Williams (2014) said. Williams' father, incredulous about his daughter's success – and paycheck – exclaimed: "You make more damn money than I have ever seen. We need to check you out! I'm callin' the police on you 'cause you got to be doing something illegal," Williams (2014) recounted with humor. Beyond a regular salary, the Burnett agency also offered profit-sharing options to its employees, thereby sweetening the financial pot and incentivizing them to continuously produce excellent work.

The Leo Burnett agency was a special place and had an impeccable reputation as perhaps the greatest place to work for creative advertising professionals. Many of the most effective and memorable themes and figures in the history of advertising came out of that agency including: "Fly the Friendly Skies" for United Airlines; Tony the Tiger for Kellogg's cornflakes cereal; the (Jolly) Green Giant for frozen vegetables; the Pillsbury Doughboy for baking products; Charlie the Tuna for canned fish; and the Marlboro Man cowboy for cigarettes. Founder Leo Burnett, who launched the agency in Chicago during the Great Depression, established the agency's philosophy as a "simple mission to create superior advertising" (Applegate, 1994, p. 80). Unlike the slick images of handsome and polished advertising executives in their grey flannel suits, Leo Burnett was described as "short, bald and paunchy" (Applegate, 1994, p. 81) and an "inarticulate curmudgeon who simply loved his work" (Applegate, 1994, p. 83). As a testimony to his creative reputation, in 1961 he was an inaugural inductee into the Copywriter's Hall of Fame and was featured on the cover of *Time* magazine in 1962 along with other important advertising practitioners (Applegate, 1994, p. 82). Although Leo Burnett perceived differences in the ways that men and women responded to the competitive pressures in the advertising industry work environment, he thought women were less capable of taking on key responsibilities; nonetheless, he was willing to give assignments to women as well as men, believing that "the best would always perform" (Applegate, 1994, p. 82). Requiring a strong work ethic, he was known to give scathing critiques to his employees' work, using coarse language and his omnipresent thick black pencil. After Burnett's "retirement" in 1967, he maintained an office at the agency so he could be close to the work he loved. After his death in 1971, the Burnett agency retained the culture that emphasized high standards for creative work.

Williams thrived in the exciting creative environment at Leo Burnett, which suited her talents and willingness to work hard. Describing the culture of the agency in her own words, Williams (2014) reflected:

> "Burnett had created at the time what I considered was the epitome of a creative agency. You were surrounded by the most creative people in the ad business. If you looked at what Burnett worked on at the time, its products were the top products in their categories. Creative thinking permeated the agency culture. Burnett had a mantra: 'If you were not selling 100%' – you could not stay in that place. It's just the way it was. Somehow Leo – and he had a methodology – identified the best of the best in the creative area. The best creatives were either at Leo Burnett or had been at Burnett. The creative philosophy was infused [into the culture] and it went viral. The creative department was a 24/7 department and no one ever went home. Everybody was always competing – but competed in such a way that you could get along. That's the way I felt. But what could I say because I was winning all the time?"

Early on, Williams' work ethic and abilities were recognized by several white males who would serve as her mentors, teachers, and advocates during her time at Burnett. Associate Creative Director Jim Gilmore initially hired her. Gilmore, who preferred staffers who were well-rounded science and liberal arts majors, immediately recognized Williams' intelligence and "hired her for her brains" (Gilmore, 2015). Williams' first boss was Don Marrs, who reported to Rudy Perz, a Creative Director. Perz was closely associated with the iconic Pillsbury Doughboy character and Perz and Williams collaborated on a number of Doughboy projects. Two weeks after starting at Burnett, Williams approached Gilmore with an idea for Pillsbury, which was one of the agency's largest accounts. With a campaign theme already in place: "Nothing's Quite as Good as Biscuits in the Morning," Williams proposed that a tagline be added, "It's Pillsbury's Best Time of Day" (Hayes, 1999). The tagline was adopted and Gilmore, recognizing a winner, recalled: "We were doing the Doughboy television spots, and when this young girl came in with that line, I knew she was going to go a long way" (Hayes, 1999, p. 184). Williams' successes led to additional opportunities with Pillsbury and other brands, and she was promoted to Copy Supervisor in 1972. Her second boss, Creative Director Charlie Blakemore, promoted her to Associate Creative Director in 1974. In 1976, the agency named Williams as a Creative Director and she was elevated to a vice-presidency by the end of the year. This promotion made her the first female Vice President and Creative Director at the Leo Burnett agency (Cuneo, 2002).

Outside of the agency, the world was experiencing tensions with respect to race relations and Civil Rights activities, and Gilmore recalls Williams being driven to work each day by her older brother when violence broke out in parts of Chicago (Hayes, 1999). In the 1960s, the advertising agency business was scrutinized for being among the least diverse industries with respect to employment of minorities. The *Chicago Reporter*, a monthly publication covering racial topics in metropolitan Chicago, published an issue in March 1975 with the cover story headline: "Blacks are Most 'Hidden Persuaders' in Chicago's Billion Dollar Advertising Business" reporting on the 15 largest general-market agencies in metro Chicago employing at least 50 people. At the time, Burnett was the largest agency in Chicago and also employed the greatest numbers of minority employees – 134. This number accounted for more than 50 percent of all minority employees among the Chicago-area agencies and blacks represented 2.8 percent of Burnett's total employees (*Chicago Reporter*, 1975, p. 1). That year, Carol Williams, who was an Associate Creative Director, and Don Richards, who was an Account Supervisor, were two of the three highest ranking black advertising professionals in the Chicago area and they both worked at Burnett. A third African-American, Ron Sampson, was the highest ranking black ad executive in a Chicago general-market agency, serving as a partner and Account Supervisor at Tatham-Laird & Kudner. The *Chicago Reporter* sharply criticized agencies' minority hiring practices, noting that only one of the 15 agencies recruited from the BAC program Williams had attended and that only 16 of the 110 graduates of the program were employed in Chicago-area agencies. The article concluded (*Chicago Reporter*, 1975, p. 1):

> "The advertising business in Chicago is an exciting, fast-paced $1 billion industry, but not for blacks and other minorities. The precise number of minority employees in the Chicago area's 367 advertising agencies is not known, but if the leading agencies are a guide, the number is small and the jobs mostly at the bottom."

In light of this background, another black woman, Suzanne Stantley, who worked at Leo Burnett around the same time as Williams, reflected on Williams' career trajectory and mentor relationships with men like Charlie Blakemore, Jim Gilmore, and Rudy Perz. Stantley (2014) remarked:

> "When you consider the times, it was remarkable for them to put aside whatever their biases were about us a people. To recognize the talent that she had and to give a young black woman that kind of responsibility is an incredible testament to her capabilities. She came up with a set of values from parents who said: 'Nobody's going to give you anything, so you work hard to get it.' When they found out she was going to work at this ad agency – a business that they were not familiar with – they said 'you do whatever you have to do to stay in the game.' She busted her ass."

Nodding in agreement, Williams (2014) added:

> "All Charlie saw was talent – as did Rudy. Those people were my bosses the entire time I was at Burnett. I would see a lot of other people at Burnett – especially African-Americans – who were being shifted all around. They would come to work and they would have different bosses every few weeks."

Stantley (2014) offered: "She was protected – but, she didn't know it." Williams (2014) acknowledged: "In retrospect, I realize that."

Remembering the caliber and character of the mentors and colleagues she was surrounded by at Leo Burnett, Williams (2014) recalls:

> "I was brought up by some white men who were brilliant, extremely creative and absolutely respectful of me. Charlie Blakemore, my mentor, had created the Duncan Hines 'Feather Cut' [campaign]. Down the hall was the brilliant Bob Noel who had created the Green Giant [animated character] and Pat Martin who created 'You've come a long way, baby' for Virginia Slims [cigarettes]. Peter Horst created Morris the Cat, and Bob Tenent created 'Nothing says loving like something from the oven – Pillsbury says it best.' Those were the men that surrounded me. They were extremely brilliant and absolutely creative. They loved what they [did] and they were immersed in what they [did]. And they never gave me any evidence [of racist or sexist attitudes] whatsoever. Those guys – and I'm not talking about those from outside – they never saw anything in me except a brilliant creative talent. Burnett treated me wonderfully."

Creative thinking

Williams' manner of thinking and relationships with her mentors allowed her to produce outstanding creative work at Leo Burnett. She had the ability to think strategically and draw on her life experiences and on observations of society in such a way that breakthrough creative ideas resulted. Her work at Burnett earned her a reputation as a professional whose creative work was effective not only in raising the profile of the brand, but also in selling products. Among her credits from the early 1970s is copy for the Pillsbury brand – "Say Hello to Poppin' Fresh Dough" – which nationally reintroduced an animated Pillsbury Doughboy – and his signature giggle – into American TV households; and "Paper Knife" for Pillsbury's frosting product featuring the tagline with a demonstration: "Frosting so smooth and creamy, you can spread it with a paper knife." Williams (2014) explained:

> "Once they put Carol H. Williams' advertising on the air, you could measure the results. That was a big thing for Burnett and everybody at that time. The big thing from the time I was at Burnett was that my advertising had measurable results. My "Paper Knife" campaign for Pillsbury frosting moved it from a non-existing position to number one in the category. Duncan Hines was the huge cake mix until we did Pillsbury Doughboy cake mix. My campaign moved Secret antiperspirant from number nine to number one in the marketplace. The advertising I put on the air was insightful and had measurable results."

Williams' manner of thinking led to the famous "Strong Enough for a Man…" campaign line for the Secret antiperspirant brand, which launched in 1974 when Williams was Associate Creative Director. Once her superiors recognized that she understood the strategic aspects of creative advertising, they assigned her – with some trepidation – to the Secret brand, which was a poor-performing product in Procter and Gamble's brand portfolio. "When I was given that brand, Charlie Blakemore, who was my Executive Creative Director, begged me not to quit. No one used the product except little blue-haired women," Williams laughed (Hayes, 1999, p. 184). Sensing an opportunity to turn the brand around, she dug into the assignment. Williams (2014) offered her perspective and thought process behind the development of the Secret campaign:

> "When I started working on that brand, the depiction of women was that they were floating with the butterflies ... in slow motion through the forests ... or hanging with the girls in the beauty shop. These girls were totally non-active and they didn't work. Birds flew out of the trees and sat on their fingers. There was no hustle. And the prevailing belief was that women didn't sweat! Well I came out of a community where women sweat. They worked like dogs and they were moving quick, fast and in a [hurry]. There wasn't any cool attached to the way a black woman had to work. She was hauling groceries, hauling babies and hauling her butt, twenty-four seven. She invented the concept of multi-tasking. That was her life. As I was assigned to these commercials, I couldn't understand the depiction of women at all. So I created this campaign called 'Jack and Shirley.' And this woman had to have an antiperspirant that was as efficacious as a man's antiperspirant, but allowed her to be feminine, beautiful and who she wanted to be."

Williams' insights produced the advertising theme: "Strong enough for a man ... but made for a woman," which positioned the Secret brand directly for female consumers. The concept was compelling and the commercials and print ads featured younger, active women in modern settings (see Figure 5.2).

Williams also thought it would be a good idea to create different versions of the concept – not limited to white models – but also featuring black models in order to appeal to black women, recognizing the shifting social climate of the era and the growing appreciation of black consumers among mainstream marketers (Davis, 2013). Williams (2014) excitedly explained:

> "Procter and Gamble approved the concept and – at that time – we were doing what was called 'pools of three' – and I cast one of the commercials black. There were a lot of questions as to whether they were going to put that commercial on the air. Questions arose: 'Who told you to cast it black?' Who approved it? They're not going to put that on the air!' And they put it on the air – in 1974! People forget there were no black commercials on the air then. That Secret commercial for Proctor and Gamble broke that ceiling. So I give my client P&G much kudos. It was 1974!"

During the period of the Secret campaign, in addition to the shifting roles of black people in society, the social roles of women were also changing. The Women's Movement had commenced and, with it, the working career woman concept was starting to emerge – particularly for white women. From Williams' perspective, working outside of the home was no big deal because black women had always gone to work. "We didn't know any stay-at-home

Figure 5.2 Print and TV advertisements with Williams' "Strong Enough for a Man … but Made for a Woman" slogan for Secret brand antiperspirant featured white and black models in modern settings.

Source: *Redbook*, May 1977, p. 30. Courtesy of the Procter & Gamble Company. Reprinted with permission.

moms," she stated matter-of-factly. Williams (2014) continued: "The ones that stayed at home were the ones who couldn't get a job. But those [working] women had to manage their houses like they were stay-at-home moms. Those were highly-disciplined, focused women." This positioning for the brand resonated with women because – although they had more responsibilities – they still wanted to be seen as attractive. Thus, Williams tapped into women's desires to manage their work and personal lives effectively – to be seen as competent – yet feminine. The impact of the Secret campaign, which moved the brand into the number one position in the marketplace within six months, became a classic case study in successful advertising. Reflecting on the campaign's achievement, Williams (2014) elaborated:

> "I don't know that that's ever been done before or again. That whole concept made a lot of people pay attention. When you look at the case on the Secret brand, it became number one among white females and number one among black females. So being number one among white and black females made it number one in the nation. I don't know what it's doing now, but for about 25 years – that was it! When we began the exercise, Right Guard was number one and Ban was number two. Both of these were positioned as efficacious antiperspirants for men. It was my opinion that antiperspirants were more important to women moving into the workplace in order to have this presentation of excellence in their persons. Men with sweaty armpits was not an issue – especially blue collar men – because men sweated all the time. But women with sweaty armpits? That was a problem!"

While some industry observers attempted to attribute Williams' success with the Secret brand campaign to good fortune, Ken Smikle, President of *Target Market News*, a respected market research publication, analyzed the campaign and concluded (Alleyne, 2004):

> "That line is simplistic genius, which often gets confused with luck ... She learned the fundamental principles of good advertising from folks who really set the bar in the industry. Couple that with the sensibilities of a young African-American woman from Chicago and she literally created a new perspective in advertising that hadn't been seen before ... Carol's ability to consistently carve out nuggets of communicative genius really puts her in a place that very few other folks have been in this industry."

Un-cocooned: life after the Leo Burnett agency

Winning Advertising Woman of the Year in 1977 marked the beginning of a major transition period in Williams' life. The award attracted national attention and "agencies all over the country came after me," Williams (2014) remarked. Among those agencies were Foote, Cone, Belding and Honig (later FCB), which had offices in a number of cities, including San Francisco, California. Having visited San Francisco on many occasions and liking the city, she was also encouraged by advertising colleague Paul Frees, the voice of the Pillsbury Doughboy, who also loved the area. Eventually, she was recruited by FCB, which offered her a senior vice-presidency and the top position leading their creative department. She accepted the position and moved to the west coast in 1980, thus becoming the highest-ranking African-American woman in a general-market advertising agency. Some of her major work involved the Clorox account, where she and her team worked on brands including Clorox Liquid and Clorox II, a non-chlorine bleach. Like Secret antiperspirant, the brands were suffering from image problems and declining sales, but her efforts and leadership contributed to a turnaround and legitimization of the brands (Hayes, 1999).

However, the climate at FCB was nothing like the Leo Burnett agency and Williams experienced culture shock: "When I left Burnett, I just assumed – naively – that this is the way the ad business functions. Creativity is the focal point," Williams (2014) commented. "And when I went to FCB, I found a totally different environment. The environment was totally controlled by suits – it was all about the money. I assume it was about the money at Burnett, but to Burnett creative and money were synonymous," she surmised. Reflecting on the new atmosphere, Williams (2014) explained:

> "At Burnett it was all about the brilliance you could put on the air. I saw that the industry outside of Burnett was that they really didn't care what you put on the air. As long as you put something on the air, you could collect funds from the client. They were all about collecting money and if the client bought it – sell it – whether it was any good or not. I've seen people sell [creative ideas] to clients that they knew were problematic. Burnett had a culture where you were working for the brilliance of the creative and the integrity of the business. The money would follow the brilliance."

Another aspect of the FCB experience was the ill-treatment Williams (2014) observed and experienced:

> "I never experienced racism at Leo Burnett. I'm not saying there were not racists at Burnett and I would not say they did not have racist feelings toward me. But I think I was such a highly productive person that I really didn't give a care about racism. So once I un-cocooned myself from those guys, I was pretty shocked at what I saw and heard. I didn't know it existed."

Only able to tolerate the culture at FCB for about two years, Williams decided to leave the agency despite her stellar reputation and accomplishments. Although disenchanted with the experience at FCB, Williams met and dated her future husband, Dr. Tipkins Hood, while working there. An orthopedic surgeon and widower with a son, Tipkins, Jr., they wed on August 8, 1981. In September 1981, *Jet* magazine reported on their lavish garden wedding in Oakland, California, which included a two-day celebration. Their daughter, Carol Hood Jr., was born in June 1983. By then, Williams had left the advertising industry and settled into life as a wife and mother in California.

Carol H. Williams, entrepreneur

Over the next few years, Williams spent time traveling and caring for her family and had no plans to return to the advertising business. "I had turned a corner and closed a chapter in my life and had no intention of opening my own agency," Williams later told a reporter (Hayes, 1999, p. 186). However, shortly after her daughter was born, she started getting calls from former clients asking her to do projects for them. "Initially I wouldn't do them, but then I accepted one, and then another...," Williams (2014) explained. One early project was from a former client at Clorox who had gone to work for Computerland, a national retail computer store chain which was popular in the early days of the personal computer (Burns, 1994). Around 1984, Williams created a campaign slogan: "All you need to know about computers is Computerland" which capitalized on average consumers' general lack of knowledge about computing technology at home. Later, men with the Armour-Dial and Clorox companies hired Williams on a project basis to help them with their brands. Under this arrangement, Williams would conduct research, develop insights, determine positioning, plan strategy, and create test campaigns to introduce new products. Once the test campaigns were proven, the companies would then give the concepts to their full-service advertising agencies. Thus, Williams earned a good income and developed a reputation with Corporate America for creating innovative advertising that yielded results. However, she began to tire of creating concepts for brands and then seeing ad agency people get credit for her ideas. "I turn on the TV and some agency has my thinking and advertising on the air and are collecting millions. These [agencies] collect millions into perpetuity!" Williams (2014) exclaimed with exasperation.

Around this time, she was approached by a man from the Pacific Bell telephone company, commonly known as Pac Bell, before the Bell companies become part of the AT&T Corporation. Williams (2014) recalls: "He came to me and asked me if I knew how to do 'targeted advertising'." Recognizing "targeted advertising" as a code term for the black consumer market, Williams thought: "I'm black and I sure know advertising," so she said, chuckling: "Yeah! I can do it!" Although all of Williams' experience up until that time had concerned general-market advertising, Pac Bell's executives assumed Williams could do the "targeted advertising" they desired because she was black and had a reputation for producing effective advertising. It was also to their benefit that she was conveniently located on the West Coast near their offices, while many of the other black advertising professionals with good track records were located in the Midwest or East Coast, in places like Chicago and New York City.

New to the practice of ethnically targeted advertising, Williams (2014) explained:

> "I found out it was a lot harder than I thought it was, because when you really want to dig deep and understand the cultural insights, it's bigger than just

> functioning on the executional level or casting a person of color. There were certain issues in the marketplace and a lot of times mass market agencies don't realize that it's much deeper."

However, Pac Bell, recognizing that African-American consumers are major consumers of telecommunications products, wanted to pursue the market aggressively. Familiarizing herself with research on black consumers and telecommunication products, Williams (2014) discovered:

> "Pac Bell wanted to recognize and pursue consumers in the world of telecommunications, where blacks are the trendsetters. They are on the forefront. Their indices when it comes to the consumption of telephones and all those applications that are viable to telephones is that they are the leading consumers. In those days, it was about call-waiting, caller identification and so on. If you were black, you had to have [those services and applications] and Pac Bell had the research to prove this. If white people spent two minutes on the telephone, African-Americans were spending eight or ten minutes. Three-way calling? That was our family reunion in those days."

The Pac Bell assignment gave Williams an opportunity to take the skills she learned as a top-level provider on general-market corporate brands and translate them to targeted advertising directed at black consumers. It also started a long and fruitful relationship with Pac Bell and Bell companies as clients. Her reputation and name – arguably the most prominent among black advertising professionals on the West Coast at the time – established the foundation for an enterprise which would expand and thrive in the years to come.

"Whose eyes?" The Carol H. Williams Agency

In 1986, Williams invested $40,000 in savings and launched CHWA, which started out in her living room with a handful of employees (Bridgeforth, 2002). Her family was supportive of the venture and her financial situation was such that she did not need to draw a salary for a couple of years and could therefore invest all the earnings back into the business (Sivulka, 2009, p. 339).

Sensing a need to communicate in innovative and insightful ways on the basis of comprehensive strategic planning, the agency's philosophy centered on meaningful understandings about brands' opportunities in the marketplace among relevant target consumers. This point of view formed the basis for the agency's motto and trademarked phrase: "Whose Eyes Are You Looking Through When You View the World?" which originated in 1991 and was communicated prominently in all of the agency's promotional materials. Believing her agency to be capable of serving the needs of all advertisers, Williams decided to position the agency as "a full service advertising agency that specializes in developing strategic marketing plans and creating breakthrough advertising for the African American market," according to an agency fact sheet (Carol H. Williams Advertising Agency, 2002). The "Whose Eyes..." platform not only provided a foundation for the development of a variety of marketing strategies within CHWA, but also served as a point of differentiation for the agency, relative to other advertising firms. The concept suggests that multicultural consumer groups, such as black consumers, often draw on attitudes, values, and behaviors which differ from those within the broader mass market consumer segments. Williams (2014) explained:

> "You are really digging deep when you target cultural markets. General-market advertising is just that – it's general. When [we] look at research, [we] look at it through our eyes and our knowledge base. Oftentimes – which is very uncomfortable for mass market people – [African-Americans] use language differently. It IS coded. And so – the deeper you go – the more it's coded. A lot of times when they are sitting in focus interview groups – they are trying to justify how to [cater to] our markets. They will ask inside a focus interview group to a black [participant] – 'would you rather see an all-black commercial or an integrated commercial?' Well of course – African-Americans in this society, in this environment, with our sensitivities, with the dangers we know and the 'watch-outs' – are going to say 'integrated commercials' because that's what's politically correct to say. But when you look at our viewing habits – other than sports and a couple of other shows – it will consistently show that [African-Americans] watch all black shows. They resonate very highly on our [viewing] lists and usually are primary shows – just like any other culture."

Explaining how creative insights are derived for purposes of targeting African-Americans and other multicultural audiences, Williams likens the understanding of consumer segments in ways similar to how anthropologists study their subjects by immersing themselves in their subjects' environments. For example, African-Americans often use common English words and expressions in inventive and unexpected ways, which are unfamiliar to those outside of black culture, in a process known as "coding." Williams (2014) reveals:

> "When we look at research – and the way that we spin [language] – the way we use it, the way we code it, and then have to decode it and re-code it to be applicable in that market, we can consistently make messages that are very powerful in the African-American community. We're just not recognized by the mass market. [General-market agencies] would rather talk in a generalized fashion to all groups and use blacks in situational [manners] coupled with whites because they believe that's who we are. So, they [convey] absolutely no awareness of the fact that blacks – like Asians and others – live inside these black and Asian and Hispanic groups and are very comfortable within them. It is not reflective of anything that is negative or necessarily racial. It just reflects how usually these cultural groups are. It is what it is."

Over time, CHWA would expand its specialization to articulate a "multicultural" and "urban" market orientation, in addition to focus on African-American consumer markets, as indicated on the agency's internet website.

The "Welcome" page of the CHWA website states the following (carolhwilliams.com, 2014):

> "Our approach seeks to understand the Multicultural perspective with product branding. As a matter of discipline, we identify both the similarities and differences between the alternative narrative and its general-market counterpart. Our work leverages the uniqueness of the Multicultural point of view in order to create the strongest affinity between the consumer and the brand, while remaining true to its essence."

In offering its services to clients and prospects, CHWA also developed a trademarked proprietary marketing approach entitled "Selling to and Through" which seeks to increase sales in the general consumer market by communicating with a core African-American consumer market (Carol H. Williams Advertising Agency, 2002, p. 2). This approach has been particularly effective in product categories where African-American and urban consumers – those who typically live in major U.S. cities – are the main consumers or trendsetters within certain brand or product categories. At the same time, CHWA's experience is that ads targeted at African-Americans are just as effective with general-market consumers, but general-market ads are less effective with African-Americans (Carol H. Williams Advertising Agency, 2002, p. 2). Using this approach, CHWA's strategy was successful in helping many clients to achieve or even exceed their marketing objectives. For example, in the late 1980s, Pacific Bell experienced a 9 percent increase in Universal telephone service customers after CHWA began targeting black consumers; and met its nine-month revenue goal in only two months after its Call Return campaign attracted a wide variety of consumers (Hayes, 1999). Moreover, a television ad for Walt Disney Parks titled "Signs" had tremendous appeal beyond the black consumer market. The touching commercial featured an African-American boy as he recounts his day at a Disney theme park with his hearing-impaired grandfather using sign language (Harris, 2008). Using sophisticated computer animation, the boy's expressiveness is so compelling that his experiences literally come alive in the grandfather's mind. Released in 2007, the spot was rated the number one commercial of the year among *all* consumers, according to IAG Research and *Advertising Age* (Fora. TV, 2008). Addressing the selling approach, Williams (2014) explains:

> "In order to find insights that particularly resonate with a target group – but that also allow you to target that group – insight must resonate *to and through* that group to other groups. That [strategy] is particularly brilliant and often happens when you target the African-American market. Many African-American agencies have been heralded for identifying insights. But even though you go through the African-American market to get it, it impacts other markets. We have seen huge results from that [approach]. The thing is, it is not top of mind necessarily or [clients] can't get it when they go through the general-market. They only get it when they go through the African-American markets."

Strategically creative: the CHWA business approach

Over the years, the agency's approaches and reputation attracted top-tier accounts, resulting in a client roster which grew in size, prestige, and billings and representing a wide variety of brands (see Table 5.1). These assignments consisted of communications aimed at African-American, multicultural, urban, and – sometimes – general-market consumers. *Black Enterprise* magazine, the leading U.S. publication covering black-owned businesses, twice named CHWA its "Advertising Agency of the Year" in 1999 and 2004 (Hayes, 1999; Alleyne, 2004). Each June, *Black Enterprise* publishes an annual issue devoted to the largest black-owned firms in the United States including the top black-owned advertising agencies. Since 1998, the year that the list of black-owned advertising firms was reinstated, CHWA was consistently listed among the top seven black-owned agencies in the country. Moreover, between 2004 and 2010, Williams' agency ranked number two on the list, trailing only GlobalHue as the nation's largest black-owned advertising firm.

Much of CHWA's success was attributed to its overall marketing approach, often referred to as "strategically creative" and infused into the agency culture by Williams. The head of a major market research firm commented: "She is a strategic creator. Many people think that creative is enough to sell a brand, but Carol is grounded in what makes brands grow and sell" (Hayes, 1999, p. 182). Williams was cited for insightful creative work and problem-solving, comprising a balance between the "magic" – the messaging aspect that resonates with consumers – and the "logic" – the component that builds the brand image and sells the product (Alleyne, 2004, p. 194). Industry observers

Table 5.1 Roster of selected Carol H. Williams Advertising accounts

AARP	Luster Products
Allstate Insurance	Marriott
California Dept. of Health Services (Tobacco Control; Black Infant Health)	McNeil Nutritionals (Lactaid Milk)
California Public Utilities Commission	McNeil Pharmaceuticals (St. Joseph Aspirin)
California State Lottery	Nationwide Insurance
Cingular Wireless	Nissan North America
Coca-Cola	Oakland Airport/Port
Colgate-Palmolive	Oakland Healthy Start
Coors Brewing Co.	Pacific Bell/SBC/Southwestern Bell
Crown Royal	Pfizer
Disney Channel/Walt Disney Company	Procter & Gamble
Frito-Lay	Starwood Hotels & Resorts
FX Network	Summit Laboratories
Gallo Winery	Universal Studios Home Entertainment
General Mills	University of California – Davis Medical Center
General Motors	U.S. Army
Hewlett-Packard	VISA
Kmart	Washington Mutual
Kraft	Wells Fargo

suggest it is rare to find individuals who are highly adept at both the creative and business sides of advertising. Regarding her work as a craft, Williams sees creativity as a highly intellectual pursuit requiring passion, communication, clarity, and courage as components of the creative process (Alleyne, 2004). She told *Black Enterprise* (Hayes, 1999, p. 188):

> "I love what I do. It's fun, but it's also extremely rough. Digging deep for the insights is one thing, coming up against clients who also struggle to recognize the vitality and viability of this market, nor invest money in it to impact the bottom line [is another]. A lot of them believe all black people want to be white and question the need for so-called African-American insight. But there's no room for a mental lapse when a client's brand is riding on your back. Nothing gets my adrenaline going more than turning a brand around. Selling a product is based on insightful thinking and breakthrough ads. If you can master that, you can master the art of advertising."

The work

The strategic approach utilized by CHWA set the agency on a long path of significant accomplishments. These included a 1996 campaign for the Nissan Maxima automobile which increased prospective customers' consideration intentions by 100 percent, according to Nissan (Hayes, 1999, p. 186). In 1997, CHWA introduced "Electric Man," a computer-generated animated character for the California Public Utilities Commission (CPUC) intended to inform black consumers about upcoming deregulation of the investor-owned utility. Given research that showed consumers regarded the utility commission as a "big, predatory governmental entity," the character was successful in humanizing the image of the brand while explaining available options for consumers (Kelly, 1997, p. 5). The "Electric Man" television commercial was so effective that CPUC decided to expand the concept to other media.

In 1998, CHWA acquired the Coors Brewing account and helped to rehabilitate the brand's reputation among African-Americans (Kelly, 1998). Suffering from flat sales and image problems related to rumors associating the brand with past bigotry (Cole and Brantley, 2014), the agency developed an effective messaging approach. It also recruited a celebrity – actor Jamie Foxx – to appear in Coors Light commercials and marketing events at a modest cost prior to him becoming an Oscar-winning megastar (Williams, 2014). Where black celebrities had been reluctant to endorse the brand given its image problems, others like wealthy hip-hop artist Dr. Dre were subsequently willing to participate in advertising for the Coors brand and Coors distributors were also enthusiastic about the agency's work (Hayes, 1999).

CHWA's successful trajectory continued into the new millennium as it attracted major corporate brands, contributing to the growth and reputation of the agency. The agency became the first black-owned agency of record for the Washington Mutual Company and several Procter & Gamble brands (Hayes, 2004). This accomplishment was important since the agency of record purchases all advertising media for clients, often on behalf of other agencies, thereby boosting its total billings and stature among agencies. The agency handled new accounts including Cingular Wireless, the Westin and Sheraton hotels, and St. Joseph's children's aspirin for McNeil Pharmaceuticals, promoting a heart health aspirin regimen for black adults (Harris, 2005; Hayes, 2004). CHWA landed an assignment for the lactose-free Lactaid brand milk in 2004, charged with persuading African-American women to try it. Although research indicated that 75 percent of the black population is lactose-intolerant, African-Americans continued to consume traditional dairy products due to their taste and sensory appeal. The agency created a test ad titled "Pass those cookies," which spoke to the problem and overcame objections in a believable way. The test concept was evaluated as the second most highly rated ad among 1,500 in a research company's database, leading to adoption of the idea by the client (Osterman, 2007, p. 44). In 2006, the agency won an Effie and a "Best in Show" award by the Insurance Marketing and Communications Association for its "Our Stand" commercial featuring actor Dennis Haysbert for Allstate. The commercial increased awareness of Allstate insurance by 72 percent among young African-Americans and significantly increased the share of those considering the brand for insurance coverage (Osterman, 2007, p. 45).

The agency scored a coup in 2002 when it landed the lucrative African-American consumer advertising account for GM Corporation, valued at $20–30 million in billings (Halladay, 2002). The GM account was three to five times the size of its Nissan client, which had to be resigned to avoid a conflict of interests. Acquisition of the GM account, with responsibility for several brands and regions, pushed the agency to another level, enabling it to generate billings consistently beyond the $100 million range each year. For a number of years beginning in 2002, CHWA was the second largest among all black-owned agencies. Thus, CHWA could utilize prominent celebrities in its advertising for high-end brands such as boxing legend Muhammad Ali for the Yukon Denali (see Figure 5.3) and entertainer Mos Def for its "Poetry in Motion" Envoy Denali campaign.

Other CHWA ads presented GM brands relevant to African-American consumers in manners consistent with their language and lifestyles (see Figure 5.4). In 2010, GM assigned CHWA its Cadillac business for African-American luxury car buyers (Wentz, 2010). Noting the agency's experience with luxury vehicles, Joel Ewanick, GM's Vice President of U.S. Marketing, commented: "We need to tell the Cadillac story to affluent, urban consumers in ways that are relevant to them" (*Target Market News*, 2010).

Committed to strategic marketing which produces results, Williams' agency typically shunned clients who merely sought to put black faces in general-market campaigns or do public relations advertising. Williams told *Black Enterprise* in 1999, "I don't want those kinds of clients or 'civil rights' ads. I am looking to build brands. Unfortunately, many clients don't come to minority agencies to do that" (Hayes, 1999, p. 188). Williams also believes

Figure 5.3 Ad for GMC Yukon Denali featuring Muhammad Ali by the Carol H. Williams Advertising agency.

Source: *Ebony*, April 2003, p. 57. Courtesy of General Motors Corporation. Reprinted with permission.

Figure 5.4 Ad for GMC Envoy featuring African-American couple by the Carol H. Williams Advertising agency.

Source: *Ebony*, March 2004, p. 38. Courtesy of General Motors Corporation. Reprinted with permission.

that like-mindedness is important to the agency–client relationship. She terminated a lucrative relationship with Bank of America when they couldn't agree on the correct approach for a campaign. Williams explained (Alleyne, 2004, p. 192): "It was not a comfortable situation. A huge client, but I have a philosophy that compatibility, and being able to advance who you are as a person is essential in my life. I don't do what I do just for the money."

CHWA culture

As the business expanded, the fledgling agency outgrew the family living room and Williams expanded staff and moved to leased office space. By the 1990s CHWA was located high in a large office building overlooking Merritt Lake in Oakland, California (Hayes, 1999). CHWA opened a second major office in 2004 in Williams' hometown of Chicago, located on Michigan Avenue in the vibrant downtown business district; and later opened satellite offices in New York and Detroit to service various accounts. According to Williams, the CHWA workplace environment represents a "celebratory, yet peaceful and intellectual environment"

(Alleyne, 2004, p. 190) conveying sophistication with a bit of whimsy, decorated in rich jewel tones like maroon, deep green, royal blue, and lots and lots of purple. Contemporary and African art adorn the walls and a modernized 1950s-style jukebox plays music of a variety of genres – R&B, jazz, soul, and rap. Photos of Williams and family members, celebrities, dignitaries, and leaders – including the President of the United States – are on prominent display. Plaques and statues representing nearly every type of advertising industry award and community service recognition are exhibited in the glass-tabled conference room.

The CHWA staff is a multicultural mix comprising peoples of various backgrounds – male and female, African-American, African, Italian, Hispanic, Asian, and from the Caribbean – who have attended schools all over the country from Harvard to Morehouse (Alleyne, 2004). Believing that creativity and keen intellect go hand-in-hand, key employees are provided a high degree of independence and are expected to meet high expectations and deliver exceptional client service (Alleyne, 2004). Some long-time staffers have been with the agency 20 years or more and several members of Williams' family work for the company. The size of the staff increased from a handful of employees at the inception of the agency to as many as 173 in 2006 according to *Black Enterprise* annual reports. That number fluctuated when clients reduced advertising budgets during a major recession around 2008 and other problems such as GM's highly publicized bankruptcy filing in 2009. GM subsequently emerged from bankruptcy with the help of a loan from the federal government. During these circumstances, the agency maintained an optimistic outlook and reputation. A global marketing officer for Procter & Gamble praised Williams and CHWA, saying:

> "She is a charismatic leader. The character of [her office], the feel, the spirit … the whole culture blew me away while I was there. There's clearly a high level of energy and engagement and rapport and harmony. It's what you need in an agency to deliver outstanding work."
>
> (Alleyne, 2004, p. 192)

The vision and legacy of Carol H. Williams

A marathon can be defined as a long-lasting or difficult task or operation of a specified kind. As CEO, Chief Creative Officer, and founder of CHWA, Williams has distinguished herself as a long-distance runner in an industry which is notoriously difficult for African-American women. One year, as an anniversary gift to her staff, Williams provided CHWA employees with signed athletic shoes, underscoring the "agility of mind and fleet of feet" prowess associated with long-term endurance and performance (Shot Callers, 2007). As such, her agency has been consistently recognized as one of the most successful black-owned agencies in the history of advertising. Regarded as an icon, Williams is recognized as an advertising industry visionary, adviser, and mentor. Her advertising agency remains the largest in the world that is 100 percent black-owned, woman-owned, *and* independent. Unlike most of the top long-surviving, black-owned agencies, Williams insisted on remaining independent, resisting the calls to sell a large share of her firm to a large media and marketing holding company or merge with another entity. However, she acknowledges the complications created by the new configurations in the advertising industry, explaining (Williams, 2014):

> "These acquisitions and alliances are creating a highly different environment, where media-impacted dollars are used to purchase relationships that cannot be forged by agencies like mine. The segmentation of media from the mass-market agencies, in which they relocated this business to their subsidiaries and holding companies, has always, in my opinion, been a strategy to block smaller agencies from being able to qualify and thus profit. It definitely makes it more difficult."

Williams has been presented with nearly every award and recognition bestowed within the advertising industry and black business community and the trade press has long taken note of her accomplishments. For example, *Advertising Age* praised Williams in a 2002 Special Section titled "Women to Watch" where she was the only African-American featured (Cuneo, 2002). *Essence*, a magazine aimed at African-American women, ran an inspirational article featuring Williams titled "How I Made a Million" (Bridgeforth, 2002). In 2009, the Minority Executive Enterprise Council named her as one of the "50 Most Powerful Minority CEOs & Corporate Executives" in the nation, which included recognition by the U.S. Congress. In 2015, the well-respected AARP (formerly the American Association of Retired Persons) organization and the *Network Journal* magazine, named her as one of 25 "Most Influential Black Women in Business" (*Network Journal*, 2015). Beyond these recognitions, Williams is also involved in community service and uses her resources to aid dozens of philanthropic organizations including the Congressional Black Caucus, the NAACP, the Rainbow/PUSH Coalition, the Oakland Bay Area Links, the U.S. Dream Academy, the National Newspaper Publishers Association, and several Chicago-area and California community groups, and religious and educational organizations, such as a Silicon Valley group which promotes STEM training for youth.

As the keynote speaker on the occasion of receiving a major honor from the respected University of Missouri School of Journalism for service to the advertising profession, Williams was introduced as having "broken through racial barriers and battled sexism to reach the pinnacle of the advertising industry, while still managing to raise wonderful and successful children and cultivate a loving marriage" (Judge, 2006). "Carol Williams is not only a brilliantly successful advertising entrepreneur and creative director, but also an inspiration" said the program's chairperson (Judge, 2006). Among the success secrets shared by the outspoken CEO, Williams (2014) comments: "Challenges are well-disguised opportunities." She encourages women to learn to handle opportunities saying: "When the door opens, you've got to move through it – bust it down if necessary!" (Bridgeforth, 2002, p. 189).

Confessions of an advertising woman

In light of the recognitions and accolades Williams has received, it would appear that she was able to circumvent most of the problems that have vexed other agencies established by African-Americans and by black women in particular. Yet, she shares some unsettling situations when her authenticity or legitimacy were questioned. For example, Williams (2014) reflects on questions regarding the status of her business:

> "I went through a period in my life – which makes me somewhat uncomfortable to talk about – where certain clients didn't hire me because I was black. They hired me because I was very good and produced results. It wasn't about civil rights duty. It wasn't about feeling good or any of that stuff. It was about that this woman here can put advertising on the air that impacts the bottom line. And its why a lot of those companies hired me and I never had to go through those [minority] portals. A black woman told me point-blank to my face one time: 'I don't think you are black-owned, because you are not registered anywhere in those minority vendor programs."

Referring to pressures from Civil Rights organizations prompting advertising agencies and their clients to utilize minority media and vendors, registries and directories were established which allowed marketers to easily identify minority-owned providers. Speaking about an incident that occurred in the late 1980s, Williams (2014) continued:

> "This woman came to my office and was asking me a bunch of questions. She had the problem that all of these companies she approached would make her fill out all of this minority paperwork to satisfy [criteria] as a minority vendor. She said to me, 'you never did that. Why don't you do that? You're not registered as a minority vendor for – hypothetically – AT& T.' And I said – 'well I've done work for AT&T (Pac Bell) for a very long time' and then I referenced my career at Burnett and Foote, Cone and Belding. That just blew right past her. She wasn't hearing that. That woman sat in my office, in my face and said, 'well I think you're just a front for some white agency. You are not black-owned, because why don't you do these things?' Then I reacted in a way that I shouldn't have. I took it as an insult and I told her to get up and get out of my office."

Williams (2014) remembers other situations when she was confronted with racist remarks or behaviors inside predominately white organizations, although her temperament allowed her to cope with such circumstances calmly. Sharing one incident and explaining her reaction, she recalls:

> "You get impacted constantly with statements of ignorance and racism which I think they really don't know is ignorant and racist. Or they may just be pushing your buttons. But whatever they are doing, whatever it is, it's not worthy of my attention. There was a woman inside this company – she was a white female – she said to me: 'Carol, don't you think blacks were happier when they were

> slaves?' And I asked: 'why do you think that?' She said: 'Well, they were always laughing and singing.' Now my thinking was – in my environment growing up, the only time I saw black people break out in song was when the preacher would call for it in church. So for her to articulate something like that was the epitome of ignorance to me. I looked at her and said: 'You need to stop watching so much television' – and I walked away. But if she actually believes that blacks were walking around picking cabbage out of a garden and singing, then that's her problem – it's not going to be mine. That is not my responsibility in life. These kinds of things are prevalent throughout these companies. Whether they are intentional, whether they are done to intimidate or insult you – I have no idea. And I really don't care. It's not my issue and I'm not fighting that battle."
>
> (Williams, 2014)

While Williams chose not to engage in conflicts concerning insensitive behaviors of individuals in marketing organizations, she is an activist for fair treatment and respect for African-American consumers and business owners in the marketplace. For example, at the 2011 annual Rainbow/PUSH convention in Chicago, she publicly criticized major brands including Nike, Visa, Burger King, and Clorox for reducing black and urban media buys and agency contracts and not supporting causes important to the black community (Hughes, 2011). She commented:

> "The big thing in the industry is that you look at certain products that are multi-million dollar lines on the shelf, and the predominant contributor to them being multi-million dollar lines are the African-Americans. But they still will not invest into the black community on any meaningful level by contributing to a black-owned agency or other black-owned business."

Williams offered firsthand insight on the Clorox brand, drawing on her observations when she worked with the company in the 1980s and noticed that they were "not preoccupied with or interested in hiring any minorities" (Williams, 2014). Indicating that African-Americans are the primary consumers for brands like Clorox, she urged attendees to make these companies more accountable to their consumer bases, arguing (Hughes, 2011):

> "Our pain is that you don't understand your power. I understand that the Clorox Company excels because we contribute to its bottom line. Who do you think buys bleach that is the multi-billion dollar product that Clorox sells? Bleach is the pillar of their whole industry. Clorox is moving billions of dollars through yet, 42 percent of bleach is bought by African Americans and another 27 percent is bought by Hispanics. When you look at the Caucasian consumption of bleach, it's less than 18 percent.
>
> Most of all, the majority of African-Americans have a bottle of Pine Sol in their homes – I don't have to look in their cabinets. I can look at the numbers. African-Americans buy 82 percent of Pine Sol. Who sells Pine Sol? Clorox. The brand manager is white; the assistant brand manager is white and [so is] the brand manager over the brand manager, the media manager. [And] you people demand nothing of

> this company. The only black person I ever saw at Clorox was me and the receptionist. We have to create a situation that supports Reverend Jackson, and we have to figure out how to do that strategically, because our community will never be uplifted if we don't demand more of these companies."

Interestingly, the Clorox Company found itself embroiled in a negative public relations firestorm in 2015 when it released a comment via the Twitter social media platform in response to the Apple company's release of racially diverse emojis — iconic representations of people used in electronic messages – featuring a variety of skin tones. Clorox's Twitter comment said: "New emojis are alright, but where's the bleach?" (Visconti and Estrada, 2015). Backlash ensued over social and traditional media, with many observers interpreting the comment as racist and questioning whether Clorox was implying that the emojis should be bleached white. At the same time, information about the lack of employee diversity within the Clorox Corporation was publicized, heightening the criticism directed at the company. In response to the incident, Clorox issued an apology: "Wish we could bleach away our last tweet. Didn't mean to offend" (Visconti and Estrada, 2015).

Williams' personality and fortitude may explain how she has been able to succeed in the advertising business over the long haul. Articulating her position, "From the time I was a very young kid, I was inundated with forces that told me what I couldn't do as a black and a woman" (Ellis, 2004). "I love kicking [that notion] in the butt!" she exclaimed. Unable to provide a response as to whether she has faced more challenges in the advertising profession as an African-American *or* as a woman, she explained (Williams, 2014): "I do not know if I can aptly answer that question since all I have ever been is a black female and there are certain areas where I don't know how to separate it." However, she believes that people of color often have difficulty fitting into advertising organizations because the industry has not been conditioned to tolerate diversity. "You have to really find yourself in the midst of some very exceptional people and exceptional men in order to find yourself a compatible fit," Williams (2014) concluded. Moreover, recently Williams was invited to participate in the 3% Conference, an organization dedicated to the advancement of women in advertising. Williams (2014) recalled:

> "At this conference I was recognized as this phenomenon because I was one of the very few women and blacks that had reached the level in the advertising industry that I had. I found out what the '3% Conference' means: of the creative directors and executives, less than three percent of them are women. Having [worked] in this business in the early '70s and fought this fight, I was pretty doggone shocked to find out in 2013 it still is that way! When I came into the business, everybody who ran the business was a man. *Mad Men* is not a figment of the imagination. They were all white males. But it was accepted because that's the way it was. So any of us who were moving through that venue as females – or anything else – were looked at very strangely. There were very few if any women. No Asians and no Hispanics that I could recognize. Now I get to this

'3% Conference' and find out that the business is still functioning that way. Although on the lower level there are more women – primarily white women. And then when you get to the top level, it's less than one percent."

Williams acknowledges the trade-offs that women – especially mothers – must make to be successful in the advertising business. She conveyed to a reporter how her daughter spent more time in her office than in play yards when CHWA was a new company. "That's hard," she admitted (Sivulka, 2009, p. 339) and lamented the fact that she did not have time to have five children like her mother. She also thinks that many of the young women coming up in the business do not really understand the passion and commitment involved in reaching the top. Williams (2014) advises: "to be a top ten talent, you are working 100%, 24-7. You've got to put the time in." On women adapting to advertising agency culture, Williams (2014) opines:

"Now there are all kinds of excuses as to why women can't make it on the upper levels: the [biological] clock gets' em – wanting to have children, get married – all that stuff. Other things become a priority to them. To get to those top levels [the work] has got to be a primary priority. There's sacrifice."

Perspectives on issues facing black-owned advertising agencies

Despite her business successes and personal triumphs, Williams is keenly aware of the challenges that confront black-owned agencies collectively and make them vulnerable as viable enterprises. Williams does not believe that minority-owned agencies *must* assume a specialist orientation in order to survive, but understands the historical context of the issue and why most have done so. "There are a multiplicity of different problems," she acknowledges, citing difficulties which are germane to black-owned agencies. One problem she identifies is talent raids – whereby general-market agencies lure away top talent from black agencies to lead multicultural efforts in their own firms – making it difficult for the black agencies to maintain consistency in terms of their creative look and output. Ironically, the individuals that are drawn away often find it difficult to progress in the new agencies and are unhappy when they run into career roadblocks. Black agencies also face the problem of losing their share of "multicultural" advertising dollars when marketing budgets are shifted away from African-American consumers in favor of those catering to Hispanics (Hayes, 2003). This problem was exacerbated after the 2000 U.S. Census showed the Hispanic population to outnumber the size of the black population. Williams (2014) notes with frustration:

"Now it is a most insidious platform if they say that this budget contains $100 million dollars – and a million of it will go to the African-American market and 10 million of it will go to the Hispanic market. I would ask – 'Why is 10 million of it going to the Hispanic market?' They answer 'Well, there are more of them.'

> And I say – 'but they aren't buying your product. You know those Hispanics are not going to buy your product.' And African-Americans are spending $1.3 trillion in consumer goods. Hispanics don't spend $1 trillion, yet. So why is their dollar more valuable? And why is it that you look at 'we vs. them'? Why isn't it us vs. whites? I'm not quite understanding this paradigm you're creating here."

Other phenomena comprise serious threats to the survival of black and minority-owned agencies. Namely, limited capital resources and financial partnerships put many black agencies at a considerable disadvantage in the modern era which is characterized by marketing and media company mergers and holding company conglomerates with significant cash and resources. Williams (2014) notes: "The model for what an agency is and does was established by the mass market companies." Therefore, if an agency is to be viable, it must have ongoing income and considerable capital resources. Lacking such resources or access through strategic partnerships puts many black-owned agencies in a vulnerable position. Williams (2014) explains:

> "The mass market [holding] companies invested in media companies, because that's how you really make money. They then set these media companies apart – which most of them own. And then they set up all of these criteria – for clients and agencies – by which [an agency] could then qualify to buy media. So in order to buy media for a hypothetical company – let's say they want to spend $10, $15 or $20 million in the African-American market. They require you to have $30 million in the bank to be able to do this. The African-American agencies don't have the resources to meet these criteria. Under these circumstances you are sufficiently pushing all of us [black agencies] out of the arena. You've got to have $350 million dollars to back [minority agencies] for running this media business through your company. That's the way they block African-Americans from playing in that game. The largest media company in the country is Starcom. Starcom is owned by Publicis which owns Burnett and other firms. Most [mass media agencies] are not doing that, but a bunch of them are. Those companies are all owned by the same people."

In addition to issues concerning capital resources, Williams (2014) describes how multicultural agencies are treated differently from general-market agencies in terms of work assignments and financial commitments from clients. Commonly, a marketing idea for minority consumers will be developed by a minority-owned agency and – once the advertiser understands the consumer behavior insights and the principles underlying the concept – will assign it to their general-market agency for incorporation into their campaigns, calling it "efficiency" (Williams, 2014). At the same time, the budget allocated for minority segments is decreased, thereby reducing the revenues earned by the minority-owned agency. Moreover, Williams maintains that advertising clients have historically had financial obligations to their general-market agencies, particularly when those firms are the agency of record. Williams (2014) explains:

> "I came up during the era when it was constantly told to me that [clients] have a responsibility to their ad agencies that they are profitable. They had reliance that their relationships on the client side were [committed] to help them grow. Our clients don't feel that responsibility for us. They really don't care if we are profitable or not. It's our problem. What I feel is that most African-American agencies haven't found a mass market company that is committed to the growth of their business. African-American [agencies] seldom get the infusion of capital from these clients that allow them to improve and increase their resources."

Williams identifies a final critical issue which potentially undermines multicultural agencies – a shift toward a marketing communications approach known as the "total market strategy." With this approach, general-market agencies cast models of all ethnicities in their marketing campaigns to provide an appeal that is diverse in appearance. Williams (2014) explains:

> "On the surface it is a strategy which has been created by mass market agencies on the basis that it is inclusive. So it is actually a very brilliant kind of 'look.' It is supposed to – instead of being general-market which primarily talks to whites/ Caucasians – be positioned as a strategy that includes the total market. So it talks to everyone. And it's very inclusive. I think it is a rebranding of the old mass market strategy. And the objective of it is to reduce the number of dollars that have moved from the mass market agencies and gone to ethnic agencies to do ethnic strategies. So its primary purpose is to keep the money where it always was – with the mass-market agencies."

Williams (2014) argues that a problem with the "total market strategy" approach is that it fails to produce cultural cues and nuances which resonate with consumers of color. However, clients may be content with this approach in that it reduces overall advertising expenditures, meets marketing objectives at a satisfactory level, and creates the appearance of diversity – which is important to the companies' images and reputations. Williams (2014) continues:

> "Instead of you seeing an all-white commercial, you will see a primarily white commercial with one black in it sitting next to a white female or an Asian. It appears to be inclusive and integrated – but the bottom line is that it says: 'Mr. Client, by casting this way we have now addressed the total market so you need not take any of this mass market budget and spend it with a minority agency in order to speak directly to them.' Now it will be argued that's not what it supposed to do, but it doesn't matter ... because the result is the same. It really is all about the money – and where the money goes. It is a very interesting and very brilliant strategy, but it can successfully negate the reason why you do business with a targeted agency."

Mentorship and advice

Williams' insider knowledge and extensive industry experience make her sought after as a counselor, teacher, and mentor. She exposes others to methods and practices which are instrumental to the practice of strategic, innovative, and effective creative work – the art and science of the advertising craft. Her staff is steeped in her business philosophy and the agency culture is regarded as one where individuals – if willing to work hard – can learn and grow. There is heavy emphasis on testing and measurement of advertising concepts and the use of technology to perform business functions. Williams has been known to offer scathing critiques of creative work and business pitches, a trait which is likely a carry-over from her Leo Burnett days and the type of feedback that was offered in that environment. A former intern advises: "Make sure you catch the vision of the Matriarch herself" (Glassdoor.com, 2014) to get the most out of the opportunity at CHWA. The agency maintains an internship program which provides opportunities to students of all backgrounds from inside and outside of the U.S. The interactive and participatory culture at the agency underscores a lesson Carol Williams once learned from her father. She recalls being at a baseball game with him in Chicago when a player got upset over a call and was subsequently thrown out of the game. Her father said: "Now that guy right there – that's a fool – because he's out of the game. No matter what the issue, don't ever get sent to the bench. Only if you stay in the game, can you ever win" he advised (Shot Callers, 2007).

In advising young people of color who are interested in advertising agency careers, Williams (2014) offers the following:

> "Making relationships that are sustainable from people who are on the client side is important. Get involved with people who are committed to your growth, that are committed to you being successful. You in turn are committed to them being successful. Exchange information that will allow them to move up the ladder. This is paramount because once you have those kinds of relationships, it becomes circular, it becomes sustainable."

Williams (2014) continued:

> "Every growing company is going to make mistakes and is going to have employees who make mistakes because we're learning the business. There are always those 'hidden problems' that you consistently run in to. If you don't have a partner as a client, it will knock the hell out of you. Usually with the minority agency – one mistake – you're out the door. They don't give you a second chance. Whereas with the mass market agency, they can screw up all kind of money, all kind of effort, but the relationship has been made on such a level that it absorbs it and moves on."

What is the legacy of Carol H. Williams? Retired agency entrepreneur Tom Burrell once commented that a problem with many small businesses is that they do not survive past the principal's departure (*Small Business Magazine*, 2008). However, Williams has carefully considered the future of her agency and has a solid plan of succession in place. She has a goal of not only continuing the CHWA as an independent minority-owned firm, but also creating a new generation of young millionaires steeped in the craft of groundbreaking strategic advertising and marketing. At this writing, the future of the CHWA seems optimistic. Over Williams' long career in advertising, she has leveraged her talents, training, and relationships to develop knowledge, understanding, and wisdom which can be imparted for the benefit of others.

Carol's daughter

Carol Hood, Jr., the only daughter of Carol H. Williams, grew up watching her mother make history and therefore knew better than to accept the white-washed version of the advertising industry conveyed via mainstream media. On Mother's Day 2014, she posted a tribute to her mother on the Facebook social media site, writing about hearing her mother's stories of the advertising business and her prescience regarding the future, stating:

> "My whole life my mother has shown foresight, brilliance, the ability to read between the lines and predict the future so frighteningly so that if this were Salem, she'd surely been burned at the stake.
>
> People ask me why I don't care for *Mad Men*. Why should I? When I can call this woman and listen to her stories and know that there is a woman – an African American woman at that – who has out Mad Man'd anything AMC could ever imagine to put on television.
>
> So if anything, Mom (Carol) thanks for ruining that show for me. I love you!"

References

Alleyne, S. (2004) 'The Magic Touch,' *Black Enterprise*, June pp. 188–194.

Applegate, E. (1994) 'Leo Noble Burnett,' in *The Ad Men and Women: A Biographical Dictionary of Advertising*. Westport, CT: Greenwood Press, pp. 79–85.

Bridgeforth, G. (2002) 'How I Made a Million,' *Essence*, October, pp. 188–189.

Burns, C. (1994) 'ComputerLand Drops Name and Retail Stores Become Service Giant,' *Network World*, March 28, p. 24.

Carol H. Williams Advertising Agency (2002) *Agency Fact Book*. Oakland, CA: Carol H. Williams, Inc.

Carolhwilliams.com (2014) 'Welcome,' Company website of the Carol H. Williams Advertising agency. Available at: www.carolhwilliams.com (Accessed: June 1, 2014).

Chambers, J. (2008) *Madison Avenue and the Color Line: African-Americans in the Advertising Industry*. Philadelphia, PA: University of Pennsylvania Press.

Chicago Reporter (1975) 'Blacks are Most Hidden Persuaders in Chicago's Billion Dollar Advertising Business,' March, p. 1.

Cole, B. and Brantley, A. (2014) 'The Coors Boycott: When a Beer Can Signaled your Politics,' October 3 [Online]. Available at: www.cpr.org/news/story/coors-boycott-when-beer-can-signaled-your-politics (Accessed: June 1, 2015).

Cuneo, A. (2002) 'Big Thinker has the Touch,' *Advertising Age*, June 3, p. s-16.
Davis, J. F. (2013) 'Realizing Marketplace Opportunity: How Research on the Black Consumer Market Influenced Mainstream Marketers, 1920–1970,' *Journal of Historical Research in Marketing*, 5(4), pp. 471–493.
Ellis, J. (2004) '"Women of Distinction" Media & Marketing: Carol H. Williams,' *East Bay Business Times*, May 21, p. E-4.
Fora.TV Conference and Event Video (2008) 'Speaker: Carol H. Williams.' Available at: http://fora.tv/speaker/16336/Carol_H_Williams (Accessed: October 2, 2013).
Gilmore, J. (2015) Telephone Interview with the Author, May 20, 2015.
Glassdoor.com (2014) 'Carol H. Williams Agency Reviews.' Available at: www.glassdoor.com/Reviews/Carol-H-Williams-Advertising-Reviews-E144101.htm (Accessed: May 26, 2015).
Halladay, J. (2002) 'Williams lands GM,' *Advertising Age*, January 7, p. 30.
Harris, W. (2005) 'Winds of Change,' *Black Enterprise*, June, pp. 159–167.
Harris, W. (2008) 'Surviving the Game,' *Black Enterprise*, June, pp. 155–158.
Hayes, C. (1999) 'Not Just an Ol' Boys Club,' *Black Enterprise*, June, pp. 180–188.
Hayes, C. (2003) 'Massacre on Madison Avenue,' *Black Enterprise*, June, pp. 177–182.
Hayes, C. (2004) 'Only the Strong Survive,' *Black Enterprise*, June, pp. 179–184.
Hughes, Z. (2011) 'Carol H. Williams, Ad Agency Maven, Puts Visa, Nike, Clorox and Burger King on Blast,' *Rolling Out*, June 21 [Online]. Available at: http://rollingout.com/entertainment/carol-h-williams-ad-agency-maven-puts-visa-nike-clorox-and-burger-king-on-blast/ (Accessed: May 15, 2014).
Jet (1981) 'Loving Couple,' September 24, p. 31.
Judge, R. (2006) 'Carol H. Williams to Receive Missouri Honor Medal, Deliver Major Address on Market Segmentation,' *Missouri School of Journalism News Release* [Online]. Available at: http://journalism.missouri.edu/2006/03/carol-h-williams-to-receive-missouri-honor-medal-deliver-major-address-on-market-segmentation/ (Accessed: May 15, 2014).
Kelly, J. (1997) 'Carol H Williams breaks CPUC Ad,' *Adweek* (Western edn.), November 24, p. 5.
Kelly, J. (1998) 'Coors taps Carol H. Williams,' *Adweek* (Western edn.), February 23, p. 3.
Network Journal (2015) '25 Influential Women in Business Awards' [Online]. Available at: www.tnj.com/25-Influential-black-women/2015 (Accessed: April 10, 2015).
Osterman, J. (2007) *Excellence in Brand Advertising*. New York: Visual Relevance Publishing.
Sharp, B. (1969) *How to be Black and Get a Job in the Advertising Business Anyway*. Self-published, Sharp Advertising.
Shot Callers (2007) 'Carol H. Williams,' Video recording by Sun Seekers TV [Online]. Available at: www.youtube.com/watch?v=zMVP6T-j740 (Accessed: March 1, 2014).
Sivulka, J. (2009) *Ad Women: How They Impact What We Need, Want, and Buy*. Amherst, NY: Prometheus Books.
Small Business Magazine (2008) 'Tom Burrell,' May 22 [Online]. Available at: www.youtube.com/watch?v=L9Kwy1sHNDk (Accessed: May 15, 2015).
Stantley, S. (2014) Telephone Interview with the Author, June.
Target Market News (2010) 'Cadillac Selects Carol H. Williams Advertising as its African-American Agency,' September 24, p. 1.

Visconti, L. and Estrada, S. (2015) 'Clorox Apologizes for Tweet about Diverse Emojis,' *Diversity Inc.* [Online]. Available at: www.diversityinc.com/news/clorox-apologizes-for-tweet-about-diverse-emojis/ (Accessed: April 16, 2015).

Wentz, L. (2010) 'GM Assigns Cadillac African-American Account to Carol H. Williams.' Available at: www.autonews.com/article/20100924/RETAIL03/100929896 (Accessed: June 8, 2015).

Williams, C. H. (2014) Personal Interviews with the Author, June.

6 African-American women and structural oppression in the advertising industry

The advertising industry, as a socioeconomic institution, is an important reflection of a society's culture, norms, and values. Historically, American society has often been stratified on the basis of such factors as gender, race, ethnicity, and socioeconomic status. Observing the role of women and minorities in advertising, sociologist Anthony Cortese (2008, p. 100) concluded, "Cultural beliefs favor whites over people of color, males over females and the privileged over the disadvantaged." Since cultural beliefs tend to pass from generation to generation and among people in organizations, the individuals who lead the establishments comprising the advertising industry – holding companies, agencies, trade groups, and advertisers – are instrumental in shaping the corporate cultures of advertising organizations. Since advertising is largely an unregulated service business which operates with little oversight, the corporate cultures of advertising organizations are typically shaped by the beliefs, preferences, attitudes, personalities, and behaviors of those in positions of power and authority.

Evidence concerning cultural conditions in advertising organizations over the nearly 150-year history of the advertising business indicates that women, African-Americans, and other people of color commonly experienced various discriminatory practices which defined their professional roles and limited their career prospects in the advertising business. Collectively, these practices are called *structural oppression* – institutional biases and barriers which limit occupational opportunities. Structural oppression, also known as institutional oppression, consists of systemic ways in which organizations' histories, cultures, ideologies, policies, and practices – combined with beliefs and behaviors of individuals – interact to maintain a power hierarchy for a particular in-group while restricting opportunities for out-group members on the basis of characteristics such as race, gender, social class, religion, and sexual orientation (Open Source Leadership, 2012). The concept of structural oppression is an appropriate theoretical orientation for this analysis since it provides understanding with respect to diversity issues in corporate and advertising workplaces and the impact concerning women and African-Americans in the advertising profession. The background literature supplied in Chapter 1, along with the biographies of the pioneering African-American adwomen provided in Chapters 2–5, indicates that the subjects of this research encountered significant structural oppression in their careers. Although each woman had an excellent college education, significant managerial experience, and the wherewithal to run a successful business – Barbara Gardner Proctor, Caroline R. Jones, Joel P. Martin, and Carol H. Williams all experienced and observed various types of structural oppression which impacted their professional opportunities and choices. Moreover, other African-American adwomen report similar experiences, as discussed in this analysis.

Aspects of structural oppression

Historically, structural oppression existed in many societal institutions including educational, legal, health care, and business sectors. In business institutions, structural oppression occurs when established policies, customs, and practices systematically produce inequities based on individuals' memberships in certain social groups. Various practices characterizing structural oppression permeate business organizations and become normalized as part of their corporate cultures. Under these circumstances, economic and social privileges typically accrue to individuals of a dominant social group at the expense of people outside of the dominant group. In Western society, the dominant, privileged group usually consists of able-bodied white Christian heterosexual males of European descent; and the oppressed groups are usually females, people of color, non-Christians, gay, lesbian, or transgendered people, the poor, non-European immigrants, and non-English speakers (Alberta Council for Global Cooperation, n.d.). Privileges associated with the dominant social group and disadvantages associated with the oppressed or marginalized group(s) tend to endure over time (Open Source Leadership, 2012). The recognition of the dominant social group can vary depending on the society in question, but oppression typically consists of at least one of a number of social categories which identifies some members as subordinate or "different" and the dominant group exploits such differences in order to maintain its position of privilege and power (Alberta Council for Global Cooperation, n.d.). Behaviors and practices stemming from structural oppression may be overt or covert, unintentional, or even unrecognized and are woven into the fabric of the institutional culture (Hinson and Bradley, n.d.). Structural oppression may be rooted in beliefs concerning inherent superiority and inferiority about social groups and is often supported by prejudices and stereotypes – widely held beliefs about certain types of people which are socially accepted (Open Source Leadership, 2012). It is important to note that stereotypes attributed to groups can be positive or negative. A critical aspect of structural oppression is that people in subordinate groups are often viewed only as part of the group – not as individuals – and as such are given limited options and choices (Open Source Leadership, 2012). Under this description, structural oppression equals bias plus power. Power is manifested in terms of the ability to exercise authority and deploy resources and set the rules and standards that others must adhere to. In society and business, power privilege belongs to individuals of the dominant group based on mere membership in the group.

Structural oppression and corporate culture

The concept of structural oppression is applicable to corporate cultures across business sectors including the advertising industry. Scholars published important studies concerning women and African-Americans in managerial roles in corporations concerning the time frames addressed in this research, indicating a number of common practices associated with various types of structural oppression. Some of the most important studies in this area were conducted by sociologist John Fernandez, a Yale Ph.D. and expert on leadership, diversity, and human resources topics. He conducted groundbreaking research regarding women and multicultural managers in corporate settings in the 1970s, 1980s, and 1990s. His first study, *Black Managers in White Corporations*, was published in 1975 using data collected in the early 1970s concerning the experiences, attitudes, and opinions of 272 black and white managers at eight large corporations including banks, public utilities, and manufacturing concerns. Of the 272 subjects, 93 were black men, 23 were black women, 23 were white women, and 133 were white men. Another study by Fernandez – *Racism and Sexism in Corporate Life* – published in 1981, was among the earliest research to analyze the attitudes and perceptions of multicultural male and female managers in corporations including whites, blacks, Native Americans, Hispanics, and Asians employed at 12 major corporations across the United States. This study involved the attitudes and opinions of a much larger sample – 4,191 managers – representing a managerial workforce of about 125,000 people. The participants included 1,728 women and 2,463 men; 248 Native Americans, 257 Asians, 907 blacks, 691 Hispanics, and 2,088 whites (Fernandez, 1981, p. 10). While the number of managers of color increased over the time frame between the 1975 and 1981 studies, Fernandez concluded that the circumstances regarding the roles and treatment of minority and female managers remained relatively unchanged. Moreover, a subsequent study showed a persistence of stereotypes attributed to people of all backgrounds in corporate workplaces (Fernandez, 1999). Studies by Fernandez and other scholars, providing valuable insights concerning corporate workplace environments for women and African-American managers from the 1960s into the 2000s, are summarized in this chapter. In addition, a typology which identifies various types of structural oppression typically experienced by women and people of color in marketing and advertising organizations appears in Table 6.1.

Structural oppression and managerial women in corporate environments

Women of all backgrounds in corporate management roles often encountered structural oppression in their career paths. Acknowledging this circumstance, a white male bank manager admitted: "The discrimination against women in the past was not apparent, and to many people it was not an obvious policy

Table 6.1 Types of structural oppression identified in marketing and advertising organizations

Type of structural oppression	*Definition*	*Articles where referenced*
"Glass ceiling," "Glasshouse Effect," and similar models referring to women's opportunities in the workplace	Vertical and/or horizontal career barriers experienced by women whereby their professional roles or opportunities are limited by the dominant organizational culture and/or norms	Alvesson, 1998; Arnberg and Svanlund, 2016; Broyles and Grow, 2008; Maclaran, Stevens, and Catterall, 1997; Mallia, 2009; Still, 1986
"Economic Detour," "Economic Racism," "Sanctioned Segregation," and similar models referring to race-based foundations of enterprise or professional endeavors in corporate settings	Business opportunities for minority-owned firms or minority professionals by which such firms or professionals are limited to serving consumers and/or interests with similar ethnic backgrounds	Butler, 1991; Cassidy and Katula, 1990; Chambers, 2008; Cuneo, 2006; Davis, 2002; Pierce, 1947; Stuart, 1940
"Simultaneous Oppression," "Concrete Ceiling," "Caste-Typing," and similar concepts referring to minority females in business settings	Terms which describe opportunity constraints driven by race *and* gender concurrently that may be experienced by minority female professionals, employees, or customers in business organizations	Bristor and Fischer, 1995; Davis, 2013a; Lach, 1999

because of [women's] conditioning. But realistically they [companies] do discriminate against women" (Fernandez, 1975, p. 71). A white woman manager at a utility company in the early 1970s noted that women had to start out in clerical positions, while males started in managerial jobs, although they all had college degrees or similar preparation (Fernandez, 1975, p. 74). Women often found themselves excluded from informal work groups and information networks, which are critical to advancement in firms (Fernandez, 1981, p. 88; Mor-Barak and Cherin, 1998); and there was some evidence that being female was viewed as a hindrance to promotion (Fernandez, 1975, p. 128). Yet, Ryan (1975) found that college-educated women of the early 1970s had similar aspirations to men and expected to assume traditional and career roles in an uninterrupted pattern, in contrast to earlier generations; in fact, only 18 percent of college women planned *not* to work after having children. However, women believed they had to work harder than men to get ahead and that they were penalized more heavily for making mistakes (Fernandez, 1981, pp. 94, 97). Reports indicated numerous circumstances and enduring perceptions in workplaces which serve to undermine women's performances and contributions. For example, women are more likely to be presumed as incompetent until they prove themselves, women are often interrupted or ignored in meetings, women in workgroups are less likely to get credit for their contributions, women are judged more harshly on appearance, and women are likely to be judged as "too emotional" (Goudreau, 2014). In addition, double standards exist with respect to the evaluation of men's and women's workplace performances, where certain behaviors or characteristics are viewed negatively when they are associated with women. For example, behaviors such as assertiveness or aggressiveness may be viewed positively when associated with men, but might cause women to be perceived as pushy or "bitchy"; talkative women are seen as less competent, while talkative men are seen as knowledgeable; men are promoted based on potential, while women are promoted based on performance (Goudreau, 2014; Goudreau, 2015; Rivers and Barnett, 2013). With respect to compensation, women tend to get lower initial offers and suffer "motherhood penalties" – including those with advanced credentials like medical degrees and MBAs – while men receive "fatherhood bonuses" (Goudreau, 2014; Rivers and Barnett, 2013). Moreover, "successful" women are often viewed as unlikeable (Goudreau, 2015). Fernandez (1981, p. 99) concluded: "Corporations must begin to recognize that it is not the fault of women that they have been limited in their corporate careers – it is primarily the fault of sexism and its assumptions of female inferiority."

Women and structural oppression in advertising firms

Similar to women's experiences in a variety of corporate environments, research on gender roles in the advertising industry also revealed structural oppression at the organizational level for adwomen. As indicated early in this book, jobs available to women entering advertising agencies were often limited to clerical roles, regardless of educational background, with opportunities in research, copywriting, or other creative areas offering escape from the clerical trap. Caroline Jones' entry into the advertising business as a secretary was consistent with this norm. During the 1960s and 1970s, women generally had limited involvement on the account side of the advertising business since those jobs required significant client contact. Joel Martin recalls an unspoken assumption that account work was to be conducted by agency "account men" (Davis, 2015). Barbara Proctor was so attuned to the prevailing taboos concerning adwomen working with accounts that she named her agency Proctor & Gardner so that prospective clients would assume that a man was involved in managing the business. Further, the main subjects of this study – Proctor, Jones, Martin, and Williams – all started their advertising careers in the 1960s and gained experience in the Creative Departments of general-market advertising agencies. However, although they were in the creative sphere – a desirable area in most agencies – they were often limited to "women's products," which served as a type of "girl jail" according to Sarah Watson, a high-ranking adwoman (Kosin, 2015). This circumstance is contrasted to the experiences of legendary adwoman Mary Wells, whose work on "hard" accounts like airlines and cars catapulted her to unprecedented levels of success as an entrepreneur. Respected adwoman and author Jane Maas, a contemporary of Wells, reflecting on the advertising women she interviewed for her book, *Mad Women*, recounted that they often felt guilty, frustrated, overwhelmed, and angry. She explained (Maas, 2012, p. 205):

> "Maybe the women who entered the advertising world of the sixties really were mad. We were probably crazy to think we could break into such a male-dominated world, where the only sure way for a woman to become a copywriter was to start as a secretary and write ads on a speculative basis nights and weekends, for free."

Over time, the variety of types of advertising jobs increased for women, and the numbers employed in creative, research, media, and account services areas began to approach or equal those of men (Mallia, 2009). By the 1990s, women made up 66 percent of the total advertising workforce with women representing about one-third of Creative Department positions (Broyles and Grow, 2008). A 4 A's survey found 73 women in senior management positions in 1994, which increased to 265 by 2005 (Bosman, 2005). Scholars also found an increased "feminization" of practices in advertising and marketing organizations, where traits and skills often associated with women such as creativity, intuition, social interaction, nurturance, helpfulness, and cooperation are valued (Alvesson, 1998; Madaran and Catterall, 2000). Women also scored high on positive leadership traits including collaboration, teamwork, high integrity, and relationship-building skills, making them suitable for leadership in advertising workplaces (Liesse, 2013). In their biographical profiles, Proctor, Jones, Martin, and Williams were each noted for their excellent social and relationship-building skills, which are important to teamwork and leadership. Given that advertising is a service profession which is notoriously relationship driven, it was predicted that the increased emphasis on feminine skills would provide more opportunities for women seeking advancement to upper-management positions in agencies. However, Alvesson's (1998) ethnographic study of gender roles in an advertising agency concluded that "male power is central in the agency" and Mallia's (2009) research showed that men still outpaced women in all executive levels in advertising, including creative management. Overall, many advertising workplaces were characterized as masculine "fraternity," "gentlemen's club," or "locker room" cultures where social activities like fishing, socializing in bars, and playing golf were common (Broyles and Grow, 2008; Goudreau, 2015; Maclaran, Stevens, and Catterall, 1997; Still, 1986). In addition, women were often excluded from venues where men conducted business in informal settings such as male-only private clubs and golf courses. For many years, women were openly discouraged from pursuing certain account management positions and working on "men's" accounts concerning products like beer and automobiles (Broyles and Grow, 2008, p. 5). Lori Hiltz, who eventually became CEO of Havas Media North America, told *Harper's Bazaar* about the overt sexism she faced in the advertising industry in the 1980s (Kosin, 2015):

> "In my career, I was born and raised in Detroit in the automotive industry, so imagine this in 1982 – I worked probably for the most chauvinistic group of professionals. I was the only woman in an entire organization. There's no technology. There's absolutely nothing but barriers. Starting in the business when media and creative and everything was still sitting together, it was, 'oh, you go over in the media department, you can't manage an account. You can't. Because you're a girl.' I swear. So that's how I got into media, because there was no room for girls at the table. It was the real essence of advertising because it was perceived that it was a man's world, especially in automotive."

Certain types of structural oppression often related to women's experiences in advertising and marketing firms. Literature concerning women's corporate careers often refers to the "Glass Ceiling," indicating circumstances where women are allowed to rise only so high in organizations. A woman in the advertising industry in the early 1970s noted the difficulty of women moving beyond the middle-management level (*Time*, 1971, p. 99). Moreover, Maclaran, Stevens, and Catterall (1997) found that the experiences of female managers in marketing organizations often comprised a "Glasshouse Effect" – concurrent vertical *and* horizontal barriers based on gender – by which professional women could only advance to certain levels and were pigeonholed into certain areas – such as creative or research departments. Women were often denied opportunities which were readily provided to men, which restricted their abilities to grow and learn other areas of the business. For example, for women restricted to the creative spheres of advertising, they might have difficulty as managers or entrepreneurs since they lacked experience with areas like account management and finance. Finally, workplace norms also impacted adwomen's compensation levels, effectively lowering their status in the organization. In advertising firms, salaries were often lower for women compared with men with comparable responsibilities. Caroline Jones' biography reveals she was increasingly distressed about pay issues throughout her advertising career and compensation and share of the business were likely reasons as to why she left Mingo-Jones to start her own agency. Although her name was on the company nameplate, she contended she was not provided the financial rewards or status at the agency comparable to her male business partner.

Another issue for advertising women was the dilemma associated with workplace-related sexual advances. Adwoman Jane Maas (2012, p. 28) indicated that sex was rampant in advertising agencies of the 1960s, due in large part to the advent of the birth control pill and the permissive culture in many agencies. However, women were more likely to suffer sexual harassment in the workplace, and laws providing protection did not yet exist. To be fair, some women used sex as a tool to advance their careers or to enter into mutually beneficial relationships with men (Maas, 2012, p. 30). Yet, openly promiscuous women were often punished in some manner and some were terminated for lack of discretion or other perceived misdeed (Maas, 2012, p. 30). African-American adwoman Sarah Burroughs, one of the early black women to work in a general-market agency, confirmed that along with heavy drinking and smoking, "hooking up" among men and women was commonplace in the advertising industry during the 1960s (Davis, 2014b). Employed at FCB in Chicago in the mid-1960s, Burroughs avoided parties since there were many adulterous relationships going on and – since she was married and the only black woman at the agency – the activities made her uncomfortable. At a work party, she instinctively punched a white man after he pinched her on her rear. Shocked, he said he did that to "all the girls." Burroughs replied: "Not this girl – don't touch me again." After that warning, he never bothered her and she perceived the incident as indicative of the ways that women were treated in the workplace.

Interestingly, Maclaran, Stevens, and Catterall (1997) found that both men and women may impede the progress of ambitious women seeking advancement in marketing organizations, upholding traditional norms of corporate culture. For example, some men and women believed that certain advertising jobs were unsuited to women. Another study found that women were held to higher performance standards in organizations by men, women, and even themselves, due to unconscious biases about women's capabilities (Silverman, 2015). Even in the creative sphere, where women tended to have significant representation, juries of national and international advertising award programs were often all male or male-dominated and tended to favor humorous ads created by men to appeal to men (Broyles and Grow, 2008). In fact, a brouhaha ensued in 2005 surrounding comments made at an industry event honoring the creative work of copywriter Neil French. Asked why there were so few women Creative Directors, French responded that the work of female creatives was "crap … and they don't make it to the top because they don't deserve to," articulating a controversial sentiment in the industry as to why women weren't advancing (Broyles and Grow, 2008, p. 4). Indeed, a mid-2000s news article showed that there were only four female Creative Directors in the flagship offices of the top 33 agencies in the United States (Bosman, 2005); and a 2006 trade publication featuring the 50 most creative people of the last 20 years included no women at all (*Creativity*, 2006). Alison Burns, Global Client Services Director of JWT, reflecting on the historical makeup of gender roles in advertising agency creative departments, commented (Kosin, 2015, p. 3):

> "I think the departmental point is quite an interesting one because it has always been very counterintuitive to me and remains to this day astonishing that the creative department should remain so male-dominated as it is today. Because, rather stereotypically, one considers women to be highly successful creative

> human beings and they tend to be very successful in environments that are intrinsically or inherently creative. And yet that's not true in advertising agencies. They're still under-represented, as are openly gay people, as are ethnically diverse people. You need diversity of imagination and you need a colliding of disparate views to be inspired in that way and yet the opposite is true. They tend to be highly structured, very male, very heterosexual and very white creative departments. And it should be the photographic negative of that."

Outside of the United States, a study of the Swedish advertising industry looked at employment patterns along gender lines between 1930 and 2012. While Sweden is known for its gender-equality policies, Arnberg and Svanlund (2016) found that men typically held managerial positions in advertising, including those in the creative area, while women were concentrated in clerical and unskilled labor positions. When a 1965 government policy shift opened advertising jobs to a greater number of practitioners, the industry became dominated by a large number of small firms, with more women participating in a wider variety of roles including creative and project management roles. However, by 2000, women employed in copywriting and art direction jobs leveled off around 30 percent, and men continued to dominate the power positions and creative work. Arnberg and Svanlund (2016, p. 17) concluded that "discriminatory structures and practices" prompted some women to leave advertising firms, including those who left to engage in self-employment. These findings are consistent with the experiences of some of the women addressed in this study, who found entrepreneurship preferable to the conditions they faced as advertising agency employees.

A 2013 IPG/*Advertising Age* survey examined gender issues among 1,000 employees which underscored persistent aspects of structural oppression in contemporary advertising workplaces concerning women, although progress relative to earlier time periods was indicated (Liesse, 2013). More than half of the women respondents cited as major barriers, biases (including unconscious biases) among current senior leaders (57 percent), career interruptions due to family responsibilities (55 percent), and their own lack of self-promotion at work (54 percent). Smaller proportions of women indicated advancement barriers including lack of mentors or sponsors (45 percent), inadequate leadership backgrounds (38 percent), and too few women aspiring to top roles (33 percent). Men dominated advertising in five areas including creative, executive management, strategy and planning, digital, and sales and marketing; and women dominated in media and account management – the latter representing a departure from past norms. Noting women's shifting roles within the advertising industry, Joyce King-Thomas, a President and Chief Creative Officer at McCann XBC, attributed slow progress to the "legacy of male leadership in the business" (Liesse, 2013, p. 10).

Finally, a number of factors were identified as hindrances to women's quests for managerial positions in the advertising industry: lack of acceptance of women in authority roles; lack of mentorship and/or role models; regard of feminine traits as weaknesses; unsupportive work environments; exclusion from informal social groups, activities, and information networks; and work–childcare conflicts compounded by long and unpredictable work hours and/or work-related travel (Broyles and Grow, 2008; Dishman, 2013; Maclaran, Stevens, and Catterall, 1997; Still, 1986). A study by IPG indicated that women in advertising believed work–life balance was an important goal more so than men (Hall, 2000). Other research suggested women lacked the commitment and motivation to "drop everything" – including family life – to end up in power positions in advertising (Broyles and Grow, 2008, p. 5; Iezzi, 2005; Kazenoff and Vagnoni, 1997, p. 19). A woman copywriter commented "maybe women just don't want to put up with the bullshit" required to advance to the upper-echelons of advertising management (Broyles and Grow, 2008, p. 4). Shelley Lazarus, who rose to top of the O&M agency in the late 1990s, made it a point to emphasize work–family balance, but noted the difficulties in doing so (Maas, 2012, p. 206).

Structural oppression and African-American managers in corporate settings

As with women, structural oppression substantially reduced professional opportunities for African-Americans in corporate environments. Prior to enactment of policies such as the Civil Rights Act of 1964, overt "conscious racism" was part of the culture of many American workplaces (Bendick and Egan, 2009, p. 51). Racial discrimination was not illegal, segregation was widespread, and society had not embraced equality as an ideal. Fernandez (1975, p. 3) explained: "Exclusion of blacks from management was considered the norm in business," and "the white corporate community's 'closed door' policy effectively kept blacks from reaching managerial ranks." However, civil rights gains opened up corporate managerial careers to African-Americans. By 1967, blacks represented 0.7 percent of all managerial positions, which increased to 1.9 percent by 1971, although none were in upper management (Fernandez, 1975, p. 67). Historically, business organizations were maintained such that mobility was generally based upon conformity to group norms imposed by the dominant group with respect to social class, education, religion, organizational and political affiliations, age, race, and gender (Caplow, 1954). When civil rights gains offered improved access to educational and job opportunities for blacks, those seeking entry into corporate employment often conformed to the in-group norms regarding style of dress, speech, social skills, behaviors, and other forms of assimilation (Cox, 1991, p. 35; Fernandez, 1975, p. 2). In fact, adoption of the norms of the corporate environment was considered a matter of survival within those organizations for women and minorities (Cox, 1991, p. 37). However, since African-Americans could not change their skin color, biases among individuals often functioned such that blacks were subject to various types of discrimination in the corporate world. They were often excluded from work activities like discussions and meetings, were marginalized as members of work groups, were not invited to informal social functions like luncheons, sporting events, and parties – and, if they were, no one socialized with them (Fernandez, 1975, p. 27; Mor-Barak, 1999, p. 53). Moreover, most white managers had little contact with blacks outside of work (Fernandez, 1981, p. 53; Mehra, Kilduff, and Brass, 1998, p. 447). Fernandez (1975, p. 82) noted an enduring "culture gap" concerning values and behaviors where "It is believed by many white managers that blacks cannot interact effectively with whites in higher business circles, particularly in social activities where much business is informally transacted." A bank manager explained: "Until blacks are accepted socially, they will never move above middle management, because senior management necessitates socialization" (Fernandez, 1975, p. 83). This is a critical problem in advertising and marketing professions, which require a great deal of socializing and client contact, in formal and informal settings.

Interpersonal relationships and informal communications are central to progress at the middle and upper management levels in corporations, since they are used to test ideas, gain secret information, and garner support of key people or make the right contacts in order to move ahead successfully. Yet, if subjected to a hostile work environment or negative attitudes by the majority, Fernandez (1975) concluded that blacks had little hope of equal treatment on the job. A black manager with light skin, straight hair, and blue eyes related that negative racial comments were often made in his presence:

> "Because most people believe I am white, they express all types of negative attitudes about blacks to me. When I disagree with them and tell them I'm black, they don't know how to act or what to say. They usually get all red and say something like they really didn't mean what they said, that they have colored friends or went to school with them."
>
> (Fernandez, 1975, p. 122)

Such ostracism cuts blacks off from important information networks related to workplace opportunities. Moreover, a study by the John J. Heldrich Center for Workforce Development (2002) found that African-Americans experienced more potent forms of bias at work compared with other ethnic minorities including Hispanics and Asians. African-Americans were perceived by all groups as being treated unfairly in terms of opportunities for training and promotion and were more likely to be considered as the targets of discrimination at work. Taken together, these circumstances undermined development of interpersonal relationships and denied black professionals certain opportunities and fulfillment in the corporate workplace.

In spite of the unwelcoming environment, some blacks were employed in managerial positions in corporations. However, research showed African-American managers were often placed in lower-management positions of limited authority and decision-making, constrained upward mobility, and were situated in race-based career roles (Collins, 1997; Fernandez, 1975, p. 66). An Equal Employment Opportunity investigator in the early 1970s noted that "subtle discrimination which may exist in a closely knit group is particularly difficult to overcome" and "tacit agreement among certain key leaders in a unit can assure that a Negro never performs work above a minimum level of skill and responsibility" (Fernandez, 1975, p. 2). Minority managers also faced severe hostility given competition for the relatively few upper and middle management advancement opportunities (Fernandez, 1981, p. 62). A study of MBAs indicated that minority members had significantly less access to mentors in corporate settings compared to whites (Cox, 1991, p. 44). Therefore, when minority managers were promoted, they had to "make their own way or hope for a white male sponsor" (Fernandez, 1981, p. 55). As indicated in the biographies of Joel P. Martin and Carol H. Williams, supportive white male mentors were critical to their nurturance and advancement early in their advertising careers while working at their first agencies.

Many African-Americans in corporate managerial positions were placed in jobs concerning ethnic employees, such as Affirmative Action managers assigned to work with minority groups within the organization and/or minority-oriented associations such as the NAACP and the Urban League. Moreover, those at relatively high levels in the organization were often placed in visible positions with limited authority, such as community or public relations, urban affairs, and personnel positions; or positions in the black sphere of the company concerning "special markets" or black consumers. These managers often had advanced college degrees and/or considerable prior work experience. A good example was the Pepsi Corporation's Negro Sales group which operated for several years following World War II catering to the black consumer market. A white supervisor justified these types of practices to a black manager, explaining that – as the first African-American manager – he should be content just to "be seen" (Freeman and Fields, 1972, p. 78). White managers also feared losing business if their "clients had to deal with a black" (Freeman and Fields, 1972, p. 78), a common scenario in marketing and advertising organizations. Taken together, these types of practices offered little hope to black managers interested in upper-management or significant client-contact roles in white corporations unrelated to "minority" aspects of the firm.

Fernandez (1981, p. 39) concluded that while blacks made significant progress in the years immediately following the Civil Rights Act, that progress seemed to slow somewhat in the 1970s and 1980s, with covert acts of oppression occurring regularly. Black managers were likely to report alienation, isolation, and criticism in their corporate lives along with difficulties in social interactions. Caroline Jones' biography, for example, indicates how she often felt lonely, isolated, and ostracized while a Vice President at the BBD&O agency. White males also shared some of these perceptions and acknowledged that discrimination existed in the business world – 89 percent believed that blacks faced obstacles, 54 percent believed minorities faced racist tendencies, and 60 percent admitted to stereotypical remarks about minorities (Fernandez, 1981, p. 65). Fernandez (1981, p. 19) concluded: "Once a minority is perceived as taking to which the dominant group feels exclusively entitled, it is subjected to all the harassment, exploitation, manipulation and oppression a dominant group can muster." Fernandez also observed that African-Americans seemed to bear the most acute forms of corporate racism, based on their darker skin tones, social norms established in slavery, and a history of overt, legally sanctioned standards such as "separate but equal" and Jim Crow laws, Black Codes, and other discriminatory and segregationist policies concerning blacks. As such, African-Americans often experienced a variety of biases within their workplaces. White managers too sometimes acknowledged unfair practices toward blacks within their industries, but were less likely to agree that such practices involved their own firms. Overall, African-Americans tended to face acute stress and isolation once they assumed middle- and senior-management roles in corporations, if indeed they were able to rise to such rarefied positions, and had to develop superior coping skills in order to survive. Often these stresses prompted black managers to leave white corporations. For example, Barbara Proctor, Caroline Jones, and Carol Williams all had extremely negative experiences at certain mainstream advertising agencies and left those companies, dissatisfied.

African-Americans in mainstream advertising firms

The types of structural oppression that African-Americans encountered in corporate environments extended to the quality of their experiences in general-market advertising firms. The historical record indicates that the limited number of blacks able to obtain positions in white advertising firms was mostly confined to low-status positions such as clerical and janitorial work or functions unrelated to the practice of advertising (Chambers, 2008, p. 126). Structural oppression even extended to advertising agency internship opportunities (Boulton, 2015). Jobs involving client contact were essentially unattainable and in the years following World War II, mainstream agencies would not hire experienced black admen like David Sullivan, Vince Cullers, and Byron Lewis, so they pursued other opportunities. As noted, among the first African-Americans hired in general-market advertising firms was Clarence Holte at BBD&O in New York in the early 1950s. Holte's employment was consistent with a type of structural oppression which became common within mainstream corporations: the practice of limiting black managers' roles to the black sphere in the organization when he was hired as a manager to help BBD&O cultivate the black consumer market for its clients (Chambers, 2008, p. 90). Later, in 1975, BBD&O hired Caroline Jones to do specialty work concerning the black consumer market. Given the rather inhospitable corporate climate with respect to business and people of color in the immediate post-World War II era, a specialty orientation was a realistic approach for black entry into the mainstream advertising industry. By 1950, research increasingly revealed black consumers as a sizeable and lucrative market segment, which appealed to the profit-seeking motives of corporate marketers (Davis, 2013b). But, given the long history of separation between blacks and whites and the proliferation of negative images of African-Americans in mainstream media, African-American consumers were outside of white marketers' scope of expertise. Therefore, they turned to black "inside men" like Sullivan, Holte, John H. Johnson, Moss Kendrix, and John Benjamin Harris for help in understanding and appealing to black consumers (Davis, 2013b). However, there was dissention among black leaders over the value of a "special markets" orientation among African-American marketing and advertising professionals. A 1963 study by the Urban League of Greater New York examined hiring practices at ten of the largest agencies: JWT; McCann Erickson; Y&R; BBD&O; Ted Bates & Company; FCB; Benton and Bowles; Compton Advertising; Grey Advertising; and Kenyon and Eckhardt (Chambers, 2008, p. 128), and findings revealed that among the more than 20,000 people employed by these agencies, only 25 blacks worked in "creative or executive" positions; of those, one-third were limited to black consumer market work. Sullivan and Holte defended such specialization, arguing that it provided employment opportunities for African-Americans in mainstream firms and allowed them to positively influence the strategies and images directed at black consumers (Chambers, 2008, p. 128). According to Chambers (2008, p. 91), in addition to BBD&O, mainstream agencies began to establish ethnic cells in the late 1960s, and these firms set about situating employees of color in those departments. However, the Urban League disagreed with this approach, saying that restricting black professionals to black-oriented assignments was a form of "segregated integration" (Chambers, 2008, p. 128). Black advertising pioneer, Roy Eaton, hired in the mid-1950s by Y&R, concurred with the Urban League's position, arguing that a black specialist orientation by black professionals would cause them to be pigeonholed, thereby leading to insufficient work opportunities in the future (Chambers, 2008, p. 100). However, historian Fox (1984, p. 278) noted that Eaton – a talented and classically trained musician – "could write and play the white man's music and so was not restricted to black ads and products." In a nod to the overt discrimination of the times, when Eaton inquired about a job at Y&R, the hiring manager told him: "If you were white, I'd hire you immediately" (Pollack, 2014). Despite the disagreement over general-market versus ethnic specialty work, the "special markets" practice remained popular in the industry, and while the labeling of the practice changed over time, many African-Americans in advertising were classified as specialty or niche marketers. Years later, at an industry event covered by *Advertising Age*, the specialty approach was attacked as "Sanctioned Segregation" and an industry insider blamed corporate advertisers for supporting and perpetuating the practice (Cuneo, 2006).

It is important to note that some African-Americans were able to obtain professional jobs in mainstream agencies in the 1960s which were not limited to black consumer marketing. In addition to Roy Eaton, other African-American admen including Georg Olden, Bill Sharp, Tom Burrell, Frank Mingo, and Doug Alligood; along with adwomen Barbara Proctor, Caroline Jones, Joel Martin, Carol Williams, and others were black pioneers in general-market agencies who honed their skills doing work on a variety of accounts. In fact, campaigns developed by Proctor, Jones, and Williams in general-market agencies were particularly praiseworthy, garnering significant industry recognition, thereby establishing their professional reputations in the advertising business. In addition, Martin and Williams had positive experiences at the McCaffrey & McCall and Leo Burnett agencies, respectively, avoiding many of the negative outcomes often associated with structural oppression and African-Americans in corporate environments. Overall, as professionals in advertising, the nature of the experiences of African-Americans varied widely depending on the organizational culture and the prevailing environment cultivated by the leadership within those particular firms.

"Stay in your lane": African-American advertising entrepreneurs

Historically, a number of African-Americans chose entrepreneurship as their path to participation in the advertising industry. They did so for a variety of reasons: some could not secure employment in white-owned advertising firms given biased hiring practices; some had poor experiences in general-market advertising agencies and decided to leave; and some believed they had the skills to be successful running their own companies. Chambers (2008, pp. 67–68) acknowledges the existence of black-owned advertising agencies as early as the 1920s, but given the circumstances of the times – overt discriminations against blacks, widespread racial segregation, and poor economic conditions such as the Great Depression – he noted: "Black agencies had virtually no chance to produce advertisements for large consumer products firms, the leading advertisers in the country." Therefore, the earliest black agencies were small, local, limited-service firms which typically produced advertisements for other black-owned businesses in their local communities. Many of these enterprises were short lived. However, the confluence of post-World War II economic prosperity, unprecedented legal, social, and economic gains for African-Americans stemming from Civil Rights legislation of the 1950s and 1960s, and keen interest in black consumers by white corporate marketers, created favorable conditions for the establishment of full-service black-owned advertising agencies (Davis, 2013b). Bates, a labor and urban studies expert, offered an optimistic view concerning enterprise development among African-Americans, based on U.S. Department of Commerce data, identifying accounting, computer programming, and advertising among key "emerging" sectors of black entrepreneurship around 1970 (Bates, 1997, p. 154). Given greater access to education, training, and capital, along with less discrimination and increased opportunities to serve government and corporate clients, Bates believed that conditions were favorable for black entrepreneurs to compete and prosper in the broader marketplace. Concurring with Bates' view, a number of African-American entrepreneurs participated in advertising agency ventures in the 1960s and 1970s, including men like Junius Edwards, Howard Sanders, John Small, Ray League, Byron Lewis, and Tom Burrell; and women including Barbara Proctor, Joan Murray, Caroline Jones, and Joel Martin.

Cognizant of the social conditions and business opportunities of the period, most late 1960s to early 1970s-era black advertising entrepreneurs engaged in black consumer market specialty work whether they wanted to or not. Howard Sanders Advertising, Byron Lewis' Uniworld, League and Murray's Zebra Associates (where Caroline Jones was involved early on), Proctor & Gardner Advertising, Burrell Advertising, and J.P. Martin Associates all willingly catered to black consumers as a market entry strategy. Since the black consumer market was underdeveloped from a corporate marketing perspective, their assignments included advertising aimed at selling products to black consumers. Some also engaged in public relations work intended to improve the image of large corporations among black consumers. Given the societal norms of the times, Chambers (2008) argued that this stance was reasonable and that the black market specialty orientation provided African-American entrepreneurs an "on ramp" into the white, corporate advertising world which had previously been off-limits to them. However, at least two of the early entrepreneurs of the period, Junius Edwards and John Small, believed that the ethnic specialty orientation was too limiting and that the route to long-term business prosperity was to service general-market accounts (Chambers, 2008, pp. 210, 215). But, they quickly found that they could not attract sufficient general-market business since Corporate America's leadership was only willing to see them as minority specialists. This situation for African-American advertising entrepreneurs comprised another form of structural oppression – the Economic Detour model of business development. Recognized in the 1940s by Stuart and Pierce, the Economic Detour model is relevant because it provides an understanding of race-based opportunities in the marketplace. This concept was first articulated by businessman Stuart (1940), upon his reflection of the business conditions typically encountered by black entrepreneurs. He argued that the legal and social practices of racial segregation drove black entrepreneurs, sometimes unwillingly, to cater exclusively to black consumers in order to have reasonable opportunities for business viability. Pierce (1947, p. 19) concurred with Stuart, illustrating quantitatively that American business operated in a dichotomous "Negro-white caste system," concluding that racial prejudice was the underpinning of such a system. There is substantial agreement that the socioeconomic conditions under segregation created a peculiar paradox for black entrepreneurs, who – denied access to the broader marketplace – benefitted from racial separation in that it created what market opportunity they had. There has also been general agreement that the most viable lines of business for black entrepreneurs were those which whites chose not to pursue (Stuart, 1940, p. xxv; Pierce, 1947; Butler, 1991, p. 74).

Historian Stephen Fox criticized African-Americans' early positioning in the advertising industry, commenting (1984, p. 278): "Most blacks aiming for an advertising career did fall into the special-markets trap: claiming expertise at selling to blacks, they were then confined to that limited category." Fox's reasoning was flawed, however, since he did not appreciate the historical context concerning how blacks came to be involved in the advertising industry and the societal conditions which constrained their ability to fully participate. Fox (1984, p. 284) continued:

> "as long as black agencies and blacks working at white agencies argued that only blacks could understand, and sell to, their fellow blacks, then white accounts could reasonably pass them by. The nationalist case logically led back to the notion that that had kept blacks off Madison Avenue for so long: that only whites could sell to whites."

The problem with Fox's conclusions is that he failed to understand the past concerning African-Americans' relationships with corporate entities and the enduring structural oppressions within them. Realistically, the black market specialist orientation was the only viable point of market entry for black advertising entrepreneurs at the time, given the historical barriers which excluded them from mainstream industry engagement. Not only were white agencies already well established and catering to white consumers, but a positioning approach calling for the acquisition of large general-market accounts by black agencies would have been rejected by Corporate America. In fact, black agency entrepreneurs Junius Edwards and John Small experienced this type of rejection. Advertising Hall of Fame member Frank Mingo (1985) acknowledged that black-owned agencies were "not about to become J. Walter Thompsons" – unless extraordinary change occurred in the industry – given historical exclusions. Simply put, African-Americans were not allowed to compete for general-market business at a level which could consistently sustain their enterprises. This was a problem not limited to black agencies in the 1950s to 1970s, but a much longer-term issue. Industry veteran Tom Burrell responded to this issue in a 1990 interview. Asked whether he believed that there was discrimination in terms of general-market accounts being awarded to black-owned agencies, Burrell replied (Cassidy and Katula, 1990, p. 103):

> "Yes. I think that 'discrimination' might suggest that in all cases it is a kind of methodical prejudice that assumes no business with any black people. First of all, to be fair and balanced about it, one of the reasons for it is that black agencies have done such a good job of positioning themselves against the black consumer market that it becomes more difficult for prospective clients to see us in any other way. Another reason is, frankly, institutionalized racism, which makes it difficult for a client to say, 'I'm going to give responsibility for all my business to this black company.'"

Another interesting aspect that Burrell spoke to was the ability of people of color to successfully develop advertising aimed at white consumers, in contrast to Fox's assertions. He argued that it was easier for people of color to construct effective advertising aimed at whites since blacks, especially in their societal roles, were immersed in white culture. Burrell explained (Cassidy and Katula, 1990, p. 99):

> "it is easier for me to sell goods and services through advertising to white consumers because I have been forced and have been compelled to be a student of white culture, because I was born and grew up in a society where I had to know white culture in order to survive. From the time that I was four years old and had to go to the store and deal with the white merchant, I have had to know white society. Similarly, when I came down out of my black neighborhood to work for a white company, I had to understand white society. We live in a white society. We are a minority in a white society, and in order to survive in that society, we have to know it. If I am going to come down and work at Leo Burnett, or wherever else I have to work, I've got to learn how to interact; I've got to understand white culture. [But] you can be white in America and live your whole life quite fully without ever having to know black culture."

African-American adwoman McGee Osse, a chief executive at Burrell Communications, and Wanla Cheng, an Asian woman who advanced to senior management roles at several general-market agencies, concurred with Tom Burrell's opinion, believing that people of color are suited to produce advertising aimed at the general market (Johnson, 2004; Smiley, 2014). Cheng explained (Johnson, 2004, p. 28): "It's hard for people of color to be in a business that is predominately about white culture. I had to work harder at fitting in to the advertising-industry culture, especially because I was born and raised in Asia." The historical record indicates that advertising by people of color and by minority-owned agencies can resonate with the general market. Work by black agencies and by black advertising professionals has been highly effective in influencing white consumers. For example, work by the Burrell agency – "I assume you drink Martell" – for Martell cognac, and – "We do chicken right!" – for Kentucky Fried Chicken by the Mingo-Jones agency, had tremendous appeal among the general market (Davis, 2002, p. 80). In addition, as their biographies indicate, Barbara Proctor, Caroline Jones, and Carol Williams produced effective, award-winning work aimed at all consumers while they were employed at large mainstream agencies. Notably, Williams' "Strong Enough for a Man – but Made for a Woman" theme for Secret antiperspirant in the 1970s became one of the top advertising campaigns of all time among all audiences. Later, a commercial for Disney Parks by CHWA titled "Signs" was voted the top TV ad by all audiences in 2007. These examples demonstrate that black professionals are capable of producing advertising that resonates beyond the black consumer market to the general market as well.

Despite the evidence concerning the competencies of black advertising professionals, over the years, conditions and practices associated with the

Sanctioned Segregation and Economic Detour types of structural oppression were widely replicated and become normalized across the advertising industry. These circumstances constrained the business activities of all advertising agencies owned by people of color, including African-Americans, Latinos, and Asians. As such, these agencies were forced to "stay in their lanes" with respect to black, "urban," Hispanic, Asian, and similar "multicultural" oriented assignments. In fact, GlobalHue's longtime dominance among black-owned agencies was rooted in the fact that owner Don Coleman embraced a "multicultural" positioning early on, and was therefore prepared to cover all the ethnic bases when black consumers waxed and waned in popularity as a target market. In addition to these circumstances, structural barriers caused African-Americans to come into the advertising industry very late – well after the period when most large agencies obtained their footholds in the business servicing large corporations. This circumstance eliminated black agencies from the wealth-building opportunities associated with servicing significant, consistent corporate accounts from the 1920s until at least the late 1960s. Butler (1991), Chambers (2008, p. 225), and Davis (2002) concurred that while an ethnic specialty orientation provided a basis for market entry for African-American entrepreneurs, a race-based business model served to limit the growth, business prospects, and general viability of black-owned agencies over the long run. This position restricts agencies to a relatively small piece of the consumer marketplace "pie" and invites stiff competition from similar specialty agencies and large general-market firms which choose to pursue black consumers or "total market strategies" as some do. In addition, the industry phenomenon whereby the most successful black agencies were partially acquired by major holding companies underscores the reality that black-owned agencies will continue to be consigned to specialty status, which limits them to niche marketing and compromises their ability to pursue accounts which provide access to the broader marketplace (Smiley, 2014). In sum, conditions imposed by structural oppression cause minority-owned agencies to start and stay relatively small. Over the years, the *collective* billings of all black-owned agencies combined have remained at about only 0.5 percent of the industry's total. As such, compared with general-market white agencies, black-owned agencies are small. This is a problem when prospective clients don't want to do business with small agencies; or when black agencies lack the resources to provide the services that corporate clients demand. Therefore, this analysis indicates that race-based enterprise development models concerning business owners of color puts their establishments in highly vulnerable positions. The long-term viability of such firms is called into question as long as structural oppressions abound in the industry.

Dual oppressions of black women in corporate and advertising jobs

African-American women have always had high rates of participation in the American labor force. Starting in the 1950s, white collar positions in certain fields become more widely available to black women, especially clerical, teaching, and government jobs, fueled by civil rights gains and a robust economy (Amott and Matthaei, 1991, p. 179). However, white collar opportunities in corporate settings came about very slowly and advancement to managerial positions was limited. In these corporate settings, the greatest degree of unfairness and exclusion was articulated by African-American women (Fernandez, 1975, p. 73; Mor-Barak, Cherin, and Berkman, 1998, p. 99). Combs (2003, p. 398) found black women faced negative workplace consequences for being "too black" for whites or "too female" for men. Black women also felt their concerns were marginalized since much of the attention regarding black problems in the workplace tended to focus on "black manhood" issues or the perceived threat of black women in business (Dewitt, 1974, p. 18; Mor-Barak, Cherin, and Berkman, 1998, p. 99). Black women also believed their problems received inadequate attention. For example, although they tend to have more education, black women consistently have higher rates of unemployment and earn less on average than black men (Fernandez, 1981, p. 73). A black woman manager at a manufacturing company explained the dual plight faced by black women: "Race and sex are unwritten employment policies. Women can't reach high positions and the same is true for blacks ... Blacks can't be too militant or aggressive" (Fernandez, 1975, p. 71). Her statements support Wilensky's (1966) view that as blacks became more educated and aware of economic rewards in American society in the post-Civil Rights era, they became more insistent in seeking workplace opportunity and equity. However, black managers in Fernandez's (1975, p. 71) study told of blacks being fired or transferred when they spoke out about discrimination or other insensitivities, resulting in them being accused of having "militant" or rebellious attitudes. An example of this was Barbara Proctor's firing from North Advertising in 1969 when she complained about an advertising concept which parodied Civil Rights protests. Another black woman felt that her company was no different from corporations in general – that white men hold the advantages and that black hiring and promoting were mere tokenism, explaining: "Government has told our company to have blacks – so they have a few blacks. Whites say blacks aren't making it because they aren't educated. I don't believe this – blacks simply aren't given the chance" (Fernandez, 1975, p. 76). U.S. Labor Department statistics showed that a higher proportion of black women in the workforce have college degrees compared to white women, but hold proportionately fewer managerial positions (Combs, 2003, p. 390). Given these circumstances, Fernandez (1981, p. 74) concluded: "black women are the most critical about the present situation and treatment of women in corporations, not only because they suffer sexist discrimination as all women do, but also because they faced the extreme form of racial discrimination that black men face."

Several studies examined the duality of race and gender for minority women in corporate settings, indicating that experiences in workplaces are different for African-American women versus white women (Blake, 1999; McCollum, 1998; Yoder and Aniakudo, 1997); and that the combination of race and gender has a negative impact for black women, such as barriers to top-level jobs, termed the "concrete ceiling" (Lach, 1999). By the 2000s, overt acts of discrimination were uncommon, but covert discrimination and subtle prejudices, including exclusion, were present and believed to contribute to reduced social support and opportunities regarding career-enhancing informal networks for African-American women (Bell and Nkomo, 1994; Bova, 2000). Combs (2003) concluded that black women in managerial and executive positions in corporations often experienced out-group status in manners which were unique compared with white females or black males in terms of access to and the quality of participation in informal social networks. As indicated, such networks are important to social support and career advancement in corporations. Moreover, in marketing and advertising organizations, such networks are also crucial to information and access regarding prospective business and account acquisition opportunities. Mehra, Kilduff, and Brass (1998) surmised that lack of access to information networks may be why African-American women – who have entered corporations in record numbers – remain underrepresented, especially in upper-management ranks. In addition, black women tended to be at the bottom of the workplace ladder in terms of advancement and earnings (Bova, 2000). Others indicate that structural inequalities driven by race and gender discrimination carry over into an organization's social systems (Greenhaus, Parasuraman, and Wormley, 1990). Feagin and Sikes (1994, p. 172) argue that white males and females are not predisposed to forego feelings of racial superiority and therefore see African-American female managers as temporary aberrations. In sum, black women face multiple simultaneous barriers in their efforts to navigate organizational social arrangements and cultures as they strive to serve successfully in managerial and executive positions.

The Madison Avenue Project

Over the long history of investigations into employment practices in the advertising industry since the early 1960s, numerous calls for increased diversity, and a variety of diversity initiatives, a significant attempt stands out. The Madison Avenue Project, initiated in 2009, was a joint effort of industry leaders, the NAACP, and the civil rights law firm of Mehri & Skalet which considered remedies – including a class-action lawsuit – seeking to alleviate the practice of "purposeful discrimination" against African-Americans in the advertising business (Elliot, 2009). What was different about this effort is that it commissioned a comprehensive study and analysis concerning the history of black employment in advertising and compared the advertising industry to employment patterns in other comparable corporate sectors using national labor statistics. Among the important findings of the 83-page report (Bendick and Egan, 2009):

1 African-Americans are under-hired in the advertising industry in professional and managerial advertising positions, which typically concern such areas as account management, research, creative, and media. Combined, only 5.3 percent overall were professionals and managers. Of these, 4.3 percent were in managerial positions and 3.2 percent were in upper management positions. However, based on national data, African-Americans should represent 9.6 percent of advertising professionals and managers. The industry would need to hire more than 7,000 additional black professionals to meet that benchmark, the study concluded.
2 Of the black professionals and managers, most were disproportionately found in ethnic specialty agencies or in peripheral areas of general-market advertising firms.
3 Stereotypes held by management often excluded African-Americans from general-market assignments, who could find work only in agencies or departments specializing in "ethnic markets."
4 About 16 percent of large advertising firms employed no black professionals or managers, a rate 60 percent higher than in the overall labor market.
5 African-American employees are under-utilized in the advertising industry; they are often believed to be uninterested, unavailable, or unprepared for advertising careers. Blacks in advertising are only 62 percent as likely as their white counterparts to work in powerful "creative" and "client contact" roles in agencies and are often assigned to work areas involving little to no client contact.
6 African-American advertising employees were underpaid in the advertising industry, earning on average about 20 percent less than white employees with comparable qualifications. Black professionals and managers were only 10 percent as likely as their white counterparts to earn more than $100,000 a year.
7 African-Americans were under-recognized among major industry individual awards, comprising only nine recipients among 196 inductees from the AAF Advertising Hall of Fame, the AAF Advertising Hall of Achievement, and the One Club Creative Hall of Fame awards, combined, between 1961 and 2008. As of 2008, no African-American had ever been inducted into the One Club (Bendick and Egan, 2009, pp. 31–32).
8 Compared with other industry sectors in the U.S. EEO (Equal Employment Opportunity) database, the advertising industry was 37.6 percent worse on eight key employment indicators including, overall representation, representation in professional and managerial positions, opportunities for promotion, occupational segregation, compensation levels, and pay disparities.

The Madison Avenue Project data and analysis showed the culmination of decades-long institutionalization of structural oppression in the advertising industry, resulting in persistent inequalities for African-Americans in particular, concerning the time frame addressed in this study. Overall, blacks in advertising were significantly worse off on key employment indicators compared with other industries. The effort was further substantiated by the involvement of prominent civil rights attorney, Cyrus Mehri, who had an excellent reputation and track record concerning discrimination lawsuits aimed at major corporations. For example, Mehri won settlements of $192.5 million, $176 million, and $46 million against Coca-Cola Corporation, Texaco, Inc., and Morgan Stanley, respectively (Carter, 2009). Reflecting on the advertising industry, Mehri commented: "Forty-five years after the passage of the Civil Rights Act of 1964, [advertising] is still a closed society where favoritism rules and merit is cast aside" (Elliott, 2009). Nancy Hill, the president of the 4 A's in 2009, explaining how the "casting" process for advertising jobs tended to eliminate blacks, commented (Carter, 2009):

> "Because we've had such a narrow point of view in terms of what the right fit is for our clients, it has automatically been said when you're looking at a résumé, it needs to do this, this, this, and this and if they don't, move on. That is what has eliminated a lot of minority candidates across the board. And by the way, not just African Americans but also Hispanics, Asian Pacifics and women."

The Madison Avenue Project sponsors sought business and employment growth in advertising, marketing, and media companies for African-Americans. While it is acknowledged that employment discrimination employment exists in other corporate sectors, many have improved over the years. However, since the advertising industry failed to keep pace with other professions on numerous critical measures, it has fallen far, far behind other industries, undermining its reputation among people those who work in the industry and those who might consider joining it. Moreover, retention rates for black employees in white agencies have been low and black agencies in general have not prospered like their white counterparts, for reasons explained in this study. These problems make employee recruitment and satisfaction problematic and cast the advertising industry in a poor light. To address these issues, ad agencies and organizations hired diversity officers at senior levels, who were frequently African-American women, similar to past corporate practices when black managers were often confined to the "minority" spheres of the organizations. The cooperation of client companies to pressure their agencies to embrace diversity in their employment policies and practices was also solicited, given that executive suites in client organizations had become more diverse than ad companies over time (Elliott, 2009). In addition, some major advertisers had supplier diversity programs in place which could provide models for other companies (Bendick and Egan, 2009, p. 70). Still, critics remained skeptical that such efforts would amount to any significant change. Examining the advertising field since the 1950s, pioneering adman and Advertising Hall of Famer Roy Eaton, now in his eighties, appeared in an *Advertising Age* video, commenting on the diversity climate in the industry (Pollack, 2014):

> "Look at every other field ... where artistic talent is prized ... You find African-Americans are doing very well. 'Why the hell should they go to where they are not wanted?' is the prevailing attitude ... The system is the system. The system is one that depends on affiliation ... Ad agencies aren't hiring more black copywriters or executives; instead they are hiring a lot of African-American diversity officers."

Boulton (2013) noted a modern system of oppression which extended into the 2000s, subjected women and minorities to unequal status, and promoted the hiring of whites on the basis of in-group fit, familiarity and friendship. An African-American woman in her thirties with a Master's degree who served in a mid-level executive role at a major advertising agency for a top-ten leading national advertiser, explained her decision to leave the industry in 2015, commenting on her frustrations with the industry culture (Davis, 2015):

> "I spent 12 years in the agency world and the lack of diversity is just absolutely crazy. Agency leadership operates based on title and perceived knowledge. I cannot tell you how many times I've witnessed someone and/or been excluded based on title, age or perceived cultural differences. I've seen accounts with 40-plus people and only one person of color. Agencies and brands alike treat diversity in advertising as a second thought. Additionally, most brands don't have diverse marketing teams. You can't have the blind leading the blind. One would think that people who have done this for 25-plus years would have a clue, but they don't nor do they seem to care. People want to work with people who look like them, talk like them, have the same experiences, and it shows in the creative. But as long as they are winning awards and brands are moving products, this diversity in agencies is a long way off."

A rare breed indeed: African-American women advertising executives

Taking into account conclusions from studies of women and African-Americans in corporate life, it is not surprising that the ranks of black women in executive roles in the advertising industry are very thin. Not only have African-American adwomen had to contend with the same challenges that women typically experience in advertising firms, but they also had to endure systemic biases which are commonly directed toward African-Americans, combined with the particularly potent and persistent forms of discrimination which seem to permeate many advertising organizations, as indicated in the Madison Avenue Project research. Interestingly, only a few studies have addressed dual oppressions of women in advertising and marketing environments concerning gender and race. Bristor and Fischer (1995) found that minority female *consumers* in the marketplace experienced "simultaneous oppressions" on the basis of gender, race, and other factors. Chambers (2008, pp. 296, 240) acknowledged sexist and racist treatments concerning Barbara Proctor and Caroline Jones during their advertising careers; and Sivulka

(2009) briefly examined the experiences of Proctor, Jones, and Carol Williams. Jones, in fact, coined the term "caste-typing" to describe the combined gender and race-related oppressions she observed in the advertising industry (Davis, 2013a, p. 327).

The main subjects of this study – Barbara Gardner Proctor, Caroline R. Jones, Joel P. Martin, and Carol H. Williams – all experienced some degree of various types of structural oppression during their advertising careers, which were unique compared with the experiences of white women or black men. Beyond these subjects, other African-American adwomen shared compelling stories of their experiences with dual gender and race-based oppression in the advertising workplace. In 1971, *Time* magazine published an article which referred to black businesswomen in managerial roles as "the rarest breed of women," recognizing that they addressed issues stemming from racism and sexism in an era where society was struggling concurrently with changes brought about by the Civil Rights *and* Women's Liberation Movements. Shirley Barnes Kalunda, a black female account executive at the JWT advertising agency – one of only a few in that position in the early 1970s – discussed her career prospects in advertising, explaining: "When white businessmen look at us, they still see a female, and how far up the ladder can a female go? That's the thing that is scary. Women cannot get beyond the middle-management level" (*Time*, 1971, p. 99). An unnamed African-American woman, who eventually served in executives roles at several black-owned advertising and marketing firms, related her "horrible" early career experiences at a major general-market ad agency in the 1970s where she was "thrown into a very bad situation without a parachute or umbrella" (Davis, 2014a). Possessing an MBA, she was hired to work in a key department where the majority of her colleagues were white males. The agency favored a collaborative approach for working on client assignments and generating ideas. However, she explained: "I always encountered dead silence when I walked into the room. I was not a part of the boy's team; I was not courted by my peers and it was a difficult thing." In the face of such ostracism, she worked extremely long hours, alone, trying to live up to the demands of the position. One day, she was rushed from work to the hospital in an ambulance, believing she was having a heart attack; however, work-related stress was found to be the source of her ailments. Observing other employees at the firm, she concluded that the only way to achieve success in that environment was to find a mentor – "white and male." Unfortunately, she had a white male mentor for only about a week – the person who hired her – but he was promoted shortly after she was hired and moved on. She lamented: "I was stuck and ended up getting a racist. It was a tough ride for me." In another example, despite her excellent track record at general-market advertising agencies, Dana Wade – who eventually left to lead ethnic specialty agency Spike DDB – believed she was not promoted because she is an African-American woman. After losing a promotion at a general-market agency for a job that she was repeatedly told was hers to "one of the golden boys," Wade explained, "Nobody could tell you it was race, but ultimately, I think it was race and gender" (Johnson, 2004, p. 28). Wade noted that there were no people of color beyond a certain level at the agency.

In contrast to the negative experiences described above, some black women had wonderful experiences in advertising firms, depending on the corporate cultures within the individual advertising companies where they worked. As indicated, Joel Martin at McCaffrey & McCall and Carol Williams at Leo Burnett, had superb experiences in these general-market agencies, with access to great mentors and ground-breaking promotions during the 1960s and 1970s. Other black women thrived in leadership positions at black-owned agencies where being African-American was not a detriment. Pioneering black adwoman Sarah Burroughs excelled in both general-market and black agency settings. Burroughs started at FCB in Chicago in 1964 right out of college with a bachelor's degree in history from Lincoln University. At the time, companies actively sought college graduates and management training opportunities were plentiful. However, Burroughs – not wanting a teaching job – found the job search "was tough for me – not only because I was black, but because I was a woman" (Davis, 2014b). Learning about a job opening at an advertising agency from a recruiter, she interviewed for an 'analytical assistant' position in the Research Department at FCB which included typing research reports, proofreading, and doing data calculations. Although the job was essentially a clerical position, she interviewed with several managers, which she thought was an unusual practice for a relatively low-level job. Later she learned that she was the first black woman hired at the firm. Ron Sampson, the first African-American hired at FCB, was already at the agency when Burroughs arrived, but took another job shortly thereafter, leaving her as the only black person at the company. Although she was initially uncomfortable as the only African-American, nothing bad happened to her at FCB. Her immediate supervisor was also a woman and she felt that her agency colleagues were "welcoming" and "overly kind," prompting her to sense that there had been some sort of preparation prior to her arrival. Employees who had nothing to do with her department came to meet and greet her. Given that this was the time when major Civil Rights legislation had passed and advertising agencies were under pressure to shore up minority employment, Burroughs speculated that perhaps FCB wanted to be seen as progressive. Burroughs commented (Davis, 2014b): "Advertising people like to think of themselves as forward-thinking, cutting-edge types. FCB was a conservative and wholesome type of place. People there – especially managers – were well-off, pillars of society types, very refined." With her Tennessee roots, Catholic church background, and disciplined upbringing, Burroughs fit in well at FCB. Knowing nothing about advertising, she took books home to read about the business. She rose up rapidly through the ranks at FCB, becoming a Vice President – the first black woman in Chicago to do so, in 1971. At one point she considered leaving to pursue a social work career, which she believed paid better, but FCB convinced her to stay and gave her a raise. Burroughs attributed her ascent to hard work and being in the right place at the right time. She believed FCB saw her as: "she can talk, she can write, she's intelligent – and she's black!" Burroughs was active in BAG – the Black Advertising Group – a networking club of Chicago-area African-American advertising professionals where she met pioneering admen Tom Burrell and Bill Sharp. She recalls they were involved in "some type of advertising class" – the BAC – and she participated as a guest lecturer on research topics in the curriculum. In 1974, Burroughs was recruited by Tom Burrell to come to his agency where she started its Research Department and served in a variety of key managerial roles over 26 years, including head of Burrell's Atlanta office, and President and Chief Operating Officer of the Chicago office, until her retirement in 2000.

Coping with structural oppression: black adwomen entrepreneurs

The main subjects of this study – Barbara Gardner Proctor, Caroline R. Jones, Joel P. Martin, and Carol H. Williams – each had common qualities which helped them deal with the challenges of the advertising business and set them on the path toward entrepreneurship. They each had high-quality college educations, solid work experience gained in the creative departments of respected general-market agency agencies, professional appearances and carriage suitable for the corporate environment, and excellent interpersonal skills. In addition, they had traits such as optimism, resiliency, comfort in high stress situations, high intelligence and abundant energy, which are consistent with characteristics associated with women who fare well in corporate and marketing settings (Goudreau, 2015; Maclaran, Stevens, and Catterall, 1997; Vinnicombe and Banks, 2003). Many successful women in Corporate America adapt to and conform to the behavior patterns of the dominant group. Caroline Jones, for example, found support at JWT among the senior executive women at the agency where she mimicked their style of dress – including hats and white gloves – in order to fit in with them. High-achieving women also enhance their skills through professional development opportunities including networking activities and organizations, career-oriented seminars, and/or attainment of advanced degrees or professional certificates. For example, Proctor attended events and participated with a multitude of business and civic organizations in the Chicago area, often in leadership roles. Both Jones and Martin participated in GAP, a networking and educational association for African-American ad professionals in the New York area, and other trade groups, including the NAMD. Carol Williams learned about advertising careers as a student in the BAC in the Chicago area in the late 1960s, becoming one of its all-time most successful graduates, as well as participating in numerous industry and civic events and organizations throughout her career. Finally, if they felt they could do better, successful women often chose to exit organizations to fulfill their potential with respect to career or personal interests (Mallia, 2009). Proctor and Jones' departures from several agencies before launching their own firms are good examples of this approach; and Williams and Martin each made significant worklife changes – including exiting the advertising business – although Williams ultimately returned to the industry as an entrepreneur and Martin earned a Ph.D. before launching another venture.

Mallia (2009) identified factors in the advertising business which contributed to women's success – particularly at the executive level – and found that tenacity, a competitive personality, support at home – including spousal support or full-time childcare help – and the capability to start one's own agency were essential. Advertising Hall of Famer Linda Kaplan Thaler, a white agency CEO, tired of the long hours associated with the traditional agency business, explained her desire to embrace entrepreneurship as a means of changing the agency culture (Bosman, 2005):

> "I started my own shop because I wanted to rewrite my own rules about how business was run. The policy of 'you need to work till 12 o'clock at night or you're not doing your job' is going by the wayside. We get to work early, we work through lunch, we work collaboratively and we shrink the clock. Women are very well poised to do it because we want to go home and take care of our families."

Family and childcare issue were very important since all subjects of this study were working mothers. Martin's family was highly supportive with respect to her daughter's childcare arrangements; and the others managed family responsibilities as best they could using various approaches. In fact, motherhood shaped a lot of Proctor's business decisions, prompting her to pursue business in the local vicinity in order to be regularly present for her son. But, like many working mothers, Proctor, Jones, and Williams all acknowledged the challenges of coordinating family life with the demands of a high-powered advertising career.

It is noteworthy that the subjects had highly varied experiences early in their advertising careers. For Proctor, who entered the advertising industry in the early 1960s, the climate was less hospitable – even hostile – and, as the first black woman, she had no role models or mentors for guidance. She had to learn the business, learn how to navigate the white corporate culture, and build relationships on her own. Although Jones was required to enter the business as a secretary, she benefitted shortly thereafter from opportunities created by the social climate of the early 1960s when New York advertising agencies were being pressured by civil rights advocates to place more African-Americans in professional advertising positions, allowing her to learn copywriting and research skills. By the time Martin and Williams entered the advertising business in the late 1960s, the climate had improved somewhat, since the Civil Rights Act had passed a few years earlier and the advertising industry was still under pressure to hire minorities. Therefore, the more "progressive" agencies seemed receptive to the development and advancement of minorities in professional roles. Under these conditions, Martin and Williams fortuitously had white male mentors at their first agencies who nurtured them and helped them to flourish in the corporate environment, which helped them to obtain executive positions in their respective agencies.

Proctor, Jones, Martin, and Williams each eventually launched her own agency for various reasons and under different circumstances. Since individual advertising firms have different organizational cultures which are largely dependent on their leaders' personas, preferences, and priorities, entrepreneurship provided them the opportunity to create favorable workplace environments which reflected their personal standards and values. Davis and Watson (1982, p. 150) noted that black women – even those who are successful in corporate settings – are the most likely to seek alternatives to corporate workplaces because they are more concerned with quality of life, rather than getting ahead for the sake of getting ahead. Proctor, for example, articulated early on the need to establish an environment that she could control. This behavior concurs with Fernandez's (1975, p. 169) research, which found that black women in white corporations were the most likely to be dissatisfied with the overall work environment and subsequently make career decisions which offer opportunities for personal growth. Proctor, as one of the earliest pioneers in a new area of entrepreneurship for African-Americans – advertising – started her company as an escape from the inhospitable workplace culture in general-market agencies where she felt disrespected and unable to do work which fit her standards. Entrepreneurship also gave Proctor opportunity to cultivate the types of accounts she wanted to work with, which aligned with her personal and moral values. For Martin, Jones, and Williams, entrepreneurship provided the opportunity to live up to their potential while exercising their talents under circumstances affording a high degree of autonomy. As entrepreneurs, however, they faced several significant issues. As women in general-market advertising firms, they had been subject to Glasshouse Effect aspects of structural oppression which placed them in the creative department, but hindered them from learning other sides of the business such as account management and finance. This could be a significant problem when they moved into CEO roles and had to take responsibility for administrative and client functions of their agencies. For example, Martin – an artist who preferred creative work – mentioned difficulty in getting acclimated to the account and business aspects of the agency, and relied heavily on her husband for help in that regard. Moreover, Proctor and Jones' agencies each suffered bankruptcies, where cash flow and accounts receivable problems were encountered and contributed to the demise of their firms. Of the four women, Williams appeared the most comfortable with the business *and* creative aspects of managing an agency, and doing so successfully over the long run. Another important issue for these entrepreneurs is that, whether by choice or by circumstance, most of their agencies' assignments concerned black consumers or "urban" market work, consistent with the Economic

Detour models of business development. Although providing a viable foot-in-the-door to the advertising business in some cases, ultimately this position limited the growth potential of their agencies over the long term. While Proctor and Martin set out to cater to the black consumer market when they launched their agencies in the early and mid-1970s – a practical stance at the time – Jones and Williams each sought lucrative general-market work beyond the ethnic market niche. In fact, Williams' firm has done and continues to do some general-market work. But when Pac Bell approached Carol Williams in the late 1980s, they assumed she could do black-targeted advertising because she is African-American, although she lacked experience with that market. It is ironic that these entrepreneurs were not provided general-market opportunities on a wider basis, given that they had done highly effective and award-winning work for mainstream brands – such as Campbell's Soup and Secret antiperspirant – prior to establishing their own agencies. Therefore, being largely excluded from general-market opportunities appears to be the most unjust aspect of these women's experiences with structural oppression, given that they had already proven themselves and established track records at large mainstream agencies.

The legacy of pioneering African-American madwomen

Viewed through the prism of historical analysis, these pioneering black women's stories are intriguing, triumphant, bittersweet, and sometimes tragic. They experienced concurrent and extreme forms of gender- and race-based structural oppression, yet applied coping strategies which allowed them to persevere in their endeavors. They learned to navigate in a corporate industry climate which was not conditioned to welcome their involvement or perspectives. Moreover, as advertising executives and entrepreneurs, they had to consistently prove their worth to members of the dominant corporate culture.

Cortese (2008, p. 92) observed that ethnic agencies walk a fine line between creating positive imagery out of a sense of community responsibility and securing the bottom line. For these pioneering adwomen, their efforts had greater meaning beyond the mere practice of advertising and deriving revenue, but often extended into the realm of social responsibility and community uplift. As entrepreneurs, they were sensitive to their role as cultural producers, committed to creating ideas and images which were socially relevant and impactful. Hence, many of the themes in their advertising work depicted strong black families, well-nurtured children, economic achievement, pride in cultural history, and other aspects of human enrichment. Jones' contributions, which underscored high aspirations and upward mobility for people of color, helped corporate marketers avoid blunders by providing sensitive insights into consumers' mindsets. Williams' work cultivated social relevance while at the same time garnering effective outcomes on behalf of clients' brands. Martin's compelling and thought-provoking images and copy were examples of mindful activism. Moreover, she had the courage to change direction, to reject labels put on her by others, and move onto a new career path many would consider unorthodox. Yet, she found more fulfillment in her post-advertising career helping company leaders develop ideas and strategies so that their firms can be improved from the top down. Proctor's sense of integrity explains why she was so outspoken and involved in social responsibility activities throughout her career. She was not afraid to advise clients from an ethical perspective. Perhaps her reputation in this regard became problematic and ultimately cost Proctor her business and recognition among industry peers, especially when black advertising agencies became less of a novelty. However, she left the business knowing her purpose, ultimately providing peace of mind.

For each of these trailblazers, it was important for them to serve as mentors and role models, helping young people, people of color, and other women. As CEOs of their own agencies, each woman employed multicultural staffs, nurtured young people, and engaged in encouraging future generations of diverse advertising professionals. Today, Carol Williams remains as the only subject still active as head of her own agency – the only 100 percent black- and woman-owned independent advertising agency in the world. She resisted the call to sell part of the CHWA to a large holding company partner out of a desire to control what will be left to the next generation of agency leadership. In view of the overall history of African-American women in the advertising industry, one can appreciate the importance of maintaining the privilege of ownership, which provides individuals the authority to lead the direction and corporate culture of their enterprises, like those who came before them.

References

Alberta Council for Global Cooperation (n.d.) 'Stage Left Workshop for Canada World Youth: Oppression and Privilege Framework' [Online]. www.acgc.ca/09/images/file/resources/Youth%20Action%20Resources/Oppression%20and%20Privilege%20Framework.pdf (Accessed: October 1, 2015).

Alvesson, M. (1998) 'Gender Relations and Identity at Work: A Case Study of Masculinities and Femininities in an Advertising Agency,' *Human Relations*, 51(8), pp. 969–1005.

Amott, T. and Matthaei, J. (1991) *Race, Gender and Work: A Multicultural Economic History of Women in the United States*. Boston, MA: South End Press.

Arnberg, K. and Svanlund, J. (2016) 'Mad Women: Gendered Divisions in the Swedish Advertising Industry, 1930–2012,' *Business History*, 58 [Online]. Available at: www.tandfonline.com/doi/abs/10.1080/00076791.2016.1182158 (Accessed: May 25, 2016).

Bates, T. (1997) *Race, Self-Employment and Upward Mobility: An Illusive Dream*. Washington, D.C.: Woodrow Wilson Press.

Bell, E. and Nkomo, S. (1994) *Barriers to Workplace Advancement Experienced by African-Americans*. Cambridge, MA: MIT Press.

Bendick, M. and Egan, M. (2009) *Research Perspectives on Race and Employment in the Advertising Industry*. Washington, D.C.: Bendick and Egan Economic Consultants, Inc.

Blake, S. (1999) 'At the Crossroads of Race and Gender: Lessons from the Mentoring Experiences of Professional Black Women,' in A. Murrell, F. Crosby, and R. Ely (eds.) *Mentoring Dilemmas: Development Relationships with Multicultural Organizations*. Mahwah, NJ: Lawrence Erlbaum, pp. 77–98.

Bosman, J. (2005) 'Stuck at the Edges of the Ad Game,' *New York Times*, November 22 [Online]. Available at: www.nytimes.com/2005/11/22/business/media/stuck-at-the-edges-of-the-ad-game.html (Accessed: October 27, 2015).

Boulton, C. (2013) 'The Ghosts of Mad Men: Race and Gender Inequality inside American Advertising Agencies,' in M. McAllister and E. Vest (eds.) *The Routledge Companion to Advertising and Promotion Culture*. New York: Routledge, pp. 252–266.

Boulton, C. (2015) 'Under the Cloak of Whiteness: A Circuit of Culture Analysis of Opportunity Hoarding and Colour-blind Racism Inside U.S. Advertising Internship Programs,' *Triple C: Communication, Capitalism & Critique: Journal for a Global Sustainable Information Society*. Available at: www.triple-c.at/index.php/tripleC/article/viewFile/592/741 (Accessed: November 29, 2015).

Bova, B. (2000) 'Mentoring Revisited: The Black Woman's Experience,' *Mentoring and Tutoring*, 8(1), pp. 5–16.

Bristor, J. and Fischer, E. (1995) 'Exploring Simultaneous Oppressions: Toward the Development of Consumer Research in the Interest of Diverse Women,' *American Behavioral Scientist*, 38(4), pp. 526–536.

Broyles, S. and Grow, J. (2008) 'Creative Women in Advertising Agencies: Why so Few "Babes in Boyland"?' *Journal of Consumer Marketing*, 25(1), pp. 4–6.

Butler, J. S. (1991) *Entrepreneurship and Self-help Among Black Americans: A Reconsideration of Race and Economics*. Albany, NY: State University of New York.

Caplow, T. (1954) *The Sociology of Work*. New York: McGraw-Hill.

Carter, K. (2009) 'Resistance to Changing the Status Quo,' Black Enterprise.com [Online]. Available at: www.blackenterprise.com/mag/resistance-to-changing-the-status-quo-2 (Accessed: May 23, 2015).

Cassidy, M. and Katula, R. (1990) 'The Black Experience in Advertising: An Interview with Thomas J. Burrell,' *Journal of Communication Inquiry*, 14, pp. 93–104.

Chambers, J. (2008) *Madison Avenue and the Color Line: African-Americans in the Advertising Industry*. Philadelphia, PA: University of Pennsylvania Press.

Collins, S. (1997) *Black Corporate Executives*. Philadelphia, PA: Temple University Press.

Combs, G. (2003) 'The Duality of Race and Gender for Managerial African American Women: Implications of Informal Social Networks on Career Advancement,' *Human Resource Development Review*, 2(4), pp. 385–405.

Cortese, A. (2008) *Provocateur: Images of Women and Minorities in Advertising*. New York: Rowman & Littlefield.

Cox, T. (1991) 'The Multicultural Organization,' *Executive*, 5(2), pp. 34–47.

Creativity (2006) 'The Creativity 50: The Most Influential Creative People of the Last Two Decades,' March, pp. 38–52.

Cuneo, A. (2006) 'Ad Industry Blasted for "Sanctioned Segregation,"' *Advertising Age*, May 8 [Online]. Available at: http://adage.com/article/news/ad-industry-blasted-sanctioned-segregation/109096/ (Accessed: October 27, 2015).

Davis, G. and Watson, G. (1982) *Black Life in Corporate America*. New York: Anchor Books.

Davis, J. F. (2002) 'Enterprise Development under an Economic Detour? Black-Owned Advertising Agencies, 1940–2000,' *Journal of Macromarketing*, 22(1), pp. 75–85.

Davis, J. F. (2013a) 'Beyond "Caste-Typing"? Caroline Robinson Jones, Advertising Pioneer and Trailblazer,' *Journal of Historical Research in Marketing*, 5(3), pp. 308–333.
Davis, J. F. (2013b) 'Realizing Marketplace Opportunity: How Research on the Black Consumer Market Influenced Mainstream Markers, 1920–1970,' *Journal of Historical Research in Marketing*, 5(4), pp. 471–493.
Davis, J. F. (2014a) Interview with anonymous subject.
Davis, J. F. (2014b) Interview with Sarah Burroughs.
Davis, J. F. (2015) Interview with anonymous subject.
Dewitt, K. (1974) 'Black Women in Business,' *Black Enterprise*, August, pp. 14–19.
Dishman, L. (2013) 'Where are All the Women Creative Directors?' *Fast Company* [Online]. Available at: www.fastcompany.com/3006255/where-are-all-women-creative-directors (Accessed: November 9, 2015).
Elliott, S. (2009) 'A Lawyer's Call for a Greater Black Presence in Agencies,' *New York Times*, January 8 [Online]. Available at: www.nytimes.com/2009/01/09/business/media/09adco.html (Accessed: July 2, 2014).
Feagin, J. and Sikes, M. (1994) *Living with Racism: The Black Middle-Class Experience*. Boston, MA: Beacon Press.
Fernandez, J. (1975) *Black Managers in White Corporations*. New York: John Wiley & Sons.
Fernandez, J. (1981) *Racism and Sexism in Corporate Life*. Lexington, MA: Lexington Books.
Fernandez, J. (1999) *Race, Gender & Rhetoric*. New York: McGraw-Hill.
Fox, S. (1984) *The Mirror Makers*. Chicago, IL: University of Illinois Press.
Freeman, E. and Fields, C. (1972) *A Study of Black Male Professionals in Industry*. Washington, D.C.: U.S. Department of Labor.
Goudreau, J. (2014) '13 Subtle Ways Women are Treated Differently at Work,' *Business Insider*, June 27 [Online]. Available at: www.businessinsider.com/subtle-ways-women-treated-differently-work-2014-6 (Accessed: June 31, 2015).
Goudreau, J. (2015) '6 Personality Traits of High-Performing Women,' *Business Insider*, January 21 [Online]. Available at: www.businessinsider.com/personality-traits-of-high-performing-women-2015-1 (Accessed: June 31, 2015).
Greenhaus, J., Parasuraman, S., and Wormley, W. (1990) 'Effects of Race on Organizational Experiences, Job Performance Evaluations, and Career Outcomes,' *Academy of Management Journal*, 33(1), pp. 64–86.
Hall, E. (2000) 'The Myth and the Reality: Emma Hall Reports on the IPA's Second Landmark Report into Women and the Work–Life Balance in Advertising,' *Campaign*, p. 32.
Hinson, S. and Bradley, A. (n.d.) 'A Structural Analysis of Oppression.' *Grassroots Policy Project* [Online]. Available at: www.strategicpractice.org/system/files/structural_analysis_oppression.pdf (Accessed: September 9, 2015).
Iezzi, T. (2005) 'In Ad World, Boys vs Girls isn't Black-and-White Issue,' *Advertising Age*, October 31 [Online]. Available at: http://adage.com/article/news/ad-world-boys-girls-black-white-issue/105054/ (Accessed: October 12, 2015).
John J. Heldrich Center for Workforce Development (2002) *Work Trends Survey Report. A Workplace Divided: How Americans View Discrimination and Race on the Job*. New Brunswick, NJ: Rutgers University.
Johnson, A. (2004) 'Adapting to Change?' *Diversity Inc.*, August/September, pp. 27–34.
Kazenoff, I. and Vagnoni, A. (1997) 'Babes in Boyland,' *Advertising Age's Creativity*, 5(8), pp. 18–20.

Kosin, J. (2015) 'Ad Women: 4 Women in Advertising on "Madmen" and the Industry today,' *Harper's Bazaar* [Online]. Available at: www.harpersbazaar.com/culture/film-tv/a10907/women-in-advertising-mad-men/ (Accessed: November 9, 2015).

Lach, J. (1999) 'Minority Women Hit a "Concrete Ceiling,"' *Advertising Age* [Online]. Available at: http://adage.com/article/american-demographics/minority-women-hit-a-concrete-ceiling/42683 (Accessed: November 1, 2015).

Liesse, J. (2013) 'Women in Advertising: The Agency Challenge,' *Advertising Age*, July 22, pp. 10–11.

Maclaran, P., Stevens, L., and Catterall, M. (1997) 'The "Glasshouse Effect": Women in Marketing Management,' *Marketing Intelligence and Planning*, 15(7), pp. 309–317.

McCollum, V. (1998) 'Career Development Issues and Strategies for Counseling African Americans,' *Journal of Career Development*, 25(1), pp. 41–52.

Madaran, P. and Catterall, M. (2000) 'Bridging the Knowledge Divide: Issues on the Feminisation of Marketing Practice,' *Journal of Marketing Management*, 16(6), pp. 635–646.

Mallia, K. (2009) 'Rare Birds: Why So Few Women Become Ad Agency Creative Directors,' *Advertising and Society Review*, 10(3). Available at: www.aef.com/on_campus/asr/contents (Accessed: February 12, 2012).

Mehra, A., Kilduff, M., and Brass, D. (1998) 'A Distinctiveness Approach to the Social Identity and Social Networks of Underrepresented Groups,' *Academy of Management Journal*, 41(4), pp. 441–452.

Mingo, F. (1985) 'Blacks in Advertising' [audio recording]. Interview with John Hansen for *In Black America*, University of Texas-Austin, November 8.

Mor-Barak, M. (1999) 'Beyond Affirmative Action,' *Administration in Social Work*, 2(3–4), pp. 47–68.

Mor-Barak, M. and Cherin, D. (1998) 'A Tool to Expand Organizational Understanding of Workforce Diversity,' *Administration in Social Work*, 22(1), pp. 47–64.

Mor-Barak, M., Cherin, D., and Berkman, C. (1998) 'Organizational and Personal Dimensions in Diversity Climate,' *Journal of Applied Behavioral Science*, 34(1), pp. 82–104.

Open Source Leadership (2012) 'The Dynamic System of Power, Privilege and Oppression,' a White Paper [Online]. Available at: www.opensourceleadership.com (Accessed: September 20, 2012).

Pierce, J. (1947) *Negro Business and Business Education*. New York: Harper & Bros.

Pollack, J. (2014) 'The Real "Man Men" Diaries: Roy Eaton,' *Advertising Age*, September 24 [Online]. Available at: http://adage.com/article/special-report-mad-men/real-mad-men-diaries-roy-eaton/295110/ (Accessed: June 15, 2015).

Rivers, C. and Barnett, R. (2013) *The New Soft War on Women: How the Myth of Female Ascendance is Hurting Women, Men – and Our Economy*. New York: Penguin.

Ryan, M. (1975) *Womanhood in America: From Colonial Times to the Present*. New York: New Viewpoints.

Silverman, R. (2015) 'Managers: Watch Your Language,' *Wall Street Journal*, September 30, p. R9.

Sivulka, J. (2009) *Ad Women: How They Impact What We Need, Want, and Buy*. Amherst, NY: Prometheus Books.

Smiley, T. (2014) 'RIP Black Ad Agencies…?' TavisSmileyRadio.com, June 9 [Online]. Available at: www.tavissmileyradio.com/panel-discussion-the-decline-of-black-owned-advertising-agencies/ (Accessed: June 15, 2014).

Still, L. V. (1986) 'Women Managers in Advertising: An Exploratory Study,' *Media International Australia*, 40(1), pp. 24–30.

Stuart, M. (1940) *An Economic Detour: A History of Insurance in the Lives of American Negroes*. New York: Wendell Malliet & Company.

Time (1971) 'The Rarest Breed of Women: Black Women in the Executive Suite,' November 8, pp. 98–102.

Vinnicombe, S. and Bank, J. (2003) *Women with Attitude: Lessons on Career Management*. New York: Routledge.

Wilensky, H. L. (1966) 'Measures and Effects of Social Mobility,' in N. J. Smelser and S. M. Lipset (eds.) *Social Structure, Social Mobility, and Economic Development*. Chicago, IL: Aldine, pp. 98–140.

Yoder, J. and Aniakudo, A. (1997) '"Outsider Within" the Firehouse: Subordination and Difference in the Social Interactions of African-American Women Firefighters,' *Gender and Society*, 11(3), pp. 324–341.

Epilogue

Extraordinary women

The advertising business has undergone tremendous change over its 150-year history. The configuration of the industry, the nature of technology, and the media landscape changed dramatically. Compared with the 1960s *Mad Men* era, the industry is more inclusive regarding diversity and the roles of individuals in the business. Yet, a major shortcoming of *Mad Men* is that it completely ignored the presence of professional black admen and adwomen *who were there*, including those in white-owned agencies. Nonetheless, this study illustrates how social, economic, and political conditions within society and advertising impacted black women's opportunities and choices in the industry. While progress was made, advancement was protracted and there were simultaneous challenges which were unique to black women. Therefore, considering the background and context of the participation of African-American women in the advertising industry, what the pioneers highlighted in this study were able to accomplish is remarkable. Intelligent, resourceful, and talented, these award-winning adwomen served in groundbreaking roles in white and black advertising agencies, rising to establish their own firms. Their biographies reveal the boldness and grit of Barbara Gardner Proctor, who entered advertising as an experienced businesswoman with a unique sense of purpose; the steadfast tenacity of Caroline R. Jones, which was complimented by her charismatic personality; the creative activism of Joel P. Martin, which was motivated by her resilient spirit; and the brilliance of Carol H. Williams, whose business acumen rivals that of top corporate executives. Rarities in the advertising field, these black women CEOs stood out as important leaders, role models, and spokespeople in business and cultural communities. They led their companies with their own sets of values. That they could address such a myriad of challenges with grace and professionalism is a resounding testament to their fortitude. Perhaps one day some will be included in the Advertising Hall of Fame, a fitting tribute which would affirm the legacies of these trailblazing African-American women for the benefit and inspiration of others in the years to come.

Repercussions of structural oppression

As indicated in Chapter 6, behaviors and practices stemming from structural oppression may be blatant, clandestine, inadvertent, or even unrecognized – yet can become endemic to the essence of an institution's culture. However, the most insidious aspects occur when such practices become normalized and widely accepted in culture of the workplace. These practices may be illustrated by declarations such as: "this is the way we have always done it" or "this is how things are here." Such behaviors may be even be couched in humorous terms or treated as tomfoolery – i.e., mischief intended to create fun in the workplace environment. These actions may appear innocuous, but over time they establish standards and patterns of behavior which may go unquestioned and are widely accepted throughout the workplace. Under these conditions, individuals or ideas which do not conform to the institutional norms may be viewed as strange or problematic. However, jokes, pranks, and similar activities often come at the expense of other's pride or dignity. In some workplaces, structural oppression has manifested in such a way that it produces systemic discrimination, marginalization, and even ridicule toward those viewed as "outsiders." Unfortunately, biased and insensitive behaviors abound in some organizations.

Examples of how structural oppression is exhibited in the advertising business are illustrated throughout this study. In addition, several recent high-profile examples – which occurred while this book was being written – created backlash and cast the reputations of advertising organizations in a poor light. For example in the fall of 2015, a Creative Director at the San Antonio office of the Campbell Ewald agency sent a company email to staffers promoting "Ghetto Day" at the office, which read (Coffee, 2016a):

> "Please share with the teams that today is officially Ghetto Day in the SA [San Antonio], and we're inviting our Big D homebitches to cycle in and pop a freak with us.
>
> Ghetto music, Malt 45s at lunch, ghetto terminology, and of course, drugs and prostitution are legal all day until close of business. Word, my cerebral gangsters."

The text of the email was accompanied by an image of two African-American men standing on a littered sidewalk outside of a liquor store. The message was condemned by some staffers at the agency as racist and offensive, but was concealed within the office for several months. When eventually disclosed to IPG, the parent company of Campbell Ewald, the office's CEO and the email's author were terminated. In light of the situation, the agency also lost several clients – the Edward Jones investment company, Henry Ford Health Systems, and USAA Financial – the latter which left in order to search for "a new agency that aligns with USAA's culture and core values" (Coffee, 2016a; Coffee, 2016b).

Another high-profile episode prompted observers to question the character of the entire advertising industry. Although charges concerning the industry's poor record on diversity have been levied regularly for nearly 50 years, this incident took on enormous significance since it involved the top executive of one of the oldest, largest, and most respected advertising firms in the world. In March 2016, a white woman executive at JWT filed a discrimination and harassment lawsuit in New York federal court alleging "racist and sexist" remarks and behaviors against the Worldwide Chairman and CEO of JWT, Gustavo Martinez (Morrison, 2016). The suit named Martinez, JWT, and its holding company parent, London-based WPP Group. The plaintiff, Erin Johnson, claimed Martinez had touched her inappropriately at work, repeatedly joked about raping female employees, and routinely made slurs against African-Americans and Jewish people (Morrison, 2016). Moreover, Johnson asserted that Martinez's comments were made publicly in the presence of other JWT employees, company executives, and a reporter and that there was email and video documentation supporting her claims (Morrison, 2016; Vranica and Tadena, 2016). Johnson asserted that the lawsuit was filed after her complaints to senior management about the behaviors went unanswered. As news about the lawsuit rapidly spread, Martinez denied the charges and WPP Group responded that it had found "nothing to substantiate these charges" and informed clients that the allegations were untrue (Schultz and Bruell, 2016). Controversy followed these events, with some insiders applauding Johnson's actions and others claiming that Martinez's behavior did not diminish the workplace environment (Morrison, 2016). However, within a week, Martinez – who had been with JWT for about two years – resigned from the agency citing "mutual agreement" with WPP leadership (Vranica and Tadena, 2016).

To many observers, the lawsuit and circumstances surrounding it suggested that a culture of sexual harassment and race discrimination had been allowed to permeate JWT, with support from top management. This was a departure from the agency's reputation, where JWT was considered relatively progressive and women-friendly. After all, this was the storied agency that Stanley and Helen Resor built into a global powerhouse, where the celebrated Women's Editorial Department was a major part of the company's success, and where women were vice presidents in the 1960s. Therefore, for a company of JWT's stature to be publicly associated with such allegations sent shock waves across the industry. Moreover, Johnson's allegations touched a raw nerve and reopened significant discussions throughout the industry concerning workplace culture and treatment of women and minorities. Top leadership of agency holding companies became involved in the discussions. In light of the JWT lawsuit, Sir Martin Sorrell, CEO of WPP Group, acknowledged that the industry had "a major problem with racism and sexism" at a major industry conference (Birkner, 2016). However, Maurice Levy, CEO of rival holding company Publicis Groupe, defended Martinez, calling his actions a "one-time mistake" saying "I don't believe what happened at JWT is endemic of what's happening in our industry" (Birkner, 2016). But Sorrell replied that he violently disagreed with Levy, arguing (Birkner, 2016):

> "Maurice has a habit of ignoring the facts. When we get to senior levels of management, the number of women drops, unacceptably, to a third [of all executives]. We're putting in programs for improvement, training people internally and externally on gender and race bias. It's not just looking at the charges against Gustavo Martinez, it's looking elsewhere in the industry."

While the uproar continued, conversations quickly shifted toward topics concerning sexism in the industry, with women sharing personal stories of their experiences, suggesting that the circumstances had finally reached an "inflection" point (Wohl and Stein, 2016). Immediately after Martinez's departure, Tamara Ingram, a white woman, was named as his replacement. One of the highest-ranking women in advertising, Ingram was known for her team-building and client-handling skills, had managed over $6 billion of JWT global business overseeing 45 account teams and 38,000 employees, and had previous executive experience with other major agencies (Morrison, 2016; Stein, 2016). However, as the discourse about diversity issues in advertising workplace cultures carried on, topics regarding sexism began to dominate the conversation while issues concerning racism were given short shrift. Wheaton (2016), a columnist for *Advertising Age*, argued that race discrimination against African-Americans in advertising was a highly problematic issue which should be given prime attention. In light of these concerns, JWT management created a diversity and inclusion council and established an internal communications "hotline" so that employees could report troublesome situations (Stein, 2016). In the meantime, observers waited to learn the outcome of the lawsuit.

Promoting diversity and inclusion in the advertising industry

The lawsuit against JWT and other incidents once again shined a harsh light on the advertising industry, raising questions as to why it was not more hospitable to women and minorities, especially given the creation of a number of programs, panels, internships, and other platforms intended to foster diversity. Over the decades, a variety of initiatives were established to address structural oppression and spur opportunities for women and people of color. Early initiatives like the NAMD, the BAC, and GAP were developed in the 1950s and 1960s and provided mixed results in terms of benefit to minorities. Later, trade industry trade groups, educational institutions, corporations, and individuals launched their own initiatives. The 4 A's introduced one of the oldest intern programs, the Multicultural Advertising Internship Program (MAIP), in the early 1970s and a spate of other programs were introduced in the 2000s. I'MPART was founded by the Advertising Club of New York in 2012 to promote, attract, retain, and train diverse advertising talent; and the 3% Conference, also launched in 2012, is dedicated to the advancement of managerial women in advertising. Colleges launched their own programs, including Howard University's Center for Excellence in Advertising in 2008, and City University of New York's Group M Professional Development

Initiative established in 2010. Publicis Groupe's Starcom MediaVest (SMG) agency introduced its own programs around 2010, providing a diversity week, a diversity supplier program, and the establishment of a diversity council; and BBD&O launched its Creative Residency program in 2015. The Marcus Graham Project – named after the lead character in the movie *Boomerang* – was founded by activist Lincoln Stephens in 2008 as a career development program for young men and women of color. These and other efforts served to provide exposure, training, and mentorship for diverse youth interested in advertising; and to improve retention, advancement, and job satisfaction for diverse individuals involved in advertising careers.

Major industry holding companies and trade associations also established their own diversity initiatives. IPG, Omnicom, and Publicis created senior executive positions in their organizations to address diversity and inclusion issues, often hiring African-American women for these roles. For example, IPG was the first major holding company to do so, hiring Heide Gardner in 2003 to develop inclusion management strategies and multicultural marketing programs for its agency brands worldwide, such as InterAct – an effort to cultivate diverse talent at IPG companies. Prior to coming to IPG, Gardner was with the AAF where she launched an intern program for diverse students – the Most Promising Multicultural Students (MPMS) program in 1997 – and the Mosaic Awards in 2001, which celebrate excellence in marketing techniques and business practices regarding multicultural audiences. The AAF also introduced a MOSAIC council, with representation from industry and academia (AAF.org, 2014). Tiffany Warren founded ADCOLOR in 2005, a set of programs and awards to promote diversity and inclusion in advertising and was hired by holding company Omnicom as its chief diversity officer in 2009; by 2013, she had co-founded the Roundtable of Advertising Diversity Executives (Hammer, 2013). Similarly, agencies including O&M, Deutsche, McCann, and DraftFCB all maintained diversity officer positions and/or diversity councils by 2014 (AAF.org, 2014).

With so much attention and energy surrounding diversity efforts, programs, and appointments of executives, what has been the outcome of these initiatives in terms of addressing structural oppression? Have they made a real difference or do they mainly serve public relations purposes to ease the industry's conscience regarding discriminatory practices? Advertising companies have been typically reluctant to release data, but observers suggest that more young people of color have come into the advertising industry and that white women have been major beneficiaries. While these are commendable outcomes, there is acknowledgment that African-Americans – regardless of gender – still bear the brunt of the most extreme inequities in advertising workplaces. In the meantime, women's advocates stress that meaningful change in advertising workplace cultures should include benefits such as childcare assistance or on-site daycare, flex time, pay equity, bias training, mentorships, and greater respect for women's accomplishments (Bond, 2016; Wohl and Stein, 2016). Historical evidence indicates that considerable effort and fundamental transformation within advertising workplace cultures are required in order for the ideals of diversity to be achieved. Namely, diversity objectives must be clearly articulated and embraced from the top down throughout the organizations, put into meaningful practice, and measured. Concerning people of color, given the industry's background, top leaders must be involved and willing to embrace diversity and incentivize it within their organizational cultures in order for substantive progress to occur and be maintained.

Looking forward by looking back: notable African-American madwomen

Over the years, African-American women continued to persevere in the advertising business against a background of ongoing structural oppression. Some benefitted from diversity initiatives and others found different paths into the industry. As such, this study would not be complete without recognizing other noteworthy African-American adwomen who served in executive capacities in advertising firms who have not already been discussed in this study. Although they were not subject to full examination for this research, their presences are an important part of the historical account on black women in advertising. Apologies are offered in advance to those whose names are not mentioned directly, with the understanding that their contributions are acknowledged and appreciated.

Black women executives in general-market agencies

Considering the careers of white trailblazers like Charlotte Beers and Shelly Lazarus, who led O&M in the 1990s, Ann Fudge's appointment as the Chairman and CEO of advertising powerhouse Y&R, part of the WPP Group holding company, was lauded as a watershed moment in advertising history. With a Harvard MBA and extensive client-side brand management experience, the former Kraft General Foods President became the highest-ranking African-American woman ever in the advertising business at a general-market agency in 2003. With a long career managing major food and beverage brands, Fudge had a stellar reputation as one of the most successful and high-ranking women in corporate America and was often praised in the business press. At the time of her appointment, the president of the Association of National Advertisers commented (Sanders, 2003, p. 4):

> "It's sensational news. Not only do we have another woman now breaking through the glass ceiling, but one of color, and one who is extraordinarily talented. I hope this is the beginning of more talented people from the multicultural communities landing top roles."

Early on, however, reports suggested that Fudge would have difficulty at Y&R. They acknowledged cost and profit issues at the agency, compared with JWT and O&M, which were also part of the WPP agency network; and challenges implementing innovative integrated marketing communications strategies at the agency (Sanders, 2003, p. 143). Moreover, Fudge was new to the agency side of the business and Y&R was regarded as one of the "staunchest, most WASPiest old-boy networks" where her presence by some was likely unwelcomed (Johnson, 2004, p. 34). Unfortunately, by 2005, Y&R lost several important clients including Burger King, Sony Electronics, and the Jaguar automobile brand and Fudge moved into another position at the agency (*Wall Street Journal*, 2005). Account losses continued and Fudge retired in 2006 after three years with Y&R to devote her time to work on corporate and nonprofit boards (*Advertising Age*, 2012, p. 32).

Another prominent black female CEO in a general-market advertising firm was Renetta McCann, who served as President and Worldwide Chief Executive of the media agency SMG from October 2005 through June 2008 (Kirk, 2008). The Northwestern University graduate started her career at the Leo Burnett agency in Chicago in 1978 and rose through the media ranks assuming a variety of managerial positions, including serving as the agency's first African-American Media Director in 1989. A merger between Burnett's media unit and other entities created SMG, a subsidiary of the Publicis agency network, specializing in media buying. As one of the largest customer contact agencies in the world, the firm handled about $30 billion annually in media purchases for such clients as Kraft Foods, GM, and Procter & Gamble (Kirk, 2008). As CEO, McCann's responsibilities included strategic planning, financial management, and client maintenance in the United States, Canada, and Latin America. During a time of tremendous change in the media and advertising landscapes in the late 1990s, McCann championed the idea of placing the media buying function in a separate entity. She also served as a member of the AAF's Multicultural Business Practices Leadership Council. A recipient of numerous advertising industry awards and citations from the trade press, McCann surprised the advertising community when she stepped down in 2008, citing unspecified family and personal reasons (Kirk, 2008). After taking time off, McCann rejoined Leo Burnett in 2012 to serve as its Chief Talent Officer, and remains as one of the most influential women in the advertising business (*Advertising Age*, 2012, p. 32).

In the new millennium, other African-American women were appointed to high-level positions in general-market advertising firms. For example, at SMG, Esther Franklin, a pioneering expert in cultural communications anthropology, was promoted to Executive Vice President and Head of SMG Americas Experience Strategy in 2011 (*HistoryMakers*, 2014). Kendra Hatcher King served as Worldwide Director of Insight and Innovation at Initiative, an IPG media agency (*Black Enterprise*, 2011). Vita Harris was named Global Chief Strategy Officer at DraftFCB in 2011 (4 A's, 2011). By 2013, Traci Dinkins was Managing Director and a senior partner at Mindshare, a WPP agency; Barbara Delfyette Hester was Strategic Planning Director at Maxus; Deidre Smalls-Landau was Executive Vice President and Managing Director of Identity at Interpublic's Mediabrand multicultural agency; Gina Christie was Executive Vice President at BBD&O Worldwide; Joya Harris was Senior Vice President and Robbyn Ennis was Media Director, both at Carat; and Marissa Nance was Director of Strategic Partnerships and Multicultural Content Marketing at Omnicom Media Group, Inc. (Connley and Wilder, 2016). At O&M, Nadja Bellan-White was Senior Partner and Managing Director; and in 2014 was promoted to CEO of O&M Africa, the division of O&M dedicated to cultivating markets in 27 African countries (*Black Enterprise*, 2013; Connley and Wilder, 2016; *Morning Joe*, 2014). Amber Guild was appointed President at Collins, a brand consultancy in New York, and was named a 2016 "Woman to Watch" by *Advertising Age* (2016b). On the global front, Karen Blackett, Chairwoman of Mediacom in the United Kingdom, was named a "Woman to Watch Europe" by *Advertising Age* (2016c). At this writing, no African-American women have duplicated the accomplishments of Ann Fudge and Renetta McCann as heads of large multinational general-market agencies. However, Perry Fair, an African-American man, was chosen to lead an office of a major general-market agency – JWT-Atlanta – where he was appointed President and Chief Creative Officer in 2012 (Mather, 2015).

Black women executives in black-owned agencies

Compared with general-market agencies, opportunities for black women in leading executive roles have been far more abundant at black-owned advertising agencies, past and present. Prominent agency pioneers Vince Cullers and Tom Burrell built their agencies with the support of their wives as critical to the operations of their enterprises early on. Vince Cullers trained his wife, Marian, their two sons, and his daughter-in-law for important jobs in the firm (*Essence*, 1990). Marian Cullers was an administrative officer, serving as Vice President of the agency for many years (*HistoryMakers*, 2010). At the Burrell agency, Barbara Jones Burrell, who met Tom Burrell when they both worked at the Needham, Harper and Steers agency, joined Burrell in 1974 as its secretary-treasurer and later served as vice chair-woman of the company, even after the Burrells divorced in the early 1990s (Applegate, 1994, p. 88; Sivulka, 2009, pp. 328–329). In addition to Sarah Burroughs, who served in top positions at Burrell for many years prior to her retirement, there were numerous women in key executive roles at the Burrell agency over the years, including Alma Hopkins, Executive Vice President and long-time Director of Creative Services; Lisa McConnell and Linda Jefferson, who headed creative services and media, respectively, in 2016; along with Deborah Gray-Young, Donna Hodge, and Adele Lassere (Connley and Wilder, 2016; Jensen, 2000). Emma Young also served as Creative Director at Burrell and the Carol H. Williams agencies and also ran her own boutique agency, Emma Young Creative, Inc. At Uniworld, Valarie Graves was Senior Vice President and longtime Chief Creative Officer (Hayes, 2000) and Nakesha Holley was Vice President of integrated communications (Connley and Wilder, 2016). At

GlobalHue, Don Coleman hired Cheryl Harps from general-market BBD&O to run his media department in the early days of his agency and Tracey Jennings later served as Executive Vice President (Connley and Wilder, 2016; Hayes, 1998). Other African-American women who served in top executive roles at black-owned advertising agencies from the 1970s forward include Terri Gardner of Brainstorm Communications, Barbara Simmons of Eden Advertising and Communications, Danielle Austen of fluent360 (formerly Team Ignition), Verdia Johnson of Footsteps, Faith Morris of Merge Consumer Marketing, Tricia Clarke-Stone of Narrative, Kimberly Blackwell of PMM Agency, Leslie Wingo and Shanteka Sigers of Sanders\Wingo, and Vida Cornelius, Kirsten Atkinson, and Ayiko Broyard of Walton Isaacson (*Advertising Age*, 2003; *Black Enterprise*, 2013; Connley and Wilder, 2016; *Essence*, 1990; *New York Times*, 1975). Finally, Shante Bacon, Founder and CEO of 135th Street Agency, was named an *Advertising Age* "Woman to Watch" in 2016 (*Advertising Age*, 2016b).

The successors

An interesting development concerned the succession of leadership when prominent African-American admen decided to retire. Upon Tom Burrell's retirement in 2004, two black women executives, Fay Ferguson and McGee Willliams-Osse – former management directors at the agency – succeeded Burrell as co-CEOs and purchased 51 percent of the company (Alleyne, 2011). By 2016, Burrell Communications was ranked number two among top black-owned agencies, trailing GlobalHue (*Advertising Age*, 2016a). In a similar story of succession by a black woman, at Uniworld, Monique Nelson was named Chairman and CEO when Byron Lewis retired in 2012 (*Black Enterprise*, 2013). The agency was ranked number four among the leading black-owned agencies, behind CHWA (*Advertising Age*, 2016a). These were important developments since these women were chosen as the first generation of successors to lead top agencies founded by men from the Golden Age of black advertising companies. Preparing for the future, after she finished college, GlobalHue's Don Coleman brought his daughter, Kelli Coleman, into the firm, eventually naming her Executive Vice President and grooming her to assume leadership of the company in the future (Alleyne, 2010). To familiarize Kelli Coleman with all aspects of the agency business, Don Coleman assigned his daughter to work in various areas of the agency – starting with the Finance Committee – so that she could understand how agencies make money. In 2015, Kelli Coleman launched an empowerment initiative called "She Who Dares" focused on women's entrepreneurship (Connley, 2015).

Final thoughts

Advertising is a peculiar occupation. At its essence, it is an idea-oriented business which exists to serve the needs and whims of clients. As a white-collar profession, it typically requires no specific degrees, licenses, or certifications to practice and there are numerous entry points into an advertising career. Thus, career opportunities are often driven by individuals' reputations and personal relationships. At the same time, advertising content is an influential social intermediary which reflects and reinforces important attitudes and values about identity roles in society concerning gender, race, and ethnicity.

While debates persist concerning how to improve diversity in the advertising industry, African-American women continue to progress – slowly – in the business while supporting and encouraging others. In 2010, nearly 72 percent of all employees in black-owned advertising firms were at the five largest advertising agencies (see Chapter 1, Table 1.2). Fast-forward to 2016 and four of the five largest black-owned agencies – Burrell Communications Group, CHWA, Uniworld, and Sanders/Wingo – were headed by African-American women (*Advertising Age*, 2016a). This development underscores the capabilities of black executive women and their significance to the historical record. As the advertising industry continues to evolve, it is important to recognize and understand the experiences and impact of diverse trailblazers who overcame barriers and established pathways for future generations of advertising professionals. As such, the stories of pioneering African-American adwomen are a vital part of that narrative.

References

4 A's (2011) 'DraftFCB Names Vita Harris Global Chief Strategy Officer,' September 9 [Online]. Available at: www.aaaa.org/news/agency/Pages/090611_draftfcb_harris.aspx (Accessed: December 9, 2015).

AAF.org (2014) 'Mosaic Council' [Online]. Available at: http://76.12.169.172/default.asp?id=60 (Accessed: June 8, 2016).

Advertising Age (2003) 'Women to Watch,' June 2, pp. S-1–S-16.

Advertising Age (2012) '100 Most Influential Women in Advertising,' September 24, pp. 18–44.

Advertising Age (2016a) 'Agency Report 2016,' May 2, p. 24.

Advertising Age (2016b) 'Women to Watch,' May 30, pp. 8–15.

Advertising Age (2016c) 'Women to Watch Europe,' May 16, 29.

Alleyne, S. (2010) 'Making Cultural Connections,' *Black Enterprise*, June, pp. 162–167.

Alleyne, S. (2011) 'Growth by Reinvention,' *Black Enterprise*, July 1 [Online]. Available at: www.blackenterprise.com/mag/growth-by-reinvention-2011-be100s-ad-agency-of-the-year/ (Accessed: May 23, 2015).

Applegate, E. (1994) *The Ad Men and Women: A Biographical Dictionary of Advertising*. Westport, CT: Greenwood Press.

Birkner, C. (2016) 'Martin Sorrell Addresses JWT Lawsuit, Acknowledging Sexism is an Industrywide Problem,' *Adweek*, March 23 [Online]. Available at: www.adweek.com/news/advertising-branding/martin-sorrell-talks-jwt-lawsuit-sexism-industry-and-media-rebates-170386 (Accessed: March 23, 2016).

Black Enterprise (2011) 'Top Executives in Advertising and Marketing,' January [Online]. Available at: www.blackenterprise.com/mag/top-executives-in-advertising-marketing/4/ (Accessed: December 9, 2015).

Black Enterprise (2013) 'Top Women Executives in Advertising and Marketing,' January/February, pp. 78–90.

Bond, Y. (2016) 'For a Gender-Balanced Workplace, Think Culture, Not Quotas,' *Advertising Age*, May 30, pp. 32.

Coffee, P. (2016a) 'Campbell Ewald's CEO has been Fired Amid Fallout Over a Staffer's Racist Email,' *Adweek*, January 29 [Online]. Available at: www.adweek.com/news/advertising-branding/campbell-ewalds-ceo-has-been-fired-amid-fallout-over-staffers-racist-email-169291 (Accessed: June 10, 2016).

Coffee, P. (2016b) '2 More Clients Leave Campbell Ewald, With One Citing Agency's Racist Email Controversy,' *Adweek*, March 2 [Online]. Available at: www.adweek.com/news/advertising-branding/2-more-clients-leave-campbell-ewald-one-citing-agencys-racist-email-controversy-169960 (Accessed: June 10, 2016).

Connley, C. (2015) 'GlobalHue's Kelli Coleman Talks Female Empowerment and Being a Boss,' *Black Enterprise*, July [Online]. Available at: www.blackenterprise.com/career/globalhues-kelli-coleman-talks-female-empowerment-and-being-a-boss/ (Accessed: December 9, 2015).

Connley, C. and Wilder, K. (2016) 'Top Women in Advertising,' *Black Enterprise*, February, pp. 66–76.

Essence (1990) 'Women in Advertising,' January 1, pp. 35–40.

Hammer, M. (2013) 'The Change Agents,' *Adweek* [Online]. Available at: www.adweek.com/sa-article/change-agents-152323 (Accessed: December 11, 2015).

Hayes, C. (1998) 'A Creative Point of View,' *Black Enterprise*, June, pp. 164–170.

Hayes, C. (2000) 'Changing Culture,' *Black Enterprise*, June, pp. 188–195.

HistoryMakers (2010) 'Marian Cullers' [Online]. Available at: www.thehistorymakers.com/biography/marian-cullers-41 (Accessed: October 15, 2015).

HistoryMakers (2014) 'Esther "E.T." Franklin,' October 21 [Online]. Available at: www.thehistorymakers.com/biography/esther-et-franklin (Accessed: December 9, 2015).

Jensen, T. (2000) 'Reorganization Coming at Burrell,' *Adweek*, October 12 [Online]. Available at: www.adweek.com/news/advertising/reorganization-coming-burrell-30178 (Accessed: October 20, 2015).

Johnson, A. (2004) 'Adapting to Change?' *Diversity Inc.*, August/September, pp. 27–34.

Kirk, J. (2008) 'Renetta McCann stepping down as Starcom MediaVest CEO,' *Target Market News*, June 10 [Online]. Available at: www.targetmarketnews.com/storyid06100801.htm (Accessed: September 12, 2015).

Mather, K. (2015) 'A True Pioneer: Congratulations, Perry Fair,' March 2 [Online]. Available at: www.jwtaltanto.com/true-pioneeer-congratulations-perry-fair/ (Accessed: December 9, 2015).

Morning Joe (2014) 'A Case of Knowing Her Value,' MSNBC-TV, July 8 [Online]. Available at: www.msnbc.com/morning-joe/watch/a-case-of-knowing-her-value-299272771574 (Accessed: December 9, 2015).

Morrison, M. (2016) 'JWT Harassment Suit Shines Harsh Spotlight on Industry's Woeful Diversity Record,' *Advertising Age*, March 21 [Online]. Available at: http://adage.com/article/agency-news/jwt-wpp-scramble-wake-harassment-lawsuit/303210/ (Accessed: March 21, 2016).

New York Times (1975) 'Soul City Payment is Called Excessive,' May 18 [Online]. Available at: www.nytimes.com/1975/05/18/archives/soul-city-payment-is-called-excessive.html?_r=0 (Accessed: June 10, 2015).

Sanders, L. (2003) 'Fudge Y&R Posting Lauded as Watershed,' *Advertising Age*, May 19, p. 4.

Schultz, E. and Bruell, A. (2016) 'WPP Internal Memo: We "Found Nothing" to Substantiate Charges Against Gustavo Martinez,' *Advertising Age*, March 10 [Online]. Available at: http://adage.com/article/agency-news/wpp-found-substantiate-charges/303068/ (Accessed: March 21, 2016).

Sivulka, J. (2009) *Ad Women: How They Impact What We Need, Want, and Buy*. Amherst, NY: Prometheus Books.

Stein, L. (2016) 'JWT Creates Diversity and Inclusion Council Following Lawsuit,' *Advertising Age*, May 16, p. 8.

Vranica, S. and Tadena, N. (2016) 'JWT Chief Exits Amid Allegations,' *Wall Street Journal*, March 18, p. B-3.

Wall Street Journal (2005) 'Ad Notes,' April 18, p. B-4.

Wheaton, K. (2016) 'Black (Ad) Lives Matter: The Industry's Biggest Diversity Problem,' *Advertising Age*, May 30, p. 36.

Wohl, J. and Stein, L. (2016) 'Ad Industry Hits Inflection Point on Women: Now What?' *Advertising Age*, May 30, pp. 16–17.

Index

Page numbers in *italics* denote tables, those in **bold** denote figures.

Printed in the United States
by Baker & Taylor Publisher Services